MICROSOFT® WINDOWS®
NETWORKING

ESSENTIALS

MICROSOFT® WINDOWS® NETWORKING
ESSENTIALS

Darril Gibson

WILEY

Wiley Publishing, Inc.

Acquisitions Editor: Jeff Kellum
Development Editor: Tom Cirtin
Technical Editors: Bradley Mitchell and Naomi Alpern
Production Editor: Christine O'Connor
Copy Editor: Kim Wimpsett
Editorial Manager: Pete Gaughan
Production Manager: Tim Tate
Vice President and Executive Group Publisher: Richard Swadley
Vice President and Publisher: Neil Edde
Book Designer: Happenstance Type-O-Rama
Compositor: James D. Kramer, Happenstance Type-O-Rama
Proofreader: Publication Services, Inc.
Indexer: Robert Swanson
Project Coordinator, Cover: Katherine Crocker
Cover Designer: Ryan Sneed
Cover Image: © Andrew Holt / Getty Images

Dear Reader,

Thank you for choosing *Microsoft Windows Networking Essentials*. This book is part of a family of premium-quality Sybex books, all of which are written by outstanding authors who combine practical experience with a gift for teaching.

Sybex was founded in 1976. More than 30 years later, we're still committed to producing consistently exceptional books. With each of our titles, we're working hard to set a new standard for the industry. From the paper we print on, to the authors we work with, our goal is to bring you the best books available.

I hope you see all that reflected in these pages. I'd be very interested to hear your comments and get your feedback on how we're doing. Feel free to let me know what you think about this or any other Sybex book by sending me an email at nedde@wiley.com. If you think you've found a technical error in this book, please visit **http://sybex.custhelp.com**. Customer feedback is critical to our efforts at Sybex.

Best regards,

NEIL EDDE
Vice President and Publisher
Sybex, an Imprint of Wiley

To my wife, who brings so much joy
and happiness into my life.

ACKNOWLEDGMENTS

Books are massive projects that succeed only with the cooperation and help of several people. My name is on the cover as the author, but many, many other people contributed to its success. First, I want to thank Jeff Kellum for thinking of me for this project—I love working with the Wiley team. I'm grateful for all the efforts of the technical editor, Bradley Mitchell, who provided some great feedback; I only wish there was more room in this book to implement all his suggestions. It was great to work with Tom Cirtin again, an excellent development editor who provided great editorial assistance and helped keep the book on track. I also want to thank my brother, a knowledgeable networking expert named Duane Gibson, who provided input on many of the chapters in this book. Last, thanks to Production Editor Christine O'Connor and Production Assistant Nicholas Moran, who helped make sure the final production looked as good as it does.

About the Author

Darril Gibson is the CEO of Security Consulting and Training, LLC. He has written, coauthored, and contributed to more than a dozen books, and he regularly consults and teaches on a wide variety of IT topics. Most of the books he's been involved with are available on Amazon by searching for *Darril Gibson*. He has been a Microsoft Certified Trainer (MCT) since 1999 and holds a multitude of certifications including MCSE (NT 4.0, Windows 2000, and Windows 2003), MCITP (Windows 7, Windows Server 2008, and SQL Server), Security+, CISSP, and ITIL Foundations. Darril lives in Virginia Beach with his wife of more than 18 years and two dogs. Whenever possible, they escape to their cabin in the country with more than 20 acres of land where his dogs wear themselves out chasing rabbits and deer.

You can reach the author by writing to darril@mcitpsuccess.com.

Contents at a Glance

CONTENTS

CHAPTER 14   Troubleshooting TCP/IP   283

APPENDIX A   Answers to Review Questions   309

APPENDIX B   Microsoft's Certification Program   319

INTRODUCTION

Computers are very common today, and just about any computer is connected to a network. People with the knowledge and expertise to configure and maintain networks are needed in any organization.

IT administration starts with network administration in most organizations. If the computers can't communicate on the network, nothing else matters. Network administrators need to be able to quickly identify any communication problems and resolve them. Of course, to do this, administrators need to understand how the network works under normal conditions.

The Microsoft Technology Associate (MTA) certification is a new certification level. It includes three separate tracks: Information Technology (IT) Professional, Developer, and Database. The IT Professional track is for individuals pursuing work as administrators. The Developer track is for individuals pursuing work as programmers and software engineers. The Database track is for individuals pursuing work as database administrators and database developers.

The IT Professional series includes three certifications:

Networking Fundamentals This is the first certification in the MTA IT Professional track. It lays a solid foundation of basic networking knowledge needed for the other MTA certifications and also for the more advanced Microsoft Certified Technology Specialist (MCTS) and Microsoft Certified IT Professional (MCITP) tracks. This book covers the objectives for exam 98-366. You earn this certification by taking and passing exam 98-366.

Security Fundamentals Security Fundamentals is the second certification in the MTA IT Professional track. It builds on the knowledge learned in the Networking Fundamentals certification and adds fundamental security knowledge needed by administrators. IT administrators in any environment need to be aware of the risks with IT systems. You earn this certification by taking and passing exam 98-367.

Windows Server Administration Fundamentals This certification builds on the knowledge gained in the Networking Fundamentals and Security Fundamentals certifications. It digs deeper into knowledge and skills needed by Windows Server administrators. You earn this certification by taking and passing exam 98-365.

Each of these certifications can serve as a stepping-stone to Microsoft's next levels of certifications: Microsoft Certified Technology Specialist (MCTS) and Microsoft Certified IT Professional (MCITP).

We have included an Appendix at the back of this book that highlights the Microsoft certification program, as well as lists the exam objectives for Exam 98-366, and how they map to this book's content.

Who Should Read This Book

This book is for current or aspiring professionals seeking a quick grounding in the fundamentals of networking in a Microsoft environment. The goal is to provide quick, focused coverage of fundamental skills.

If you want to break into networking or are already working in networking and want to fill in some gaps on fundamental networking, this book is for you. You can use the knowledge gained from this book as a foundation for more advanced studies.

This book is focused on the objectives of the Microsoft Technology Associates (MTA) Networking Fundamentals certification. This is the first certification in the MTA IT Professional series. After mastering this material, you can move onto the Security Fundamentals and Windows Server Administration Fundamentals MTA certifications.

You can read more about the MTA certifications and MTA exam certification paths at **www.microsoft.com/learning/en/us/certification/mta.aspx**.

What You Will Learn

You will learn the essentials of networking in a Microsoft environment. In addition, this book covers all the objectives of the Microsoft Technology Associates Networking Fundamentals exam (exam 98-366).

What You Need

Since this book is focused on providing you with only the essentials, the biggest requirement is a desire to learn. You aren't expected to have a lot of knowledge or experience in networking before starting the book. It starts with the basics in Chapter 1 and steadily builds on the knowledge through the end of the book.

Ideally, you'll have some hardware that you can use. Since this is a Microsoft book, it would be good to have a system running Microsoft Windows Server 2008 or Windows Server 2008 R2.

If you're running another operating system, such as Windows 7, you can create a virtual server running Windows Server 2008. I have included an optional lab for this book, which can be downloaded at: **www.sybex.com/go/networking essentials**. It will lead you through the following steps:

> ► Configuring Windows 7 with virtualization

> ► Locating and downloading an evaluation copy of Windows Server 2008

> ► Installing Windows Server 2008

> ► Promoting it to a domain controller

You can then use this virtual lab environment to experiment with Windows Server 2008 while going through the book.

What Is Covered in This Book

Microsoft Windows Networking Essentials is organized to provide you with the knowledge needed to master the basics of networking in a Microsoft environment.

Chapter 1, "Introduction to Networking"   Identifies the names of many of the physical and logical components of a network and then introduces the networking components included in networks of all sizes.

Chapter 2, "Overview of Networking Components"   Presents a big-picture view of networking components and how they work together. The chapter starts by explaining basic transmission methods used within networks such as unicast, broadcast, and multicast, and then it introduces basic hardware components used in networks.

Chapter 3, "Understanding the OSI Model"   Presents the Open Systems Interconnect (OSI) and TCP/IP models commonly referenced by many IT professionals. You'll learn the layers of these models, what occurs at each layer, what networking hardware is used on which layer, and which protocols operate on different layers.

Chapter 4, "Core TCP/IP Protocols"   Presents many of the protocols contained in the TCP/IP protocol suite. You'll learn about key protocols such as TCP and UDP and also how systems use well-known ports to identify a protocol.

Chapter 5, "Exploring IPv4"   Identifies the different components of IPv4 addresses. Once you understand the components of the addresses, it becomes much easier to troubleshoot basic problems. You'll also learn how the Dynamic Host Configuration Protocol (DHCP) automatically assigns IP addresses and other TCP/IP configuration information.

Chapter 6, "Exploring IPv6"   Explains why IPv6 is needed, compares the differences between IPv4 and IPv6, and provides information on how IPv4 and IPv6 coexist.

Chapter 7, "Connecting Computers to a Network"   Presents the different types of media used to connect computers and some of the common problems that can interfere with the transmission of data.

Chapter 8, "Networking Computers with Switches"   Compares hubs and switches, managed and unmanaged switches, and layer 2 and layer 3 switches. You'll also learn how a switch is used to create a virtual LAN.

Chapter 9, "Connecting Networks with Routers"   Explains the use of routers in a network. The chapter includes information on routing tables and how routing tables are updated.

Chapter 10, "Resolving Names to IP Addresses"   Presents the two types of computer names—host names and NetBIOS names—and how these names are resolved to IP addresses. Name resolution methods included in this chapter are the Domain Name System (DNS), the Windows Internet Naming System (WINS), the hosts file, the lmhosts file, and cache.

Chapter 11, "Understanding Network Security Zones"   Presents the different areas of a network as security zones. Varying levels of security are required in different zones. The Internet is the riskiest zone. Internal networks, or intranets, are the safest. Between these two, you can create perimeter networks as a buffer zone.

Chapter 12, "Understanding Wireless Networking"   Covers the common protocols used for wireless networks in the IEEE 802.11 family. You'll also learn about the different methods you can use to secure wireless networks.

Chapter 13, "Understanding Internet Access Methods and Wide Area Networks"   Covers the different types of methods used for Internet access. You'll also learn how enterprises use wide area networks (WANs) to connect remote offices.

Chapter 14, "Troubleshooting TCP/IP"   Shows you how to use several different tools to check and verify basic connectivity issues. Tools include `ipconfig`, `ping`, `tracert`, `pathping`, and `netstat`.

Appendix A, "Answers to Review Questions"   Includes all of the answers to the review questions found in "The Essentials and Beyond" section at the end of every chapter.

Appendix B, "Microsoft's Certification Program"   Maps the objectives in the MTA Networking Essentials exam (exam 98-366) to each specific chapter where the objective is covered.

In addition, we have created an online Glossary, as well as the suggested or recommended answers to the additional exercises we have included at end of each chapter. You can download these at **www.sybex.com/go/networkingessentials**.

Sybex strives to keep you supplied with the latest tools and information you need for your work. Please check its website at **www.sybex.com/go/networkingessentials**, where we'll post additional content and updates that supplement this book if the need arises. Enter **networking essentials** in the Search box (or type the book's ISBN—978-1-118-01685-5), and click Go to get to the book's update page.

## CHAPTER 1

Introduction to Networking

Just about any computer you'll use today is on a network. Networked computers are so common it's easy to take them for granted. However, many components and technologies are working together behind the scenes to ensure a networked computer can access resources on the network.

In this chapter, I start by identifying the names of many of the physical and logical components of a network. I then introduce the components included in very small networks and show you how additional components are added as a network grows. I conclude with information on some standards organizations that help ensure all of these computers can work together no matter who manufactured them or where they're operating.

▶ **Comparing logical and physical networks**

▶ **Networking home computers**

▶ **Networking small offices and home offices**

▶ **Networking large offices**

▶ **Networking enterprises**

▶ **Understanding standards organizations**

Comparing Logical and Physical Networks

A network is a group of computers and other devices connected together. These connections can be with cables, wireless connections, or both. Networks are discussed in both logical and physical terms.

The *logical* organization of a network identifies the overall design of a network. It differentiates between local area networks (LANs) and wide area networks (WANs). The logical design of the network provides a high-level overview of the entire network and may not show smaller components such as all the switches, routers, and firewalls. By contrast, the *physical* network infrastructure includes the details of the physical components. The physical components are the devices and cabling that you can touch and feel.

This chapter presents concepts on logical network organization. You'll learn about the different types of network designs that you may find in home networks, small offices, larger offices or organizations, and enterprises.

Chapter 2 provides an overview of these physical components, and later chapters in the book (such as Chapters 7, 8, and 9) dig deeper into how these devices work.

It's important to understand how devices in a logical structure work to fully understand how data moves through a network. Once you understand how the data moves through the network, you are better prepared to maintain it and troubleshoot it when problems occur.

Networking Home Computers

Most home computers are part of a network today. At the very least, home computers have the ability to connect to the Internet, which is a massive network of networks. Figure 1.1 shows a simple networked home computer.

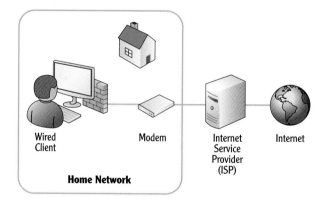

FIGURE 1.1 Home computer with access to Internet

In the figure, the computer has access to the Internet through a modem to an Internet service provider (ISP). This could be a cable modem used in a broadband connection or a modem used for dial-up connections. Broadband connections are widely available in urban areas. This includes connections through cable TV systems, fiber-optic lines, and even phone connections such as ISDN and 3G/4G data services.

Even if a broadband connection isn't available, home users can connect to the Internet through a phone line, also known as a dial-up system. Dial-up connections are much slower but are used in rural areas where broadband connections are not available. Internet access via satellites is becoming available in more rural areas, providing better connections than dial-up but still not comparable in speed to broadband connections.

ENABLE THE LOCAL FIREWALL

When a computer connects directly to the Internet through an ISP (without going through an internal router or wireless access point), it is at significant risk. The computer has a public IP address and is accessible from any other computer on the Internet, anywhere in the world. Attackers often prowl the Internet looking for unprotected computers. Enabling the software firewall on this computer provides a layer of protection.

When home users add additional computers into their home, they typically want to network these computers. Users on the network are then able to share resources. For example, consider Figure 1.2, which shows a typical home network connected to each other and the Internet using both wired and wireless connections.

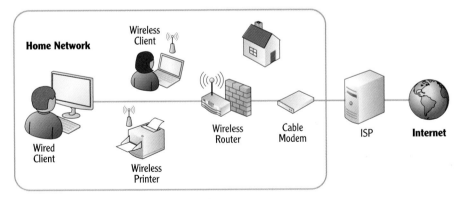

FIGURE 1.2 Typical home network

In the figure, the wired user is connected to a wireless router directly with a cable, and another user is connected via a wireless connection. A wireless printer is added that can be shared by any users with access to the wired network. An

ISP provides connectivity to the Internet, just as it would for a single user. A single cable modem connects to the ISP, and then the cable modem connects to a wireless router.

Without a network, each individual computer would need to connect to the Internet separately, incurring individual access charges. However, the single Internet connection can be shared by adding the wireless router. A great benefit of wireless is that you don't have to install cables to each computer.

Most wireless routers include several additional capabilities. For example, it's common for a wireless router used in most home networks to include the following:

Wireless Access Point (WAP)   The core purpose of the wireless device is to support connectivity for wireless clients. The WAP provides this connectivity.

Routing Capabilities   A built-in router will route data from the internal network to the Internet and from Internet data back to the internal network. Chapter 2 provides an overview of routers, and Chapter 9 includes in-depth details on routers.

Network Address Translation (NAT)   NAT translates the public IP addresses used on the Internet to private IP addresses on the internal network, and vice versa. If NAT wasn't used, you'd have to purchase or lease public IP addresses for each internal computer. Additionally, each computer would be directly on the Internet and exposed to unnecessary risks. NAT hides the internal computers from Internet attackers.

Dynamic Host Configuration Protocol (DHCP)   DHCP provides clients with IP addresses and other TCP/IP configuration information. The other TCP/IP information includes the address of the DNS server and the address of the router that provides a path to the Internet. The router address is also known as the *default gateway*.

Firewall   A WAP will provide basic firewall capabilities. This blocks unwanted traffic from the Internet, providing a layer of protection for internal clients.

Networking Small Offices and Home Offices

Small offices and home offices (SOHOs) are very similar to the sophisticated home network. They are both considered LANs. SOHOs have access to the Internet and can have either wireless clients, wired clients, or both. Figure 1.3 shows the configuration of sample SOHO network.

▶
Some ISPs provide a router instead of a cable modem. A wireless router can connect to a router just as easily as it can connect to a cable modem.

▶
Chapter 9 covers routers and NAT in more depth.

▶
Chapter 5 covers DHCP and IP addressing schemes.

▶
Chapter 11 covers more advanced configurations of the firewall. Chapter 12 includes important wireless security concepts.

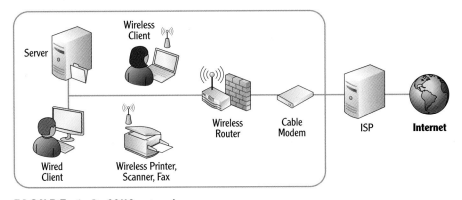

FIGURE 1.3 SOHO network

The primary difference is that a SOHO will typically have a server to provide additional capabilities for the office. For example, the server can be used as a file server to store files used within the business.

Although most offices will have a server, it's not necessary. Important files could be stored on a primary user's computer and shared to other users from there if needed. However, if important files are stored on multiple computers, it becomes harder to back up these files.

Additionally, a business may have a wireless multifunction printer that can print, scan, and fax documents to meet the needs of the business. It's not necessary to have a wireless printer. However, these are becoming more popular in SOHOs because they are easier to share between the network users.

The WAP used in a SOHO can be the same as the WAP used in the home network.

SOHOs typically have up to 10 workers but may have as many as 100.

SECURE WIRELESS NETWORKS

It's very important to lock down wireless networks with the best security available. The primary method of security for wireless networks is WPA2 (or 802.11i), which is discussed in greater depth in Chapter 12. If the network is not locked down, an attacker can use a simple laptop with a wireless NIC while driving by in a car to compromise it. This "war driving" technique allows an attacker to tap into the network and access the network's resources if the network isn't secured. Historically, wireless networks were notoriously insecure. However, technologies available today make it possible to provide sufficient security for most wireless networks.

Similarly, the WAP used in the SOHO will provide many of the same capabilities to the office as a WAP provides for a home network. This includes routing, NAT, DHCP, and a firewall.

Understanding Local Area Networks

> **A LAN is a group of computers in the same geographical location. It can include multiple subnetworks.**

The home network shown earlier (in Figure 1.2) and the SOHO (shown in Figure 1.3) are both considered *local area networks*. A LAN is a group of computers and/or other devices that are connected in a single physical location (such as a home, office, or corporate building). LANs can be much bigger than the networks shown so far. As you go through the book, you'll see how many different devices are used within the LAN.

LANs have fast network connectivity between the different devices in the LAN. Common speeds of wired LANs today are 100 Mbps or 1000 Mbps (also called 1 Gbps) and 54 Mbps or 300 Mbps for wireless.

MEGABIT AND GIGABIT

LAN speeds identify how much data they can transfer. Mbps is short for megabit per second, and a megabit represents a million bits. A LAN with a speed of 100 Mbps can transfer data at a rate of 100 million bits per second. A gigabit LAN (1 Gbps or 1000 Mbps) transfers data at a rate of 1 billion bits per second.

Occasionally, data is measured in bytes instead of bits. A byte consists of 8 bits. When bytes are mentioned, a capital *B* is used. For example, a system may have 4 gigabytes (GB) of random access memory (RAM). This is commonly listed as 4 GB. It is not accurate to list this as 4 Gb (with a lowercase *b*). Similarly, it not accurate to list a 100 Mbps LAN as 100 MBps (with a capital *B*).

A LAN is an internal network. Most LANs will have connectivity to the Internet through a router or firewall, but the LAN itself is internal. Traffic back and forth through a firewall to the Internet is filtered for security purposes. However, traffic within the LAN itself is usually not filtered. The internal network is considered a high trust area, so any traffic on the network is allowed.

Comparing Workgroups and Domains

A SOHO will typically include from one to ten workers and will usually be configured as a *workgroup*. A workgroup is a group of networked computers that share a common workgroup name. The default name of a Microsoft workgroup is simply *Workgroup*, and all computers in the workgroup will share the same workgroup name. User accounts are located on each individual computer.

Consider Figure 1.4, which shows an office with four users. Each of the users has their own computer, and an additional server is available to them. For Sally to log onto her computer, she needs a computer account on her computer. However, this account won't work on Bob's, Alice's, or Joe's computers. If Sally needs to log onto any other computer in the workgroup, she must have a separate account on that computer.

◄

Even though Internet access is not shown here, a SOHO configured as a workgroup will typically have Internet access. The focus here is the internal LAN.

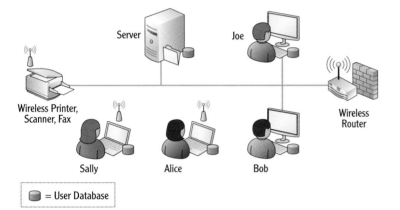

FIGURE 1.4 SOHO as a workgroup

In this scenario, there are five separate user databases—one on the server and one on each of the four computers. Similarly, each user would need to remember five usernames and five passwords to log onto each of the five computers.

However, most users in a SOHO will typically log onto only one computer in the network and will need only one user account. If users had to remember five usernames and five passwords, they would probably break a cardinal rule of security. They would probably start writing down the usernames and passwords.

When offices get larger than 10 computers or whenever offices need to have more centralized user and computer management, they move into a *domain* configuration. You can add a server and promote it to a domain controller or promote an existing server to a domain controller.

In Microsoft domains, the domain controller hosts Active Directory Domain Services (AD DS). AD DS includes objects such as user and computer accounts. Each user would have one user account in the domain, and each computer would have one computer account.

Figure 1.5 shows a SOHO configured as a domain. It has eight users with nine computers connected to the LAN. The server has been promoted to a domain controller and is hosting Active Directory. Instead of requiring users to memorize passwords for each computer, each user has a single account hosted on the domain controller.

> **A Microsoft Windows domain includes a domain controller hosting AD DS.**

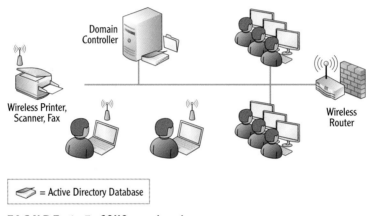

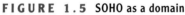
= Active Directory Database

FIGURE 1.5 SOHO as a domain

This supports *single sign-on (SSO)* where a user needs to sign on only once. All access to domain resources for the user is granted using this single account. Additionally, this one account is used to log onto almost any computer in the domain.

By default, domain users are authorized to log onto any computer in the domain except for domain controllers. Administrators are granted the right to log onto domain controllers. However, it is possible to restrict users from logging onto other computers within the domain if necessary.

Even though the server has been promoted to a domain controller, it can still perform other functions on the network. For example, a domain controller can still host files as a file server.

WHEN TO SWITCH FROM A WORKGROUP TO A DOMAIN

There isn't a specific number defining when networks must change from a workgroup to a domain. It's based on preference and usability. However, most offices switch over when the number of users reaches between 10 and 20. Multiple reasons encourage the switch.

The primary reason to switch is when users have to remember multiple user accounts to perform their job. The domain provides single sign-on capabilities where users need to remember only a single user account to log on.

A secondary reason is to help administrators reduce their workload. A domain provides centralized administration through Active Directory. It also includes advanced administration tools such as Group Policy. Group Policy allows an administrator to configure a setting once in a domain and have it apply to many or all of the computers and users.

Another reason is to allow more concurrent connections from other devices on the LAN. In older operating systems such as Windows XP, each computer was restricted to only 10 concurrent connections. For example, if a computer shared a printer, only 10 other users could send print jobs to it at a time. The 11th connection was refused. This worked the same if a computer hosted a shared application. Ten users could connect, but the 11th connection was refused. This became a logical reason to switch to a domain when the office had more than 10 computers. Windows 7 Professional and Ultimate editions support 20 concurrent connections.

Exploring the Benefits of Domains and Domain Controllers

Promoting a server to a domain controller provides several benefits beyond single sign-on. These include the following:

Simplified Management   Managing accounts in a domain is done with a group of centralized tools. For example, Active Directory Users and Computers is used to perform common administration tasks for all the users and computers in the domain. Additionally, user and computer accounts are organized in organizational units within the domain.

Group Policy   Group Policy is used in a domain to configure, control, and manage users and computers. For example, Group Policy can be used to configure password-protected screen savers for all computers in the domain. An administrator can configure the setting one time in Group Policy, and the setting is configured on all the computers in the domain. It doesn't matter if the organization has 20 users or 20,000 users; the setting is configured once, and Group Policy does the rest. Thousands of settings can be configured through Group Policy.

Built-in Redundancy and Fault Tolerance   If you have at least two domain controllers, the domain data is automatically replicated to each domain controller. If an account is added on one domain controller, it's copied to the other. If a user changes a password, the change is copied. This ensures you always have a redundant copy of Active Directory providing fault tolerance. In other words, if one domain controller develops a fault or fails, the domain can tolerate the fault. The other domain controller will carry the load.

> ▶
> **Chapter 10 covers DNS and other name resolution methods.**

Microsoft domains require a Domain Name System (DNS) server. DNS is used primarily to resolve computer names to IP addresses, but it's also used to locate domain controllers within a domain. If you don't have DNS or DNS fails, Active Directory fails.

Networking Large Offices

> ▶
> **A *subnet* is a group of computers separated from other computers by one or more routers.**

Large offices include more people, more end user computers, and more users. Although you can network thousands of people in a single LAN, you do have to take additional steps to improve the performance of the LAN. The primary difference is that you subdivide groups of computers into different *subnets*.

Figure 1.6 shows a diagram for a larger office. Notice that the office includes multiple subnets and each subnet is separated by a router. The computers are separated on the different subnets so that each subnet has less traffic. Notice that subnet A has only servers while other subnets have users. Placing the servers on separate subnets is common in larger networks.

Traffic on a network is similar to traffic on roads and highways. When there are fewer cars, traffic runs smoother. When there are more cars, traffic becomes congested, and the potential for collisions increases. You can improve traffic flow by adding more roads and highways, providing multiple paths to common destinations, and widening commonly used roads.

Similarly, more computers on a network results in more network traffic and more congestion. You can improve performance by adding subnets to control and limit traffic in different areas.

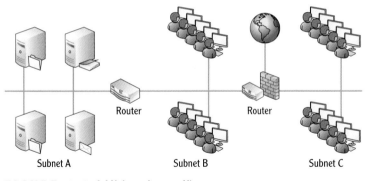

FIGURE 1.6 LAN for a large office

Just as cars can have collisions on a road, data packets sent on a network can collide, resulting in collisions. When two computers on the same subnet send data at the same time, the data collides and is unreadable. Both computers must then send the data again. They both wait a random amount of time and send the data again. If the network is very busy, the data can collide again when it's resent.

Of course, every time data has to be resent, it makes the network that much busier since there is more traffic. More traffic results in more collisions, and more collisions results in even more traffic. If the network isn't optimized, the network performance can slow to a crawl. This is similar to rush-hour traffic in a city where it may take you an hour to get somewhere that normally takes only 10 minutes.

ROUTERS AND SWITCHES

Although Figure 1.6 shows how routers are used to subnet the LAN, the diagram doesn't fully show how computers are connected within each subnet. Switches or hubs connect computers to each other within a subnet. Routers connect the subnets together.

For example, all the servers in subnet A could be connected with a switch. Similarly, all the computers in subnet B could be connected with a second switch, and all the computers in subnet C could be connected with a third switch.

Switches are used to connect computers within a subnet. Routers are used to connect subnets. These two important points are repeated and expanded on throughout this book.

Networking Enterprises

There is no formal definition of an enterprise, but it generally implies an organization with multiple locations. Occasionally, documentation defines an enterprise as an organization with more than 250 users to differentiate it from a large office, while other documentation defines it as more than 5,000 users.

From an IT professional's perspective, the biggest difference between a large office and an enterprise is the number of IT professionals supporting the network. Some offices with as many as 50 users are supported by only one or two administrators. These administrators do a little of everything.

In contrast, an enterprise may have dozens of IT professionals, with many of them having specialized knowledge. Some may be experts on email systems such as Microsoft Exchange. Others may be experts on database systems such as Microsoft SQL Server. End user help-desk professionals are experts on Windows 7 and other desktop operating systems and provide direct support to the users.

Another significant difference with enterprises is the method used to connect the different locations. Instead of just a single LAN in a single location, the organization is connected using different WAN technologies. WANs can be used to connect large offices to large offices. WANs can also connect smaller branch offices to the larger main offices.

Last, many workers are mobile. For example, salespeople are often traveling to meet customers. These mobile workers still need access to resources on the main network. Remote access technologies allow mobile workers to connect to the main network from remote locations.

> **While remote access technologies are more common in enterprises, they can be used anywhere, including SOHOs.**
>
> ▶

Understanding Wide Area Networks

> ▶
>
> **A LAN has one or more subnets in the same geographic location. A WAN is two or more LANS connected in different geographical locations.**

A *WAN* is created when two or more LANs in separate geographical locations are connected. The connection between the LANs is almost always slower than the speed of the LANs themselves. For example, consider Figure 1.7. The organization headquarters has a high-speed 1000 Mbps (1 Gbps) LAN connecting all the computers and other devices. Similarly, the regional office also has a high-speed 100 Mbps LAN.

The T1 WAN link connects the two LANs at a much slower connection speed of 1.544 Mbps. Although a speed of 1.544 Mbps is much quicker than a dial-up speed of 56 Kbps, it is significantly slower than the internal speeds of the LANs (100 Mbps and 1 Gbps).

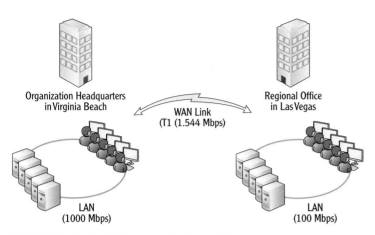

FIGURE 1.7 WAN connecting two LANs

When a WAN is created, users are able to access resources in the other LAN. For example, users in the Virginia Beach LAN can access resources such as files on servers in the Las Vegas LAN. Similarly, users in Las Vegas can access servers in Virginia Beach.

Many organizations lease the WAN links they use. This is similar to people leasing phone lines for telephone access. It's not reasonable for phone users to run their own phone lines to everyone they want to call. Similarly, it's too expensive for most organizations to run their own cables to their different locations.

Leasing the lines from telecommunications companies can be expensive. These lines usually need to carry more data than a typical phone connection. For example, a regular phone connection can carry about 50 Kbps of data and may cost $30 to $50 a month. A T1 carries about 30 times that much data with a bandwidth of 1.544 Mbps. The cost isn't quite 30 times as much, but it often runs in the hundreds of dollars per month.

◄

Other alternatives to leased lines include WAN DSL and WAN Ethernet. Chapter 13 covers the alternatives in more depth.

Understanding Branch Offices

Large organizations often have branch offices. This allows the organization to have a broader reach and allows their employees to be closer to their customers.

Branch offices are often much smaller than the main headquarters of the organization. They have fewer people and limited local computing resources. Individuals will have computers, but the branch office may not have any servers on site. However, employees still need to access organizational resources such as servers at the headquarters location. It's common for a branch office to be connected to either a headquarters or a regional office using a WAN link.

Consider Figure 1.8, which shows a branch office connected to the main head-quarters of the organization and another branch office connected to the regional office. An organization can have as many branch offices as desired. However, each WAN link costs additional money.

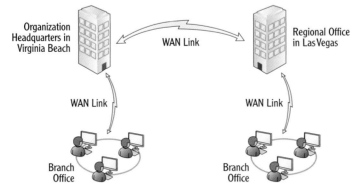

FIGURE 1.8 Branch offices connected in an organization

Since a branch office has fewer people, they have limited support. In other words, the headquarters' location will have many information technology (IT) professionals, but a branch office may not have any. Instead, the IT staff often provides remote support via the phone or using remote technologies.

Several remote assistance technologies are available to help users remotely. For example, Microsoft includes Remote Assistance. This allows administrators in one location to take control of the user's desktop (with the user's permission) to resolve a problem or show the user how to accomplish a task.

Accessing Networks Remotely

Many organizations also set up remote access capabilities. Remote access allows individuals working outside the company to be able to access resources internal to the company. These are the two primary methods of remote access:

Dial-up   A client uses a modem and phone line to connect to a remote access server that also has a modem and a phone line. After authenticating with the server, the server provides connectivity to the internal network. A dial-up remote access server is accessible to any client that has access to phone lines. Figure 1.9 shows a dial-up connection.

> **Chapter 13 presents remote access services in more depth.**

Virtual Private Network (VPN)   A VPN provides access to an internal network over a public network such as the Internet. The client accesses the Internet using any available means. The client then connects to the VPN server, which is reachable through the Internet. After authenticating with the server, the VPN server provides connectivity to the internal network. The VPN server is accessible to any client that has access to the Internet. Figure 1.10 shows a VPN connection.

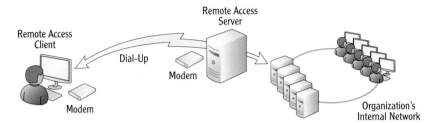

FIGURE 1.9 Remote access via dial-up

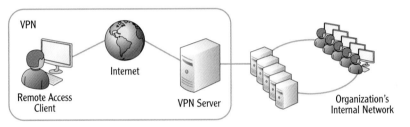

FIGURE 1.10 Remote access via VPN

REMOTE ACCESS OR VPN SERVER

The terms *remote access server* and *VPN server* have subtle differences. In short, a VPN server is a remote access server. However, not all remote access servers are VPN servers. Some remote access servers can use dial-up technologies only. If it's a remote access server using dial-up only, it's not correct to call it a VPN server.

Understanding Standards Organizations

Several standards organizations are important in networking, because they develop different types of standards to meet specific needs. For example, the IETF has created standards for the Internet communications. Without a central authority creating standards used by everyone, there is no way the Internet would be the valuable global resource it is today.

These organizations include the following:

▶ Internet Engineering Task Force

▶ World Wide Web Consortium

▶ Institute of Electrical and Electronics Engineers

▶ International Telecommunication Union

Understanding the Internet Engineering Task Force

The *Internet Engineering Task Force (IETF)* defines Internet communications standards. Its goal is to make the Internet work better. It does so by creating high-quality, relevant technical documents used by designers, managers, and users of the Internet.

Transmission Control Protocol/Internet Protocol (TCP/IP) is the protocol suite used on the Internet. It's also the primary protocol suite used within Microsoft networks. The IETF has produced a wide range of documents that define how the different protocols are used.

Chapter 3 introduces many of the protocols in the TCP/IP suite. Chapter 4 covers them in more depth.

Most documents created by the IETF are known as RFCs. *RFC* is short for *request for comments*. RFCs are written and then released to the world for comments. Many RFCs are assigned to the Standards Track category and go through a standards track. There are four primary stages for an RFC in the Standards Track category:

Proposed Standard (PS)   An RFC starts at the PS stage, the first official stage where the standard is introduced. Many standards never progress beyond this level.

Draft Standard (DS)   The second official stage is DS. At this stage, the standard has been tested and verified to work as expected. It is on the track to become an actual standard but isn't yet.

Standard (STD)   The final stage of an RFC is STD. RFCs at this stage are widely used.

Best Current Practice (BCP)   BCP is a single-stage alternative to the previous stages. A BCP provides operational specifications.

When an RFC is released, it is given a number. This number stays with the RFC, and the RFC is never changed once it's assigned a number. If a change is desired or required, a new RFC is created, and the new RFC starts over at the proposed standard stage.

As an example, RFC 791 describes the 32-bit IPv4. Even though this was created in 1981, it's still in use today. The IETF recognized that the Internet was running out of IPv4 addresses, so it tasked a working group with creating a solution. The working group first came up with RFC 1819 (commonly called the 64-bit IPv5). However, comments on RFC 1819 made it apparent that if 64-bits were used for IPv5, then the Internet would probably run out of IP addresses again in about 10 years or so. RFC 1819 was scrapped. The IETF ultimately released RFC 2460, defining 128-bit IPv6 addressing. RFC 2460 is on the standards track and currently has a status as a DS.

You can view the full RFC 2460 document at **www.ietf.org/rfc/rfc2460.txt**.

You'll read about many different protocols associated with TCP/IP throughout this book. Each of these protocols is defined in its own RFC.

For more information on the IETF, you can view its website at **www.ietf.org**. The IETF also has a page devoted to newcomers at **www.ietf.org/newcomers.html**.

◄

Some RFCs are Informational or Experimental and do not follow the standard track stages.

Understanding the World Wide Web Consortium

The *World Wide Web Consortium (W3C)* defines standards for the World Wide Web (WWW). As an example, the Hypertext Transfer Protocol (HTTP) was defined by the W3C. HTTP is the primary protocol used to transfer WWW information over the Internet. Membership of the W3C consists of organizations rather than individuals. At the time of this writing, the W3C currently has 323 members.

Most web pages are created in a Hypertext Markup Language (HTML) format. It started as an Internet-based hypermedia initiative for global information and grew into what it is today. Tim Berners-Lee invented HTML and the World Wide Web. (His proper title is Sir Berners-Lee since he was knighted in 2004.) At the time of this writing, he is the director of the W3C.

Note that although the WWW runs on the Internet, it isn't the Internet itself. The Internet is a huge network of millions of networks and includes all the networking infrastructure hardware. The WWW is one of many methods used to access information over the Internet. The Internet also supports transferring files using the File Transfer Protocol (FTP) and sharing information through newsgroups, such as Usenet newsgroups.

Understanding the Institute of Electrical and Electronics Engineers

The *Institute of Electrical and Electronics Engineers (IEEE)* is a professional association dedicated to advancing technical innovation. It has more than 375,000 members in 160 different countries. A primary function of the IEEE is defining lower-level network standards.

IEEE standards are identified as IEEE (pronounced as I triple E) with a number. The IEEE has defined many different standards that you'll read about in this book. For example, IEEE 802.3 defines various standards for wired Ethernet networks. IEEE 802.11 defines various standards for wireless networks.

Understanding the International Telecommunication Union

The *International Telecommunication Union (ITU)* is a United Nations agency that includes members from 192 countries. It is focused on information and communication technology issues. It has contributed to shared global use of the radio spectrum and international cooperation in assigning satellite orbits. It has also helped improve telecommunication infrastructure throughout the world.

Many of the telephony standards used by computers today have been defined by the ITU. This includes standards used for modem communications and video conferencing.

THE ESSENTIALS AND BEYOND

The logical network organization identifies the overall layout of LANs and WANs. A local area network is a group of computers and computing devices in a single high-speed layout. It can include one or more subnets. A wide area network is a group of two or more LANs connected with a slower WAN link. WAN links can also connect branch offices.

ADDITIONAL EXERCISES

▶ If you are in a networked classroom environment, draw a diagram of the network. See whether you can identify the path to the Internet.

▶ If you have a home network, draw a diagram of it. Are computers connected with wires, or do they use a wireless access point? Does it have a dial-up or a broadband connection?

(Continues)

THE ESSENTIALS AND BEYOND *(Continued)*

▶ Use the Internet to look up RFC 1918, which defines the private IP addresses used in internal networks. List the three private IP ranges defined by RFC 1918.

▶ Use the Internet to identify at least five different network standards in the IEEE 802 series (such as 802.3).

To compare your answers to the author's, please visit **www.sybex.com/go/ networkingessentials**.

REVIEW QUESTIONS

1. What should be enabled on a computer that has direct connection to the Internet?

   A. Router   **C.** Firewall
   B. Switch   **D.** VPN

2. True or false. A WAP often provides access to the Internet.

3. A group of computers are connected in a single location. What is this called?

   A. LAN   **C.** VLAN
   B. WAN   **D.** VPN

4. A network is connected using high-speed components rated at 1 Gbps. What does the *b* represent in Gbps?

5. Users in the network have to remember an average of five usernames and passwords to access different computers. How can you reduce the number of passwords remembered by users?

   A. Change the network to a workgroup   **C.** Create a WAN
   B. Change the network to domain   **D.** Create a VPN

6. Define a LAN.

7. Define a WAN.

8. An employee is able to connect to the employer's private network over the Internet. What is the employee using?

   A. Domain controller   **C.** WAP
   B. LAN   **D.** VPN

9. What are two types of remote access servers? (Choose two.)

   A. Dial-up   **C.** VPN
   B. WAP   **D.** Domain controller

10. True or false. All RFCs are known as standards.

## CHAPTER 2

Overview of Networking Components

Every network includes different components that connect them together. Although it's important to understand how each of these components works individually, it's easier to grasp the details if you first understand how they work together.

This chapter presents a big-picture view of all the components and how they work together. It starts by explaining basic transmission methods used within networks such as unicast, broadcast, and multicast. It also introduces basic hardware components, but later chapters such as Chapter 8 and Chapter 9 cover some of these hardware components in much more depth.

A network uses protocols as the rules of communication, and this chapter introduces the basics of network protocols. It also introduces some basic network zones such as the Internet, an intranet, an extranet, and perimeter networks.

▶ **Comparing unicast, broadcast, and multicast traffic**

▶ **Understanding network hardware**

▶ **Exploring protocols and services**

▶ **Understanding basic topologies**

Comparing Unicast, Broadcast, and Multicast Traffic

Before digging in too deep into the different physical devices used on networks, it's important to understand the different types of data transmission. Data is transmitted to and from hosts on networks using one of three transmission types:

▶ Unicast

▶ Broadcast

▶ Multicast

Chapter 5 explains IPv4, and Chapter 6 explains IPv6 addresses in more depth.

Further, data is transmitted using IP addresses. Regular mail uses home and business addresses to address letters and other correspondence. As long as the address is correct, the correspondence arrives. Similarly, computers and other network devices use IP addresses. A typical IPv4 address used in an internal network looks like this: 192.168.1.10.

Chapter 1 introduced IEEE standards. The primary standard used in Microsoft networks is *Ethernet*, defined by IEEE 802.3 (and the associated subsections of 802.3). Ethernet is a group of technologies used to connect networks using media such as twisted-pair and fiber-optic connections. Wireless connections are defined by 802.11. Although many more networking standards exist, the focus in this chapter is on Ethernet, with a little bit of wireless. The transmission types described in this section apply to Ethernet.

Understanding Unicast Traffic

Unicast traffic is one-to-one traffic.

Unicast traffic is traffic sent from one computer to one other computer. On a typical organization's network, most other computers won't even receive the unicast traffic that isn't addressed to them. For example, consider two computers connected with a switch. The data sent from one computer goes to the switch, and the switch then sends it to only the destination computer.

If a hub is used to connect the computers, the traffic will go to all the computers connected to that hub since the hub isn't as sophisticated as the switch. However, the network interface card (NIC) on the computers will recognize the unicast traffic is not addressed to them, and they won't process the data.

Depending on the type of traffic that is being transmitted, you could call the traffic a protocol data unit (PDU), segment, packet or datagram, or frame. For simplicity sake, this section limits the discussion to packets.

Consider Figure 2.1, which shows four computers on the network. If Bob's computer sends a unicast packet to Sally's computer, the packet won't reach Joe or Maria's computers or won't be processed by these other computers. Bob's computer transmits the unicast packet. Only Sally's computer will process the unicast transmission.

When the packet reaches a computer, the network interface card examines the packet to determine whether it is addressed to it. Even if the traffic reaches one of the other computers (Joe's or Maria's), the network interface card will determine the traffic is not addressed to the computer and the packet won't be processed.

Different devices such as routers and switches within a network also examine the packet to ensure it reaches its ultimate destination. These devices are presented later in this chapter with some basic information on how they handle unicast traffic.

Packets, Frames, Datagrams, and PDUs

Data is packaged together in a specific format before it's transmitted. You'll often hear the term *packets* to refer to this packaged data. Although the term *packets* is common, it is not always technically accurate.

Chapter 3 presents the Open Systems Interconnection (OSI) model, which has seven layers: Application, Presentation, Session, Transport, Network, Data-Link, and Physical. Technically, a packet is only data transferred on the Network layer of the OSI model. Similarly, data transferred on the Data-Link layer is a frame. Data transferred on the Transport layer is a segment. Data transferred on the upper three layers (Application, Presentation, and Session) is a protocol data unit (PDU).

As you dig deeper into your network studies, you'll need to be able to differentiate between packets, frames, datagrams, and PDUs. For now, the terms packet and packets refer to any data transferred on the network.

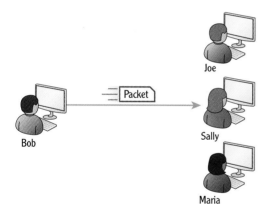

FIGURE 2.1 Unicast: one to one

Understanding Broadcast Traffic

Broadcast traffic is transmitted by one computer and goes to all computers within a subnet. Notice the clarification, though. A broadcast packet doesn't go to all computers in the world, but instead it goes to all the computers in a subnet.

You may remember from Chapter 1 that a subnet is a group of computers separated from other computers by one or more routers. Another way of saying this is that broadcast traffic goes to all computers on the same side of a router.

◄

Broadcast traffic is one-to-all traffic, on a subnet.

For example, consider Figure 2.2. Bob's computer is broadcasting a packet on the network, and each of the computers on the subnet will receive and process the packet.

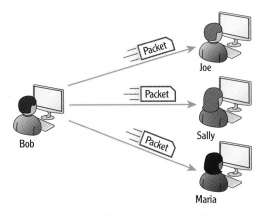

FIGURE 2.2 Broadcast: one to all

Notice that there is a slight difference in the language defining a unicast packet and a broadcast packet. This difference is important.

▶ Unicast traffic is one-to-one traffic between two computers on a network (not just on a subnet).

▶ Broadcast traffic is traffic sent from one computer to all other computers on a subnet (not the entire network).

ROUTERS AND BROADCAST EXCEPTIONS

What is consistent with almost all rules is that there are exceptions. This is true with routers and broadcast transmissions.

First, let's repeat the rule. Routers do not pass broadcasts. Routers separate subnets, and broadcasts in one subnet will not reach computers in another subnet.

Except...it is possible to program a router to pass broadcasts.

For example, consider the Dynamic Host Configuration Protocol (DHCP). A DHCP server provides IP addresses and other information to DHCP clients. Both the DHCP clients and DHCP server use a special type of broadcast known as a BootP broadcast. Routers can be programmed to pass these broadcasts on UDP ports 67 and 68. This allows a single DHCP server to serve multiple DHCP clients even if they are on separate subnets.

All the computers on the subnet will receive a broadcast packet. However, if the network has more than one subnet, all the computers on the network will not receive the packet. In other words, broadcast traffic does not cross subnets. Routers separate subnets, so another way of saying this is that routers do not forward broadcasts.

Computers are connected within a subnet using hubs or switches. Both hubs and switches *do* pass broadcast traffic.

You can think of a broadcast similar to how one person in a room can yell something and everyone in the room can hear it. Compare this to a unicast message, where one person whispers something so that only one other person hears it.

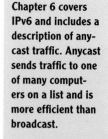

Chapter 6 covers IPv6 and includes a description of any-cast traffic. Anycast sends traffic to one of many comput-ers on a list and is more efficient than broadcast.

Understanding Multicast Traffic

Multicast traffic is transmitted from one computer to many other computers. When a computer joins a multicast group, the NIC is internally configured to process traffic using the multicast group's IP address. Now, when traffic is multi-cast to the multicast group, any computers that have joined the multicast group will receive and process the packet. Multicast traffic will pass to different subnets.

Multicast traffic is one-to-many traffic on a network.

Consider Figure 2.3. Multicast traffic sent by Bob's computer will reach multiple computers. In this scenario, Joe and Maria's computers have joined the multicast group, and they will receive the traffic. Sally's computer has not joined the multi-cast group and will not receive the traffic.

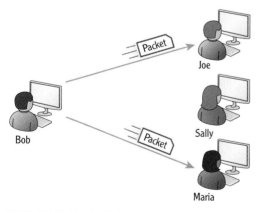

FIGURE 2.3 Multicast: one to many

In most network configurations, the multicast traffic won't even reach Sally's computer. However, even if it does, the NIC will determine that the traffic is not destined for Sally's computer, and the packet won't be processed.

Internet Group Multicast Protocol (IGMP) is the primary protocol used to transmit and process multicast traffic.

Understanding Network Hardware

▶

Networks can be either wired or wireless. Wired networks have cables, but wireless networks connect using radio frequency broadcasts.

Computers are connected within a network using several networking components. Computers have network interface cards. Cables connect the wired network interface cards on the computers to network devices such as switches. Routers connect the different subnets on a network.

Before going too far, it's important to understand some basic terms:

Collision Domain   A *collision domain* is group of devices on the same segment that are subject to collisions. Collisions occur when two devices on the same segment send traffic at the same time. In other words, only one device can send data at any given time. If a collision occurs, both devices must then resend the data. Collisions are not good, and excessive collisions degrade the network performance.

▶

In this context, a *segment* is a common connection between multiple computers.

Broadcast Domain   A *broadcast domain* is a group of devices on a network that can receive broadcast traffic from each other. In other words, if one device sends a broadcast packet, all other devices in the broadcast domain will receive it. Broadcasts are necessary, but it's useful to limit the number of computers in a broadcast domain.

Different devices are used to create separate collision domains and separate broadcast domains. Although the following sections cover many devices, it's important to understand how switches and routers are related to collision and broadcast domains:

Switches   *Switches* connect computers in a network. Switches create separate collision domains. A switch passes broadcast traffic to all connections so it does not separate broadcast domains.

Routers   *Routers* connect networks. Routers do not pass broadcast traffic. Routers create both separate collision domains and separate broadcast domains.

This section covers the following devices and components:

- ▶ Hubs
- ▶ Switches
- ▶ Bridges
- ▶ Routers
- ▶ Firewalls
- ▶ Media (such as cables)

Understanding Hubs

Hubs provide basic connectivity for devices in a network. Although these were once common devices on Ethernet networks, switches have replaced them in most networks today. A hub doesn't have any intelligence, and any data that is sent to one port is forwarded to all ports.

A port in this context is a physical connection. You plug one end of the cable into the port of the hub, and you plug the other end of the cable into the network interface card on the computer.

Consider Figure 2.4, which shows a four-port hub with different computers connected to the different ports. If Bob's computer sends a unicast packet to Sally's computer, the same packet will also reach Joe and Maria's computers. The NIC on Joe's and Maria's computers will recognize the packet is not destined for them, so the traffic won't be processed by their computers. However, the traffic can cause collisions if either Joe or Maria is trying to send data at the same time.

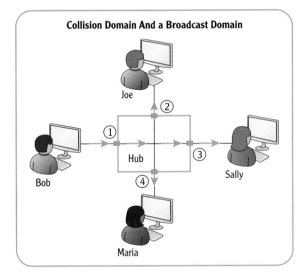

FIGURE 2.4 Four-port hub

This is a result of all these computers being in the same collision domain. Also, hubs forward broadcasts so all of these computers are in the same broadcast domain.

As mentioned previously, collision domains and broadcast domains are important topics. If you can reduce the number of collisions in a network, it performs better.

You may still see some hubs in networks today. For example, some USB hubs are popular in smaller networks.

Ports can be physical or logical. A physical port is a physical connection on a network device. A logical port is a number used to identify a protocol or service.

Switches allow you to create more collision domains, reduce collisions, and improve network performance.

Figure 2.4 shows a four-port hub, so there really isn't that much extra traffic on this network. However, when hubs were popular in production environments, they would often have 24 or more ports. Additionally, it was common to daisy-chain multiple hubs together on the same network which would create large collision domains.

Understanding Switches

▶

Switches have multiple capabilities that can provide significant performance enhancements for any network. Chapter 8 presents switches in more depth.

Switches connect computers within a network similar to how hubs connect the computers. However, switches improve the performance of a network since they isolate the computers into separate collision domains.

Consider Figure 2.5, which shows a switch replacing the hub from Figure 2.4 (shown previously). Now, when Bob sends a unicast packet to Sally, the traffic reaches only Sally's computer. The packet will not reach either Joe's or Maria's computer, so it can't collide with data sent by these other computers.

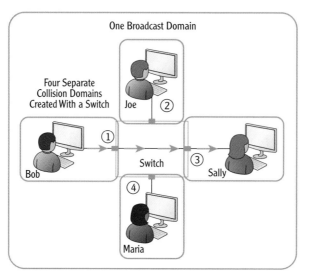

FIGURE 2.5 Four-port switch

The switch dynamically determines the destination port as traffic is received. In the first example, it determines that the traffic should flow from port 1 to port 3. However, if Maria's computer sends unicast traffic to Bob's computer, the switch makes a different determination and instead sends traffic from port 4 to port 1.

Since the switch can dynamically determine which port to send traffic through, it effectively has separated the computers into four separate collision domains. Since a switch passes broadcasts, all the computers connected via the switch are in a single broadcast domain.

Switches learn which computer is connected to which port. Chapter 8 explains the technical details of how this is done, but in short, the switch tracks the location of the computers. As each computer sends packets on the network through the switch, the switch then identifies the computer and the port that it's using. It maintains a table identifying the computers and their ports.

Switches track the location of computers connected on the switch's ports.

Understanding Bridges

A bridge is a network device that connects two or more network segments together. Any of the segments can have one or more computers on it. For example, one segment could have 10 computers connected together with a hub, and another segment could have another 5 computers connected together with a different hub.

Bridges aren't as common in networks anymore, but you may still run across them. A bridge is similar to a switch in that it will learn which port a computer is connected to and will internally switch traffic to the right port. The separate ports create separate collision domains.

However, multiple computers are connected to each port on a bridge. Separate hubs connect these computers together, and then the hub is connected to the bridge. The alternative is to daisy-chain each of the hubs together to create a single collision domain.

For example, imagine that four 24 port hubs are used to connect 96 computers in a single network. This results in a collision domain of 96 computers where 96 computers are all competing to send their data on the network.

Instead, a bridge can connect these four hubs, as shown in Figure 2.6. The bridge creates four separate collision domains of 24 computers each. Computers on each of these separate collision domains are only competing with 23 other computers to send their data, instead of 95 other computers.

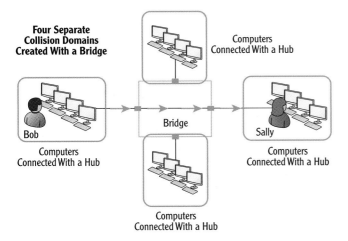

FIGURE 2.6 Four-port bridge creating four collision domains

Another benefit of bridges is that they can connect dissimilar physical topologies. For example, one port can connect computers using twisted-pair cables, and another port can connect computers using fiber-optic connections. Both wired and wireless bridges also exist. Wireless bridges are commonly used to connect a wireless access point (WAP) to another type of device on a wired network.

Understanding Routers

Routers track subnets within a network. In comparison, switches track computers on a subnet.

Routers are used to move packets between networks or subnets. Switches (or hubs) connect the devices within the subnet, and routers connect the subnets. You may remember from the previous section that switches track computers. However, routers do not track individual computers but instead track networks or subnets within a network.

Consider Figure 2.7, which shows subnet A with two computers connected via a hub. Subnet B has four computers connected with a switch.

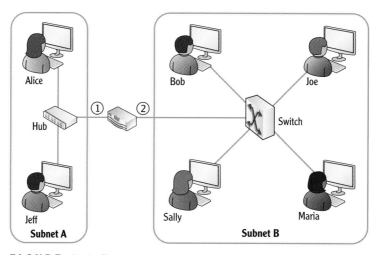

FIGURE 2.7 Two subnets connected by a router

Can you tell how many collision domains and how many broadcast domains are in this figure?

All the computers connected via the hub are on one collision domain. Each of the users connected to the switch makes up four more collision domains. Last, the connection between the router and the switch make up a sixth collision domain. There are two subnets (subnet A and subnet B), and each subnet is a separate broadcast domain.

Routers direct, or route, traffic throughout a network. When a router receives a packet, it identifies the best path for the packet to take in order for it to arrive at the final destination. In Figure 2.7, there are only two subnets, so the router doesn't have to make many decisions.

However, consider Figure 2.8, which is a multiple subnet network connected via several routers. The routers learn the locations of all the subnets and determine the best path to take to get traffic to its destination.

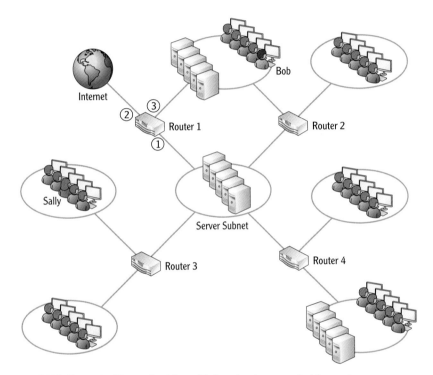

FIGURE 2.8 Network with multiple subnets separated by routers

For example, what if Sally wants to access the Internet? How many routers will she have to go through to get to the Internet? How about Bob? Notice Sally has to go through two routers (router 3 and router 1), while Bob has to go through only one router. Although that's easy to see in the diagram, the routers do a lot of work to learn these paths.

One way that routers determine the best path to take is by talking to each other. Routers use different types of routing protocols that help them learn the network and the paths to different subnets. Some routing protocols are used only in internal networks, while other routing protocols are used only on the Internet.

Chapter 9 covers routers in more depth, including the use of routing protocols.

ROUTERS AND DEFAULT GATEWAYS

Each computer on a subnet is configured with an IP address of the router. However, in this context it isn't called a router but is instead called the *default gateway.*

If you look at Figure 2.7, computers on subnet A use the IP address of port 1 of the router as their default gateway. Computers on subnet B use the IP address of port 2 of the router as their default gateway.

Figure 2.8 shows multiple routers with a subnet in the center (labeled as a server subnet). The server subnet connects with four separate subnets. However, computers can be configured with only one default gateway.

The default gateway often provides a path to the Internet. Therefore, computers in the server subnet will most likely be configured with the IP address of port 1 of router 1.

Understanding Firewalls

Firewalls provide a layer of protection for computers and networks by keeping malicious or unwanted traffic from flowing in or out of a network. The most basic *firewall* is simply a router with rules. These rules control both inbound and outbound traffic.

Consider a firewall in an automobile. It's located between the engine compartment and the passenger compartment. If a fire starts in the engine, the firewall prevents the fire from coming into the passenger compartment, or at least slows it down. Similarly, firewall rules prevent undesirable traffic from entering or leaving a network.

Firewalls can be network-based or host-based. Look at Figure 2.9 as you review these two types:

Network-Based Firewall   A network-based firewall provides protection for an entire network. Most networks have at least one firewall between the Internet and the internal network. This firewall filters all traffic in and out of the network. Network-based firewalls are a combination of hardware and software.

Host-Based Firewall   Many systems include individual firewalls also known as host-based firewalls. For example, Microsoft Windows 7 and Microsoft Windows Server 2008 servers (and many other desktop and server operating systems) include a software firewall. This software firewall filters traffic that passes in or out of the system. Additionally, security software suites often include software-based firewalls.

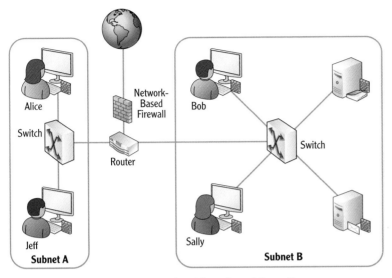

FIGURE 2.9 Network-based and host-based firewalls

NETWORK-BASED FIREWALL, HOST-BASED FIREWALL, OR BOTH?

As a best practice, most organizations enable both network-based and host-based firewalls. A common question is, "Is a host-based firewall really needed if a network-based firewall is used?" The answer is yes.

Not all malicious traffic comes from the Internet. If someone inadvertently releases malicious software on an internal network (perhaps by plugging in an infected USB), the network-based firewall doesn't provide any protection.

However, if each internal computer has a host-based firewall, the internal computers have an added layer of protection. This is a common security principle known as *defense in depth*.

Basic firewalls filter traffic based on the contents of packets such as source and destination IP addresses. Advanced firewalls can examine all the traffic in a session and make decisions based on the session traffic. Chapter 11 digs into firewalls in more depth, including advanced firewalls. Advanced firewalls can examine all of the packets within a session and analyze the conversation. Basic firewalls can only analyze individual packets.

Understanding Media

Routers connect networks together. Switches and hubs connect computing devices together. All of these devices are connected together using some type of transmission media.

Today's networks use twisted-pair, fiber-optic, and wireless connections. Both twisted-pair and fiber-optic media are cables you can touch. However, wireless connections use transceivers to transmit and receive radio frequency transmissions over the air.

Twisted pair is used for short distances up to 100 meters. Fiber-optic runs can be as long as 2 km for multimode fiber and up to 40 km for single-mode fiber. Wireless networks are primarily used within buildings.

The most common type of transmission media is twisted pair. Twisted-pair cables can be wired as either a straight-through cable or a crossover cable.

Straight-Through Cable   Wires are connected to the same pins on both connectors of a *straight-through* cable. A straight-through cable connects computers to networking devices. For example, it would connect a computer to a hub or a computer to a switch.

Figure 2.10 shows the wiring diagram of a straight-through cable. Just as the name implies, the connections are straight through end to end and each wire is connected on the same pins on both ends. The colors of the cable are based on the T568B standard.

Crossover Cable   Specific wires are crossed on opposite connectors of the *crossover cable*. A crossover cable connects similar devices to each other. For example, you would use a crossover cable to connect any two networking devices together such as the following:

- ▶ A switch and a switch
- ▶ A switch and a hub
- ▶ A switch and a router
- ▶ A computer and a computer

Figure 2.11 shows the wiring diagram for a crossover twisted-pair cable. The straight-through cable has the pairs connected from the same pins on one side to the same pins on the other side. However, the crossover cable crosses over some key wires so that transmit signals on one side go to receive on the other side.

You can easily identify a crossover cable by placing both connectors of the same cable side by side. If the orange and green pairs are swapped, it's a crossover cable.

▶

Chapter 7 covers the details of twisted-pair and fiber connections. Chapter 12 covers the details of wireless networking.

▶

Many modern routers and switches autosense the connection. In other words, if the connection needs a crossover cable, the wiring is internally changed.

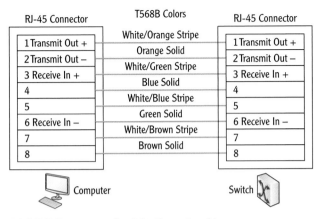

FIGURE 2.10 Straight-through cable

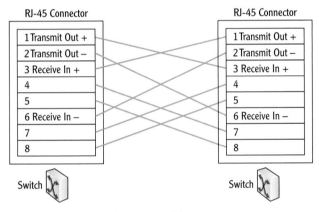

FIGURE 2.11 Crossover cable

T568A or T568B

An older wiring standard is T568A. The primary difference between T568A and T568B is that the colored pairs go to different pins. In T568A, the orange and green pairs are located on different pins than they are with T568B. Specifically, the orange pair is moved to pins 3 and 6 (pin 3 is white/orange, and pin 6 is orange), and the green pair is moved to pins 1 and 2 (pin 1 is white/green, and pin 2 is green).

It really doesn't matter which standard you use as long as the same standard is used on both ends of the cable. If you have one end wired as T568A and the other end as T568B, you have created a crossover cable.

Exploring Protocols and Services

Protocols provide the rules that computers and other devices use to communicate with other computers and devices on networks. As long as the computers are able to follow the rules, they can access resources on the network.

If devices don't follow the rules of the protocols, they simply aren't able to communicate properly on the network. Obviously, computers don't "break the rules" of the protocols just to see what they can get away with. However, if users or administrators accidentally misconfigure the protocols, it has the same effect— the misconfigured system won't function properly on the network.

Services are processes that run on a computer without any user interaction. In comparison, a user launches an application. Many of the services will start when a computer is first started and before the user is able to do anything. Other services start later either based on a delay or when needed.

Exploring Protocols

> As a reminder, the Internet Engineering Task Force (IETF) defines the protocols used on the Internet using requests for comments (RFCs) documents.

Network protocols are formally defined in official documents by standards organizations. For example, RFC 791 defines the IPv4 protocol used on the Internet and internal networks.

The primary protocol suite in use today is *Transmission Control Protocol/Internet Protocol (TCP/IP)*. It is used on the Internet and most internal networks including Microsoft networks.

Notice that this isn't a single protocol or even just the two protocols of TCP and IP. It's a full suite of protocols. When a computer wants to access a website on the Internet, it uses Hypertext Transfer Protocol (HTTP). Email is transferred using Simple Mail Transfer Protocol (SMTP), Post Office Protocol version 3 (POP3), or Internet Message Access Protocol version 4 (IMAP4). Similarly, there are other protocols for other uses.

Although you don't need to understand the inner workings of these protocols at this stage of your learning, you should be aware of the primary protocols used to communicate within networks and on the Internet. As your networking knowledge increases, you'll need to know what protocols should be enabled to perform specific functions and what protocols are not needed.

Administrators commonly configure many protocols on networks. For example, IP addresses are manually assigned to many devices such as routers and servers within a network. Additionally, Dynamic Host Configuration Protocol can be configured on a network to dynamically assign IP addresses and other TCP/IP information.

Chapter 3 introduces many of primary protocols you should know about and maps these protocols to the OSI model. Chapter 4 digs into these TCP/IP protocols a little deeper.

Understanding Services

Many of the services running on Windows systems provide network capabilities. For example, the DHCP client service on a DHCP client computer obtains an IP address and other TCP/IP configuration information from a DHCP server over the network.

Figure 2.12 shows the Services applet in Windows Server 2008. The Windows Firewall service is selected, and you can see that the current status is Started. Also, Startup Type is set to Automatic, meaning that it will automatically start when Windows starts.

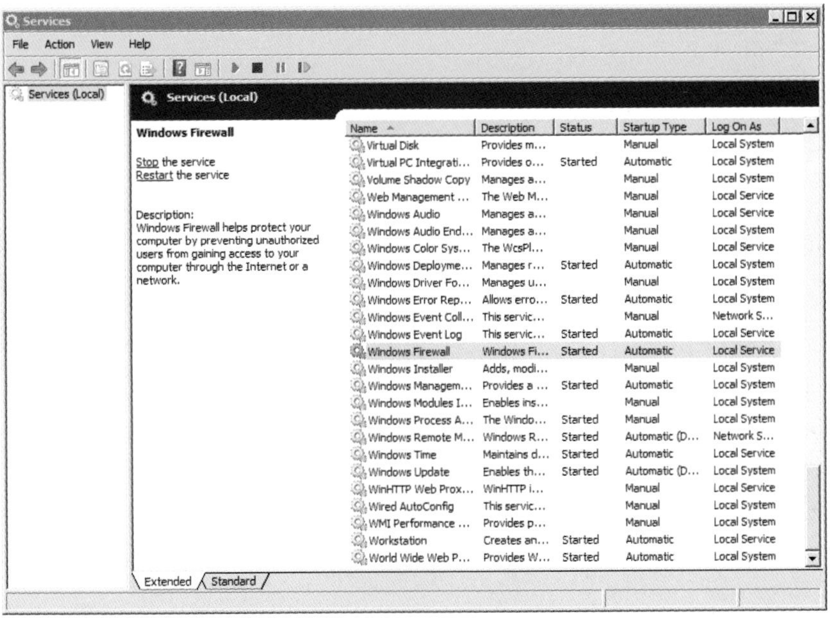

◄

Windows Server 2008 has about 120 default services, and a typical installation has more than 50 starting by default.

FIGURE 2.12 Services applet

You can access the Services applet in Windows Server 2008 by clicking Start, entering **Services** in the Start Search text box, and clicking Services.

The different startup types for services are as follows:

Automatic   The service will automatically start when the computer boots. The user is not able to interact with the system until all services set to Automatic have started.

Automatic (Delayed Start)   The service will automatically start after all services set to Automatic have started. Users are able to interact with the system before these services start.

Manual   The service starts when required. The service can be started by other services, applications, or the user.

Disabled   The service cannot start. Unneeded services are set to disabled but can be enabled if it is later determined that the service is needed.

Understanding Basic Topologies

Chapter 1 presented the terms LAN and WAN. A local area network (LAN) is a group of computers and other devices connected together in a single physical location. A wide area network (WAN) connects two or more LANs over a larger distance.

It's also important to understand the differences between an *intranet*, the Internet, a *perimeter network*, and an *extranet*. Consider Figure 2.13, which shows each of these topologies.

> Chapter 11 digs deeper into intranet, extranet, and perimeter network configurations. These different topologies create different security zones.

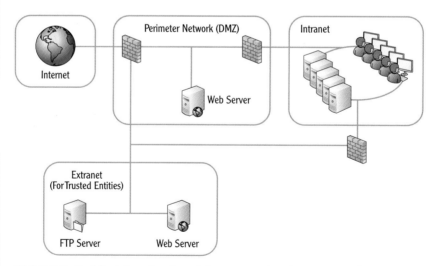

FIGURE 2.13 Internet, extranet, intranet, and perimeter network

> Computers on internal networks may be able to access the Internet, but they aren't directly connected it. These computers have a layer of protection from other computers on the Internet.

Internet   Unless you grew up in a cave, you've used the Internet. It's a massive network of computers connecting millions of smaller networks. The Internet uses the TCP/IP protocol suite. Computers connected to the Internet are able to reach any other computer on the Internet no matter where they are in the world.

Intranet   An intranet is an internal network using the TCP/IP protocol suite. The primary difference between an intranet and the Internet is that an intranet is private. Users on the Internet are not able to communicate directly with computers in an intranet. Computers within an intranet have a higher level of trust amongst themselves than computers on the Internet.

Perimeter network   A *perimeter network* is a network between the Internet and the intranet. Firewalls filter the traffic to servers in the perimeter network. Servers in the perimeter network may be accessible by a user on the Internet. However, the firewall does limit the type of traffic allowed to these servers.

◀

A perimeter network is also called a *demilitarized zone* (DMZ).

Extranet   An extranet is similar to a perimeter network. However, the biggest difference is in the intent. Servers on the extranet are accessible only to trusted entities such as trusted business partners or specific customers or vendors. These trusted entities can access the extranet via the Internet. Different methods and technologies ensure that nontrusted entities are not able to access servers on the extranet. Notice that users in the intranet also have access to resources in the extranet. However, the firewall will prevent users in the extranet from accessing resources in the intranet.

THE ESSENTIALS AND BEYOND

This chapter provided an overview of many basic networking components. You learned the basics of unicast, broadcast, and multicast transmissions. You also learned basics on how hubs and switches connect computers and how routers connect networks. Networks are connected using different types of media such as twisted pair, fiber optic, or wireless. Protocols are the rules used by devices to communicate. The protocol suite used on the Internet and Microsoft networks is TCP/IP.

ADDITIONAL EXERCISES

▶ Identify the type of media used in your network. Is it fiber optic, twisted pair, or wireless?

▶ Identify the types of network devices used in your network.

▶ Draw a logical network diagram. The diagram should include servers that are available to trusted partners via the Internet.

▶ Identify whether a computer you are using has a firewall enabled.

To compare your answers to the author's, please visit **www.sybex.com/go/ networkingessentials**.

(Continues)

THE ESSENTIALS AND BEYOND *(Continued)*

REVIEW QUESTIONS

1. What type of traffic always goes to all devices in a subnet?

    A. Unicast   **C.** Broadcast

    B. Multicast   **D.** Allcast

2. True or false. A switch blocks broadcasts.

3. What is the difference between a switch and a router?

    A. Nothing. They are the same.

    B. Switches do not pass broadcasts, but routers do.

    C. A switch connects devices together, and a router connects subnets together.

    D. A switch connects subnets together, and a router connects devices together.

4. True or false. Bridges can connect dissimilar physical topologies.

5. A firewall uses _____ to filter both inbound and outbound traffic.

6. A network-based firewall is a hardware device that provides protection for a network. What is a host-based firewall?

7. True or False. A crossover cable is used to connect a computer to a switch.

8. Which of the following standards define how twisted-pair cables should be wired?

    A. IEEE 802.3   **C.** Extranet wiring practices

    B. RFC 791   **D.** T568B

9. A company wants to host a web server for Internet users. The web server should be placed in _____.

10. What is used to provide access to a company's resources via the Internet to trusted partners?

## CHAPTER 3

Understanding the OSI Model

The Open Systems Interconnection (OSI) Model is one of the most referenced models in networking. It includes seven layers with specific activities, protocols, and devices working on each. Many network exams test your knowledge of the different elements of the OSI Model, and even some hiring managers quiz potential network employees on their knowledge. The TCP/IP Model is similar but includes only four layers instead of seven. This chapter introduces both models.

▶ **Understanding the OSI Model**

▶ **Understanding the TCP/IP Model**

▶ **Mapping devices on the OSI and TCP/IP models**

▶ **Mapping protocols on the OSI and TCP/IP models**

Understanding the OSI Model

> ▶
>
> **The OSI Model is a framework for network communication. The ISO created it, and it includes seven layers.**

The seven-layer *Open Systems Interconnection (OSI)* model is a general framework, or set of guidelines, for network communication. It defines how data is handled at several different layers. It also identifies the framework of TCP/IP protocols and hardware used on networks. There is no single standard or compliance test for the OSI Model itself. Instead, many standards have been created based on the different elements of the model.

Figure 3.1 shows the seven layers of the OSI Model. One of the primary goals of the OSI Model is operating system independence. In other words, the OSI Model allows computers running any operating system to communicate with other computers.

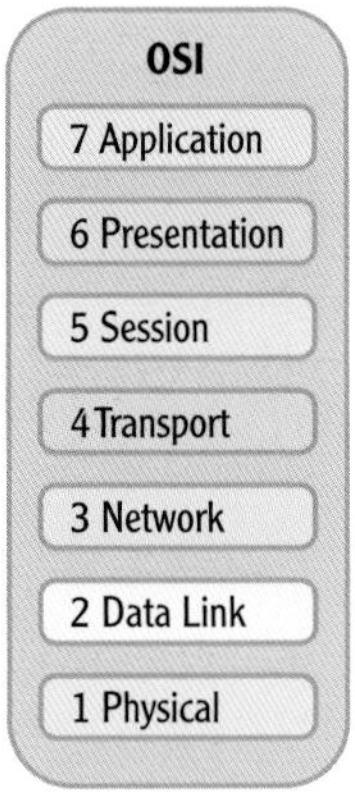

FIGURE 3.1 The OSI Model

The ISO may look like a typo. However, it's not an acronym for the International Organization for Standardization. Instead, ISO is derived from *isos*, which is Greek for equal.

The OSI Model was created by the International Organization for Standardization (ISO). The following are many advantages to the OSI Model:

Layers Interact Only with Adjoining Layers   For example, the Transport layer interacts with the Session and Network layers only. It doesn't matter to the Session layer what applications are used on the Application layer. Similarly, it doesn't matter to the Session layer what type of cable media is used to transmit the data on the Physical layer.

It Has Encouraged Creation of Industry Standards   Functions at each layer are standardized. Development of network components by different vendors is simplified, and different operating systems are able to communicate with other.

Network Communication Processes Are Segmented   Instead of a single protocol that does everything, multiple protocols are used. Troubleshooting is easier once the OSI Model is understood.

You should know the names and number of each layer. Figure 3.2 shows two commonly used memory techniques.

Notice that one method (All People Seem To Need Data Processing) starts at layer 7 and goes to layer 1. The other method (Please Do Not Throw Sausage Pizza Away) starts on layer 1 and goes to layer 7. There are many other sayings used by technicians to memorize these layers. The technique you use isn't as important as using some method to memorize it.

Of course, just knowing the names and numbers of the layers isn't all you need to know. You should also have a basic understanding of what happens at each layer.

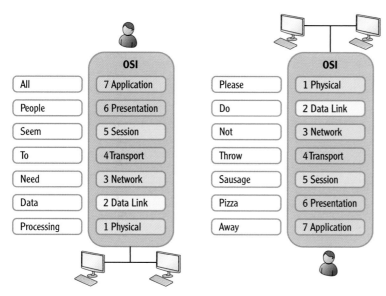

FIGURE 3.2 Mnemonics and the OSI Model

Application Layer

Layer 7 is the *Application layer*. It interacts with the Presentation layer and the end user. Several protocols operate on the Application layer:

Domain Name System (DNS)   DNS is the primary name resolution service used on the Internet and in Microsoft networks. DNS resolves host names to IP addresses. In other words, you can pass the name of a server (such as DC1) to DNS, and DNS will return the IP address. DNS is also used to locate servers running specific services within a Microsoft network.

Hypertext Transfer Protocol (HTTP)   HTTP is the primary protocol used to transmit data across the Internet for web pages. Similarly, HTTPS is a secure version of HTTP used to transmit data in an encrypted format.

File Transfer Protocol (FTP)   FTP is the protocol used to transfer files to and from an FTP server. FTP servers are commonly hosted on the Internet. In contrast, file servers are used on internal networks to host files needed by users.

Trivial FTP (TFTP)   TFTP is a lightweight FTP protocol used to transfer smaller files. TFTP is often used to transfer files to network devices such as routers.

Dynamic Host Configuration Protocol (DHCP)   DHCP is a method of dynamically assigning TCP/IP configuration information to clients. A DHCP server assigns IP

DNS is a required service in Microsoft domains and is heavily used on the Internet. Chapter 10 presents name resolution and DNS in greater depth.

DHCP saves a lot of labor and is found in most networks. Chapter 5 covers DHCP in more depth.

addresses to systems. It also assigns the subnet mask, the address of the default gateway (a router), the address of a DNS server, the domain name, and much more.

Lightweight Directory Access Protocol (LDAP) LDAP is a protocol used to query a directory service, such as Microsoft's Active Directory Domain Services (AD DS). AD DS is hosted on domain controllers.

Post Office Protocol (POP3) POP3 is an email protocol used to retrieve email from POP3 email servers. POP3 servers are commonly hosted by Internet service providers (ISPs).

Simple Mail Transfer Protocol (SMTP) SMTP is an email protocol used to send email. Clients can send email from an email server. When a POP3 email server is used, users receive email with POP3 and send email with SMTP.

Internet Message Access Protocol (IMAP) IMAP is a protocol used to receive email messages. An IMAP server allows clients to store and manage their email on the server. Users can download the email onto their computer or organize the email in different folders on the server.

Simple Network Management Protocol (SNMP) SNMP is a protocol used to manage network devices such as routers and managed switches. It can detect and report problems before they become significant.

Server Message Block (SMB) SMB is a file transfer protocol used on Microsoft networks. It's primarily used for file and printer sharing.

The Application layer determines whether sufficient network resources are available for network access. For example, if you want to use Internet Explorer to access a web page on the Internet, the Application layer determines whether access to the Internet is available using HTTP.

It's worth pointing out that the Application layer doesn't refer to end user applications. For example, applications such as Internet Explorer are not part of this layer and aren't actually part of the OSI Model at all. However, when the user launches an application that needs network access, protocols on the Application layer ensure that the resources are available to support it.

Presentation Layer

The *Presentation layer* interacts with the Session and Application layers. In essence, it acts as a translator and determines how to format and present the data.

A common method of formatting data is with the American Standard Code for Information Interchange (ASCII) table. This table includes 128 codes to display characters such as numbers, letters, and symbols. Table 3.1 shows a partial listing of the ASCII table.

TABLE 3.1   Partial ASCII table

Character	Decimal	Hexadecimal	Octal	HTML
A	65	41	101	&#65
B	66	42	102	&#66
C	67	43	103	&#67
a	97	61	141	&#97
b	98	62	142	&#98
c	99	63	143	&#99
1	49	31	061	&#49
2	50	32	062	&#50
3	51	33	063	&#51

Many other codes beyond ASCII are defined at the Presentation layer. For example, the Extended Binary Coded Decimal Interchange Code (EBCDIC) extended the ASCII table from 128 characters to 256 characters. File types such as MP3, JPG, and GIF also have their own codes defined on this layer.

The Presentation layer is also responsible for data compression and decompression and data encryption and decryption. For example, multimedia transferred over the Internet is often compressed to conserve bandwidth. If it wasn't, the World Wide Web might be known as the World Wide Wait.

Session Layer

The *Session layer* has the responsibility of establishing, maintaining, and terminating sessions. A session is simply a lasting connection between two networking devices. For example, if you use a chat program on your computer, it will establish a session with another computer to exchange the data.

Another way of saying this is that the Session layer manages the connections. It starts the session, manages the traffic during the session, and terminates the session when appropriate.

The Session layer also ensures that data from different applications are kept separate for each application at the Application layer. This becomes critical when multiple applications are running or when applications require more than one resource.

For example, you may be having a chat session in one window, downloading music in another, and reading email in a third. Three sessions are established and maintained for three different applications. The Session layer ensures that resources are available for each session and kept separate from each other.

The Session layer also tracks the mode of transmission used by the computers. Computers can transmit data using simplex, half-duplex, or full-duplex modes:

Simplex Data can be sent only one way. This isn't commonly used today in networking applications.

Half-Duplex Data can be sent both ways but only one way at a time. This is similar to a walkie-talkie where one user can press a button to talk but cannot receive any transmissions while the button is pressed.

▶ Networking professionals sometimes use the terms *simplex* and *half-duplex* interchangeably. However, they are different.

Full-Duplex Data can be sent and received at the same time. Separate methods are used to send and receive.

The Session layer coordinates the communication and determines which mode to use. Two network protocols that operate on this layer are the Network Basic Input/Output System (NetBIOS) and Remote Procedure Call (RPC).

Transport Layer

The *Transport layer* is responsible for transporting data. It handles flow control, reliability, and error checking. The Transport layer divides data into smaller chunks, or *segments*, and then reassembles the received data.

▶ Data traveling on the Transport layer is referred to as *segments*.

For example, imagine you wanted to mail all volumes of Harry Potter to a friend in another state, but you could only use envelopes. You'd have to tear the pages from the books and mail them all separately. Your friend would then have to reassemble the books from all the envelopes.

This is similar to how data is managed on the Transport layer. Huge megabyte-sized files can't travel over the network. Instead, the Transport layer segments, or divides, these large files into smaller-sized segments. These smaller segments are transmitted over the network and then reassembled when they're received. The Transport layer also manages the ordering of the segments so that when the packets arrive, they can be returned to the same order.

Two primary protocols operate on the Transport layer:

▶ Chapter 4 covers TCP and UDP in more depth.

Transmission Control Protocol (TCP) TCP provides guaranteed delivery of data. It starts by establishing a session and will not transmit data until a session is established. TCP is commonly referred to as *connection-oriented*. This means that it establishes a session before transmitting data.

User Datagram Protocol (UDP) UDP provides a best-effort method of delivering data. It does not provide guaranteed delivery of data like TCP. UDP is referred to as *connection-less*. Again, this doesn't refer to the physical connections but instead indicates that data is sent without first verifying a connection with the other system. UDP is commonly used for media streaming and diagnostic messages. Instead of using the additional overhead to establish the connection or session, UDP accepts that there may be some data loss and simply transmits the data.

Port numbers identify details about data on the Transport layer. There are 65,536 possible TCP *ports* and another 65,536 possible UDP ports. Some protocols use both TCP and UDP ports, while others use only one or the other. In this context, a port is simply a number from 0 to 65,535 that is utilized by a protocol for connection purposes. It does not represent a physical port.

◄

Although port 0 is a valid port, it is reserved for both TCP and UDP.

For example, the HTTP protocol uses the well-known port of 80 by default. When you visit a website, you could use the HTTP address by itself as `http://www.bing.com/`. However, you could also include the port number as `http://www.bing.com:80`. Bing.com is the website, and once your request reaches the server hosting it, the TCP port of 80 identifies the data as HTTP traffic. The web server passes the data to the service handling the HTTP protocol.

In short, the IP address is used to get traffic from one computer to another. Once the traffic arrives, the port number is used to identify what application, service, or protocol should process the data.

LOGICAL AND PHYSICAL PORTS

The term *ports* means different things depending on the context. Ports can be either logical (numbers) or physical (connections on devices).

TCP and UDP ports are logical ports. They are simply numbers used to indicate how data is handled when it reaches its destination. Many ports represent specific protocols such as port 80 representing the well-known port of HTTP. Chapter 4 explores ports in greater depth.

Switches and routers have physical ports. Cables plug into these ports. A switch learns what computers are connected to each port, and a router learns what networks are connected to each port.

Network Layer

▶

Data traveling on the Network layer is referred to as *packets*.

The *Network layer* is responsible for determining the best route to a destination. It uses routing protocols to build routing tables and uses Internet Protocol (IP) as the routed protocol. IP addresses are used at this layer to ensure the data can get to its destination.

Several protocols operate at this layer:

Internet Protocol v4 (IPv4)   IPv4 is an addressing protocol using 32-bit addresses. The TCP/IP suite uses IP addressing to get traffic from one computer to another. IPv4 addresses are commonly expressed in dotted decimal format such as 192.168.1.1.

▶

Valid hexadecimal characters are 0 through 9 and A through F.

Internet Protocol v6 (IPv6)   IPv6 is an addressing protocol using 128-bit addresses. IPv6 is intended to replace IPv4 and is currently being used concurrently with IPv4 on networks throughout the world. IPv6 addresses are commonly expressed in hexadecimal format such as 2001:0000:4137:9E76:3C2B:05AD:3F57:FE98.

▶

The MAC address is a 48-bit address assigned to network interface cards. The MAC address is explained more in the "Data Link Layer" section of this chapter.

Address Resolution Protocol (ARP)   This protocol resolves IP addresses to the physical address or the Media Access Control (MAC) address. The IP address is used to route packets to the next hop's network interface card. Switches use MAC addresses to track computers connected to different physical ports. While ARP resolves the IP address to a MAC address, the Reverse Address Resolution Protocol (RARP) does the opposite. RARP can be used to resolve a MAC address to an IP address.

Internet Group Multicast Protocol (IGMP)   IGMP is used for multicasting traffic. Multicast traffic goes from one computer to multiple computers. As a reminder, unicast is one-to-one traffic, and broadcast is one-to-all traffic on the same subnet.

▶

Chapter 14 covers troubleshooting techniques using Ping, PathPing, and TraceRt.

Internet Control Message Protocol (ICMP)   ICMP is used for error messages and diagnostic reporting. Several diagnostic tools such as Ping, PathPing, TraceRt, and others use ICMP.

Internet Protocol Security (IPSec)   IPSec is a security protocol used to secure IP traffic. IPSec can encrypt traffic to protect it when it's transmitted. It also includes authentication mechanisms. IPSec authentication allows computers to ensure they communicate only with known entities.

Routing Information Protocol (RIP)   This is a basic routing protocol used by routers in internal networks. Routers use RIP to communicate with each other and share information on the network. The current version is RIPv2, though OSPF has replaced it on most networks.

Open Shortest Path First (OSPF)   OSPF is another routing protocol used by routers to communicate with each other on internal networks. OSPF is more advanced than RIP and is used in more networks.

The Network layer includes two key physical devices. The primary device working on this layer is a router. Routers are the devices that perform IP based routing functions. The router looks at the IP address and determines the best path to the destination network. Data packets are then sent to the destination using this path.

RIP and OSPF are common routing protocols used in internal networks. These two protocols determine the best route to a destination based on a metric (cost). The route with the best metric will have a lower cost and will be the selected route for IP.

This is similar to using a map for highways. You look at a map to determine the best route when traveling from point A to point B. The map provides the routing information, and you can identify the best path to get to your destination. Of course, maps are static and show only paths. They don't show construction, accidents, or other events that can slow traffic down. You may use other online tools to identify traffic congestion or areas of construction.

Routing protocols such as RIP and OSPF are dynamic protocols that can adjust to changing conditions on a network. Routers use these protocols to communicate with each other regularly. If network events occur that impact known routes or if new routes get added, the routing protocols are used to ensure that all the routers quickly learn about the impact.

◄

Layer 3 switches also operate on the Network layer (layer 3). Layer 3 switches combine the capabilities of layer 2 switches and routers. Chapter 8 covers switches in more depth.

Data Link Layer

The *Data Link layer* is concerned with data delivery on a local area network. This is where local area network (LAN) technologies such as Ethernet are defined. The Data Link layer is comprised of two sublayers.

◄

Data traveling on the Data Link layer is referred to as *frames*.

Logical Link Control (LLC) IEEE 802.2   LLC interacts directly with the network layer. It is defined by the IEEE 802.2 standard. LLC provides flow control and error control and allows multiple protocols to work simultaneously.

Media Access Control (MAC) IEEE 802.3   MAC defines how packets are placed onto the physical media at the Physical layer. IEEE 802.3 defines Carrier Sense Multiple Access/Collision Detection (CSMA/CD), which is used to handle data collisions.

MAC addresses are also defined at the Data Link layer. The MAC address is also called a *physical address, hardware address, burned-in address,* or *Ethernet address*. It used to be a permanent address that was written into, or burned into, the read-only-memory (ROM) chip on the network interface card (NIC), but it is usually stored on the NIC's firmware today.

Listing 3.1 shows the results of entering the command ipconfig /all at the command prompt of a server named DC1. This provides a lot of information including the physical address (or MAC address) of the NIC. Notice that it has an address of A4-BA-DB-FA-60-AD.

Listing 3.1 Output of ipconfig /all

```
C:\>ipconfig /all

Windows IP Configuration

    Host Name . . . . . . . . . . . . : DC1
    Primary Dns Suffix . . . . . . . : Sybex.pub
    Node Type . . . . . . . . . . . : Hybrid
    IP Routing Enabled. . . . . . . . : No
    WINS Proxy Enabled. . . . . . . . : No
    DNS Suffix Search List. . . . . . : Sybex.pub

Ethernet adapter Local Area Connection:

    Connection-specific DNS Suffix . :
    Description . . . . . . . . . . . : Realtek RTL8168C(P)/8111C(P)
Family PCI-E
    Gigabit Ethernet NIC (NDIS 6.20)
    Physical Address. . . . . . . . . : A4-BA-DB-FA-60-AD
    DHCP Enabled. . . . . . . . . . . : No
    Autoconfiguration Enabled . . . . : Yes
    IPv4 Address. . . . . . . . . . . : 192.168.1.205(Preferred)
    Subnet Mask . . . . . . . . . . . : 255.255.255.0
    Default Gateway . . . . . . . . . : 192.168.1.1
    DNS Servers . . . . . . . . . . . : 127.0.0.1
    NetBIOS over Tcpip. . . . . . . . : Disabled
```

OTHER DEVICES HAVE MAC ADDRESSES

Although the code snippet shows the physical address of a NIC on a server, other devices also have MAC addresses. For example, each interface on a router has a separate MAC address. These MAC addresses at the Data Link layer are then mapped to an IP address assigned at the Network layer.

The MAC is represented with 12 hexadecimal characters (or 6 pairs of hexadecimal characters). Four bits represent each hexadecimal character. Four bits times 12 characters shows that the MAC address is 48 bits long.

Every device on a network has a different MAC address. If MAC addresses on the network aren't unique, the computers with the same MAC address can't communicate on the network.

Organizations that manufacture NICs are assigned an organizationally unique identifier (OUI) that they use in the MAC. They then use serial numbers added to this OUI to create the MAC. Table 3.2 shows how these numbers are combined to create the MAC address of A4-BA-DB-FA-60-AD.

TABLE 3.2 MAC address

Organizationally unique identifier	Manufacturer serial number
AA-BA-DB	FA-60-AD
Six hexadecimal characters (24 bits)	Six hexadecimal characters (24 bits)

These are some of the protocols that operate on the Data Link layer:

Point-to-Point Tunneling Protocol v4 (PPTP)   PPTP is commonly used with virtual private networks (VPNs). VPNs provide remote users with access to a private network over a public connection such as the Internet.

◄ Chapter 13 covers VPNs in more depth.

Layer 2 Tunneling Protocol (L2TP)   L2TP is another protocol used with VPNs. It often uses IPSec (as L2TP/IPSec) to encrypt the traffic.

Token ring   IEEE 802.5 defines a token ring technology. A logical token is passed between the computers, and a computer can communicate on the network only when it has the token. Using the token for communication prevents collisions.

Asynchronous Transfer Mode (ATM)   ATM is a cell-based method of transferring data. Data is converted into small fixed-sized cells and transferred over the network. ATM is used in WANs.

Frame relay   Frame relay is another WAN technology. Data is converted to variable-sized frames and transferred over permanent virtual circuits.

Physical devices operating on the Data Link layer include bridges, switches, and NICs.

◄ NICs also operate on the Physical layer.

Physical Layer

The *Physical layer* defines the physical specifications of the network. This includes physical media such as cables and connectors. It also includes basic devices such as repeaters and hubs. The Physical layer converts the data stream into zeros and ones (bits) and places them onto the physical media in the form of either electrical pulses for copper cable such as twisted-pair cable or light pulses for fiber-optic cable.

The Physical layer has some simple yet unique functions. It defines the physical characteristics of cables and connectors. It is also responsible for encoding signaling types, such as converting digital signals to analog signals.

Ethernet operates on the Physical layer. IEEE 802.3 defines the different technologies used for wired local area networks. Twisted-pair or fiber-optic cables are used for connectivity. It uses CSMA/CD for collision detection.

Putting It Together

Figure 3.3 shows how the OSI Model works when two different computers are interacting. The overall process is referred to as *encapsulation* where data from higher layers is encapsulated in lower layers.

Imagine a user launching Internet Explorer to access a web search engine such as Bing. The Application layer accepts the data, and the Session, Presentation, and Application layers work together to send the request to the Transport layer.

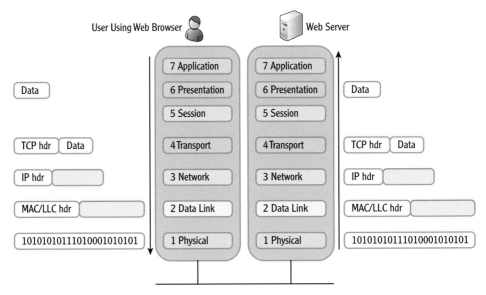

FIGURE 3.3 Data traveling up and down the OSI Model

The Transport later then adds a TCP header. This header will include port information for the source and destination computers. Websites serve data using HTTP, and HTTP uses port 80, so the destination port is set as port 80. TCP assigns a port such as 49152 to Internet Explorer as the source port. The source port is to ensure that the return traffic is returned to Internet Explorer to display the page provided by the website.

At this point, you have two TCP ports assigned and added a part of the TCP header:

▶ Destination port: 80

▶ Source port: 49152

Next, the IP addresses are added at the Network layer. The IP address of the computer running the web server is added as the destination IP address, and the IP addresses of the user's computer is added as the source IP address. This information is added as the IP header and combined with the TCP header and the data. At this point, you have the following:

▶ Destination IP address and destination port: 80

▶ Source IP address and source port: 49152

Routers on the network use the destination IP address to route the packet to the destination computer. When it arrives, the destination port is used to send the data to the service, application, or protocol associated with the port.

When the packet reaches the network where the destination computer is located, the Data Link layer discovers the MAC address of the destination computer. The MAC address is then added to the packet so that the destination computer processes the data.

The Physical layer converts the data into 1s and 0s and places it on the wire. When the data reaches the destination computer, the process is reversed. Information at the different layers is stripped off, and it's passed to the next layer.

In the example, the data will be passed to the service handling HTTP at the Application layer. The user's request is processed, and a web page is built and sent back. The entire encapsulation process is repeated on the server and then sent back to the computer that originally requested the data.

> **Notice how the packet grows as it travels down the OSI Model. Lower layers add additional information to the previous layer.**

Packets and Frames

Although the terms *packets* and *frames* are often used interchangeably, this isn't entirely accurate. The actual name depends on the layer of the OSI Model.

Figure 3.4 shows the names of the encapsulated data at the different layers of the OSI Model. Although there are multiple protocols throughout the OSI

Model, this chapter has primarily focused on the TCP and UDP protocols on the Transport layer (using port numbers) and the IP protocol (using IP addresses) on the Network layer.

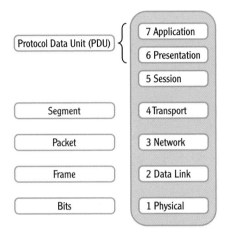

FIGURE 3.4 Encapsulated data names

Protocol Data Unit (PDU)   Data units at layers 5, 6, and 7 are called *protocol data units*.

Segment   At layer 4, the Transport layer, a TCP unit of data is called a *segment*. Remember that data is divided into smaller segments at this layer. This layer uses source and destination ports to identify the protocol, service, or application that will process the segment.

Packet   At the Network layer, a unit of data is called a *packet*. This layer uses IP addresses to get the packets from the source to the destination.

Frame   At the Data Link layer, a unit of data is called a *frame*. MAC addresses are defined here.

Bits   At the Physical layer, the data is simply bits, or ones and zeros.

Segment has two meanings. On a physical network, it's a common connection between multiple computers. On the OSI Model, it's the data at layer 4.

Some sources identify a datagram as a unit of data on the Transport layer (layer 4) using the User Datagram Protocol. Since *Datagram* is in the UDP name, this makes a lot of sense. It implies that the terms *segment* and *datagram* are interchangeable. However, official reference sources don't support this usage. At this point, you should be able to name each of the seven layers of the OSI Model and their layer number. You should also be able to identify the location of various protocols (such as TCP, UDP, and IP) on the OSI Model and the names of encapsulated data at different layers.

WHAT ABOUT DATAGRAMS?

You may come across the term *datagram* in your studies. However, depending on what source you use, the term *datagram* can mean different things. Conventional sources indicate that a datagram is simply another name for a packet.

RFC 1594 (www.faqs.org/rfcs/rfc1594.html) identifies a datagram as "A self-contained, independent entity of data carrying sufficient information to be routed from the source to the destination computer without reliance on earlier exchanges between this source and destination computer and the transporting network."

That's a mouthful. What RFC 1594 is saying is that a datagram is on the layer doing routing, which is layer 3, the Network layer. This implies that the terms *packet* and *datagram* are interchangeable.

Ideally, you should be able draw a diagram similar to Figure 3.4 (without looking at the diagram). If you can do it now, great, but it does take a little practice. Use your favorite mnemonic (All People Seem To Need Data Processing, Please Do Not Throw Sausage Pizza Away, or another one you've learned) to help.

Understanding the TCP/IP Model

The *TCP/IP Model* is a four-layer model created in the 1970s by the U.S. Department of Defense (DoD). It's also called the DoD Model. The TCP/IP Model works similarly to the OSI Model; it just has fewer layers.

Figure 3.5 shows the four layers of the TCP/IP Model in comparison with the OSI Model.

Notice that the layers on the TCP/IP Model correlate to layers of the OSI Model. The TCP/IP *Application layer* maps to layers 5, 6, and 7 of the OSI Model. The TCP/IP *Transport layer* maps to layer 4 of the OSI Model. The TCP/IP *Internet layer* maps to layer 3 of the OSI Model. The TCP/IP *Link layer* maps to layers 1 and 2 of the OSI Model.

> Note that the TCP/IP Model was created in the United States for the DoD before the OSI Model, and the OSI Model was created by the ISO as an international standard.

Application Layer   Protocols on this layer are used by applications to access network resources. Protocols include DNS, SMB, HTTP, FTP, SMTP, POP3, IMAP4, and SNMP.

> The Transport layer is also known as the host-to-host layer.

Transport Layer   Protocols on this layer control data transfer on the network by managing sessions between devices. The two primary protocols are TCP and UDP.

TCP/IP MODEL LAYERS

As you study different models, you may notice that there are different names given to the TCP/IP Model layers.

Microsoft documentation typically labels these layers as Application, Transport, Internet, and Link. For example, Microsoft online resources identified as preparation materials for the Microsoft Technology Associates (MTA) Networking Fundamentals exam (98-366) use these labels. If preparing for this exam, you should know these labels with these names.

Some networking textbooks label these layers as follows:

▶ Application

▶ Host-to-host

▶ Internet, Internetwork, or Internet Protocol

▶ Network Access or Network Interface

Many consider the IETF as the official source for these models and reference RFC 1122 (**http://tools.ietf.org/html/rfc1122**) and RFC 1123 (**http://tools.ietf.org/html/rfc1123**). These documents identify the layers as follows:

▶ Application

▶ Transport

▶ Internet Protocol

▶ Link

Internet Layer   Protocols on the Internet layer control the movement and routing of packets between networks. Protocols on this layer include IPv4, IPv6, IGMP, ICMP, and ARP.

Link Layer   This layer defines how data is transmitted onto the media. It includes multiple protocols such as Ethernet, token ring, frame relay, and ATM.

The Link layer is also known as the Network Interface or Network Access layer.

Mapping Devices on the OSI and TCP Models

The OSI and TCP/IP models are reference points for the devices used on your network. These devices may include NICs, hubs, switches, routers, and firewalls. Figure 3.6 shows these models with their associated network devices.

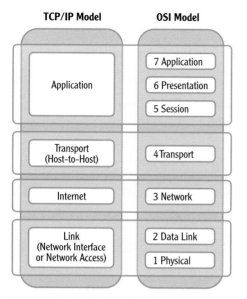

FIGURE 3.5 TCP Model

Devices on the lower levels (such as layer 1, the Data Link layer) have very little intelligence. As you move up the layers, though, the devices are more and more sophisticated. For example, an advanced firewall on the Application layer (layer 7) can analyze traffic within a session and make decisions to block or allow the traffic.

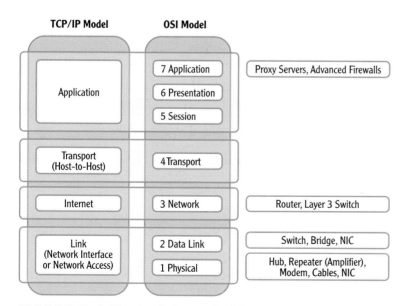

FIGURE 3.6 Mapping devices on the OSI and TCP/IP models

A hub (on layer 1) is unable to make any decisions and simply transfers all the data received on one port to all other ports of the hub. Switches (on layer 2) learn which port computers are connected to and internally switch the traffic. Routers (on layer 3) can talk to other routers and learn the best path to any subnet within a network.

If you can map devices to specific layers of the OSI or TCP/IP models, you will be a better network troubleshooter. For example, consider a problem where a computer is not communicating on the network.

There are multiple reasons why communication is not working. If there are no green lights at the NIC card or switch, you may have a layer 1 problem. The physical connection has failed. This could be a faulty cable or faulty NIC. The NIC connects to a hub or a switch, so the problem could also be a faulty network device or faulty port on the network device.

If the NIC LED is not lit, it's important to realize the problem is a layer 1 problem. There is no need to troubleshoot the configuration of TCP/IP, the operating system, or the applications that are on different layers.

This is similar in concept to troubleshooting car problems. Imagine if you turn the ignition key but nothing happens. There's no sound, no clicking, nothing. You probably won't waste your time checking the oil or gas. The problem is more likely with the battery or ignition system.

> **Some hiring managers include basic troubleshooting questions about the OSI Model and/or TCP/IP Model during interviews.**

Physical Layer

Devices at the Physical layer are concerned only with the physical aspects of communication—actual data transmission through physical connectivity. The Physical layer does not understand logical addressing with IP addresses or physical addressing with the MAC addresses.

At the Physical layer, you will find cables, cable connectors, NICs, hubs, modems, and amplifiers or repeaters.

The hub is a common device found at the Physical layer. It enables network expansion by allowing multiple devices to be plugged into a central point. As a layer 1 device, the hub is not aware of any addressing and ignores layer 2 MAC addresses and layer 3 IP addresses. It simply passes data received on one port to all other ports.

You may notice that NICs are listed on both the Physical layer and the Data Link layer. A NIC provides simple feedback with a lit LED indicating that the NIC is plugged in. This is a function performed at layer 1.

The NIC can also analyze traffic to determine whether received traffic is addressed to the computer based on the MAC address. If the traffic is addressed to the computer, the NIC processes the traffic and passes it to the internal processor. This process occurs on layer 2, making a NIC both a layer 1 and layer 2 device.

The modem is also found at layer 1 of the OSI. The modem is a modulator–demodulator; it converts digital signals from your computer into analog signals used over the telephone line. Demodulation is the conversion from an analog-to-digital signal.

Repeaters and amplifiers are sometimes referred to as the same thing, but there is a subtle difference. The repeater will regenerate a digital signal, and the amplifier will regenerate an analog signal. Both boost single strength as it travels along a cable, allowing a signal to travel further before reaching its destination. For example, if a cable is only able to carry a signal 100 meters, you can put a repeater between two 100 meter cables to extend the distance to 200 meters.

> ◀
> **Although modems aren't common in urban areas, they are still popular with rural users who don't have broadband connections.**

Data Link Layer

Devices on the Data Link layer include switches, bridges, and NICs. Switches and bridges create separate collision domains.

Switch   The switch is a layer 2 device that learns MAC addresses of devices to segment traffic. These MAC addresses tell the switch which devices are connected to which port within a subnet. The switch then internally switches traffic to create separate collision domains.

> ◀
> **Chapter 8 provides much more depth on basic layer 2 and advanced layer 3 switches.**

Bridge   The bridge learns the MAC addresses of devices that are connected to a port similar to how a switch learns these MAC addresses. However, a bridge will typically have multiple computers connected to each bridge port via a hub.

Network Interface Card   The NIC is shared between the Data Link layer and Physical layer. The NIC contains the layer 2 MAC address that is used at layer 2. It analyzes traffic at this layer and determines whether the traffic should be processed by the computer. If the traffic is addressed to the computer, it passes the traffic to the central processor.

Network Layer

The router is the primary device on the Network layer. It routes packets based on their logical IP address.

Routers route IP traffic to different subnets within a network. They can communicate with other routers using routing protocols such as RIP and OSPF. Routers use these routing protocols to learn about multiple subnets within a network.

Layer 3 switches also operate on the Network layer. They are advanced switches that have the ability to route traffic on layer 3 similar to how a router routes traffic.

> ◀
> **Chapter 9 covers routers in more depth, including how they communicate with other routers to learn new routes.**

Application Layer

Chapter 11 covers proxy servers and firewalls in more depth.

Proxy servers and advanced firewalls work on the Application layer. They have the ability to examine traffic and make decisions based on the content. For example, a proxy server can block access to specific Internet websites based on the website address.

Any firewall can block traffic based on source or destination data contained within packets. Basic firewalls do this by blocking traffic based on IP addresses or ports in each individual packet. Advanced firewalls can analyze multiple packets within a session and make decisions to block or allow the traffic to continue.

Mapping Protocols on the OSI and TCP/IP Models

It's also important to understand where protocols operate on the OSI and TCP/IP models. Figure 3.7 shows a mapping of many of the protocols introduced in this chapter.

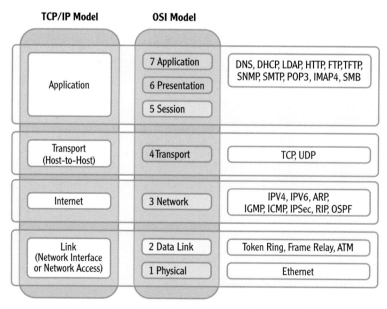

FIGURE 3.7 Mapping protocols on the OSI and TCP/IP models

You probably don't have a full grasp of the details of these protocols at this point. That's expected. These protocols have only been introduced and mapped to the different layers.

As you move through the chapters in the book, you'll learn much more about these protocols. Return to these diagrams to remind yourself where the protocols operate and where the devices operate.

◀

Chapter 4 covers
these protocols in
more depth.

THE ESSENTIALS AND BEYOND

In this chapter, you learned the basics of the OSI Model. The model is a framework, or set of guidelines, used to develop and standardize networking protocols. This model has seven layers known as the Application, Presentation, Session, Transport, Network, Data Link, and Physical layers. The TCP/IP Model includes four layers: Applications, Transport, Internet, and Link. Protocols and devices are designed to work on specific layers of the OSI and TCP/IP models, and you learned the layers associated with specific protocols and devices.

ADDITIONAL EXERCISES

▶ Draw the OSI Model, and label the seven layers with their names and numbers.

▶ Identify the ASCII decimal codes for the phrase *Networking Essentials*.

▶ Draw the TCP/IP Model, and map its layers to the OSI Model.

▶ Map as many protocols as you can to the layers of the OSI and TCP/IP models.

To compare your answers to the author's, please visit **www.sybex.com/go/networking essentials**.

REVIEW QUESTIONS

1. The OSI Model has _____ layers

2. Write down a mnemonic you use to remember the OSI Model.

3. True or false. TCP is a connectionless protocol.

4. What is a unit of data called at the Transport layer?

   A. Packet   C. Frame
   B. Segment   D. Protocol data unit (PDU)

5. Which of the following could be a valid MAC address for a server named Server 1?

   A. Server1   C. A4-BA-DB-FA-60-AD
   B. 192.168.1.5   D. G4-BA-10B-FA-60-AT

(Continues)

THE ESSENTIALS AND BEYOND *(Continued)*

6. IPv4 operates on the _____ layer of the OSI Model.

7. List the protocols that operate on the Transport layer of the OSI Model.

8. True or false. Devices that operate on layer 7 of the OSI Model are more intelligent than devices that operate on layer 1.

9. Routers operate on which of the following layers of the OSI Model?

    A. Layer 1   D. Layer 4

    B. Layer 2   E. None of the above

    C. Layer 3

10. Proxy servers operate on which of the following layers of the OSI Model?

    A. Layer 1   D. Layer 4

    B. Layer 2   E. None of the above

    C. Layer 3

Core TCP/IP Protocols

An important part of understanding networking is understanding networking protocols. TCP/IP is the primary protocol suite used in networks today, including the Internet. TCP and UDP are two important protocols that are integral to most networking communications, but there are many more.

This chapter presents many of the more popular protocols with a high-level overview of these protocols and their purpose. It's important to understand the basics of TCP and UDP, such as which one is connection-oriented and which is connection-less. However, you don't need in-depth knowledge of the common protocols other than understanding their primary purpose. Many common protocols also use specific ports identified as well-known ports. You should also have a good understanding of how ports work and the well-known ports used with specific protocols.

▶ **Understanding TCP and UDP**

▶ **Exploring Common Protocols**

▶ **Understanding Ports**

Understanding TCP and UDP

Transmission Control Protocol (TCP) and *User Datagram Protocol* (UDP) are the two primary protocols used to transport data across a network. They both operate on the Transport layer of the OSI Model, but they have distinctive differences.

The primary difference between these two is the delivery mechanism. TCP provides guaranteed delivery with acknowledgments, sequence numbers, and flow control. UDP provides best-effort delivery without a guarantee.

Chapter 3 introduced these two protocols with two important points:

TCP Is a Connection-Oriented Protocol   TCP starts with an established session using a three-way handshake process. This three-way handshake ensures a connection is established before data is transmitted.

UDP Is a Connection-less Protocol   UDP sends data using a best-effort method. It doesn't establish a session, so it doesn't provide guaranteed delivery.

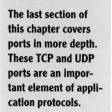

The last section of this chapter covers ports in more depth. These TCP and UDP ports are an important element of application protocols.

Application protocols use TCP, UDP, or both to transfer application data. These protocols are identified using logical ports. For example, HTTP uses TCP port 80. When a system receives data using TCP port 80, it is processed as HTTP.

Exploring TCP

TCP provides guaranteed delivery by starting with the three-way handshake process shown in Figure 4.1. Imagine that Sally's computer wants to transfer information to Bob's computer. Before the data transfer starts, the computers establish a connection with each using this three-way handshake.

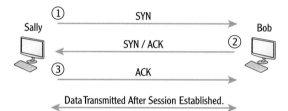

FIGURE 4.1 **TCP handshake process**

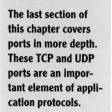

A flag is simply a single binary bit set to a 1. For example, the SYN flag is set by setting a specific bit in the packet to a 1.

Sally's computer starts by sending a packet with the *synchronize* (SYN) flag set. When Bob's computer receives the packet, it responds with another packet with both the SYN and the *acknowledge* (ACK) flags set. Sally's computer then completes the three-way handshake by sending a third packet with the ACK flag set.

At this point, both computers have an established session. They both have assurances that the other computer is operational and they are able to communicate with it. Data is then transmitted between the two computers after the session is established.

You can compare this to using different methods to get a message to a friend. One way is to make a phone call. This also uses a three-way handshake process, as follows:

1. Sally initiates the phone call to Bob.

2. Bob answers the call with "Hello, this is Bob." Sally recognizes Bob's voice and knows it's him.

3. Sally says "Hi. This is Sally." Bob recognizes Sally's voice and knows it's her.

Figure 4.2 illustrates the three steps of the phone call.

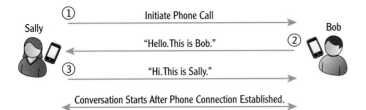

FIGURE 4.2 Phone call uses a similar handshake process

Admittedly, the phone call may not be so formal between two friends. With caller ID, Bob may recognize Sally right away and just say something like "Yo!" Still, the conversation doesn't start until the phone connection is established.

Of course, in a conversation, both people talk. If you were talking to a friend, you'd expect your friend to occasionally acknowledge what you're saying with agreement or comments. You can't just talk for an hour without your friend saying anything back. At least I hope not! Instead, you pass on your information in separate pieces.

TCP also divides the data into smaller segments. For example, the data could be a 1 MB file. TCP could divide this file into 250 segments that are 4 KB. These 4 KB segments can travel over the network more efficiently than a single 1 MB file. TCP uses sequence numbers to track these segments.

When the data is segmented, each separate segment is assigned different sequence numbers such as 1 through 250. The receiving computer then receives each of these segments and uses these sequence numbers to put the data back together in the correct order.

However, the sending computer doesn't just throw all of these segments onto the network and hope the other computer receives them. TCP coordinates this process between the two computers.

Imagine that Sally wants to download music from Bob's computer. The TCP handshake process starts the process. Next, the two computers decide on how big the individual segments can be and how many segments can be sent between acknowledgments. The number of segments that can be sent at a time is the TCP sliding window.

Figure 4.3 shows the two computers with an established session. They have negotiated a segment size of 1500 bytes and a sliding window of 3. When Sally's computer receives three segments, it verifies the data is intact and then sends an acknowledgment (ACK) message. Bob's computer then sends three more segments.

If even a single bit is lost in the transmission, the data in the segment is no longer valid. TCP uses an error checking process called a *cyclical redundancy check* (CRC). This CRC verifies the data is intact in each segment. If the three segments are received without errors, Sally's computer sends an ACK packet saying "Give me three more."

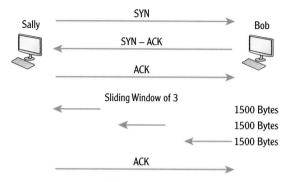

FIGURE 4.3 TCP sliding window

However, if any of the segments are missing or corrupt, Sally's computer sends a *negative acknowledge* (NACK) packet instead, requesting the missing or corrupt segment. If the sending computer receives a NACK, it retransmits the segments in the sliding window. Eventually, Sally's computer will receive all the segments and be able to reassemble them into the original MP3 file sent by Bob's computer.

Exploring UDP

UDP is a best-effort protocol. Delivery is not guaranteed like it is with TCP, but UDP will do its best to get data to its destination. UDP does not use a three-way handshake. It simply sends the data to the destination.

Imagine you have a message you want to get to your friend as soon as possible. You could call, but what if your friend doesn't answer? You could leave a message. You could send a text message. You could even send a letter through the regular mail. However, none of these methods provides any assurance that your message was received. Still, you are making a best effort to pass on the message, and these methods normally work.

This is exactly what UDP does. It makes a best effort to pass on messages, but it doesn't have any of the overhead of TCP. UDP doesn't use the TCP three-way handshake process to establish the session. It doesn't use periodic ACKs and NACKs to verify data was transmitted or request retransmissions of corrupt data.

A logical question comes to mind. If UDP is unreliable, why is it used? The reason is that some data doesn't need guaranteed delivery. In addition, some data transmissions are slowed down by the extra overhead required by TCP.

Because UDP doesn't use the guaranteed delivery mechanisms of TCP, it is referred to as unreliable. Also, it doesn't check for out-of-order messages.

▶

For example, streaming media such as streaming audio, streaming video, and Voice over IP (VoIP) all use UDP. These methods frequently lose packets here and there, but the overall message is still received. Have you ever watched a video online? It may occasionally be jumpy or miss some of the audio. This is because UDP is used and some of the packets are lost. Still, you're able to get the overall message.

If TCP was used instead, the transmission would be a lot slower. If you needed to ensure that you received the full video, you may be able to download the actual video file, instead of having it streamed to you. The file download would use TCP, and the entire file would be intact.

Even though UDP does not verify a connection before sending data or include a check for out-of-order messages, it does validate the data. UDP does use a checksum similar to how TCP uses a checksum. The checksum can indicate to the receiving computer that the data has been modified (perhaps by just dropping a single bit) and isn't valid.

Exploring Common Protocols

TCP and UDP are primary protocols used for data transmission. However, several other protocols are important to understand. Chapter 2 introduced many of these protocols and listed the OSI layer where they operate. This section provides a deeper explanation of them.

The protocols used in this section are commonly used within Microsoft networks and/or on the Internet.

Address Resolution Protocol

The *Address Resolution Protocol* (ARP) uses broadcast transmissions to identify the Media Access Control (MAC) address of computers.

The IP address routes the traffic to the correct subnet. When the destination subnet is reached, the ARP protocol broadcasts the IP address to all computers on the subnet, as shown in Figure 4.4. This ARP broadcast asks, "Who owns this IP address?"

Each computer that receives the ARP broadcast looks to see whether it has the broadcasted IP address. If so, the computer responds with its MAC address.

When a computer resolves a MAC address using ARP, it stores it in a cache for two to ten minutes, depending on the operating system. If it wants to communicate with the computer again, it doesn't have to send another ARP broadcast to get the MAC address but instead retrieves it from cache.

The MAC address is also known as the physical address. It is expressed in hexadecimal characters such as 01-23-45-AB-CD-EF.

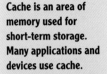

Cache is an area of memory used for short-term storage. Many applications and devices use cache.

Maria
Jose
"Who owns this IP?"
IP 192.168.1.11 255.255.255.0
MAC: FF-FF-FF-FF-FF-FF
"Here's my MAC"
IP 192.168.1.11 255.255.255.0
MAC: 00-03-FF-9C-02-00

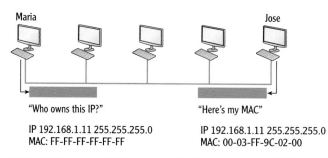

FIGURE 4.4 **ARP translates the IP address to a MAC address.**

These steps will work on a variety of Windows systems, including Windows 7 and Windows Server 2008.

The ARP protocol is part of the TCP/IP protocol suite, but there is also a command-line tool named arp. You can view the ARP cache from the command line by following these steps in a Windows system:

1. Click Start ➢ Run.
2. Type **cmd** in the Run box, and press Enter.
3. At the command prompt, type **arp -a**, and press Enter.

Figure 4.5 shows the arp command (specifically arp -a) used to show the contents of the ARP cache.

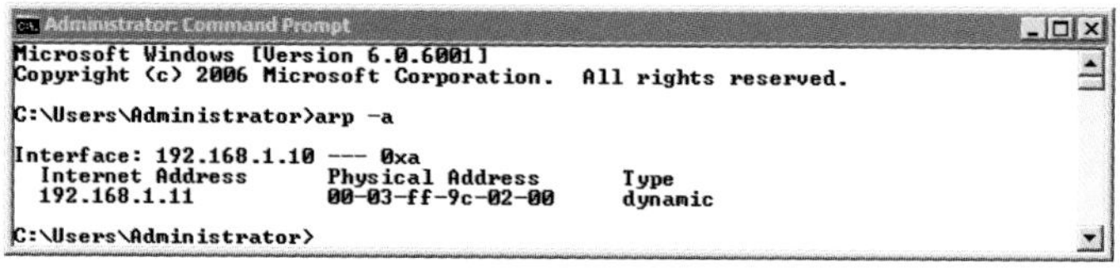

Administrator: Command Prompt
Microsoft Windows [Version 6.0.6001]
Copyright (c) 2006 Microsoft Corporation. All rights reserved.
C:\Users\Administrator>arp -a
Interface: 192.168.1.10 --- 0xa
Internet Address Physical Address Type
192.168.1.11 00-03-ff-9c-02-00 dynamic
C:\Users\Administrator>

FIGURE 4.5 **Viewing the ARP cache**

Hypertext Transfer Protocol

HTTP is different from Hypertext Markup Language (HTML). **HTML is the Internet standard for formatting and displaying documents on the Internet.**

Hypertext Transfer Protocol (HTTP) defines how files on the World Wide Web (WWW) are formatted, transmitted, and rendered in web browsers. Figure 4.6 shows Internet Explorer accessing the site **bing.com**. The address bar shows the Uniform Resource Locator (URL) as **http://www.bing.com**.

Some sites use encryption to protect the data transmission. For example, if you purchase something over the Internet, you'll provide information such as your name, address, and maybe credit card data. This needs to be protected as it goes over the Internet. HTTP over Secure Sockets Layer (SSL), or HTTPS, provides this protection.

FIGURE 4.6 Web browser accessing a web page with the URL

You can tell whether HTTPS is being used from the URL. Instead of HTTP, it will list it as HTTPS. Additionally, most web browsers include a lock icon somewhere on the page. For example, Internet Explorer 8 shows a lock icon at the end of the URL.

If HTTPS is not in the URL or the lock icon is not displayed, information you enter and submit to websites can be intercepted and read by eavesdroppers on the Internet.

HTTP uses TCP port 80 by default. HTTPS uses TCP port 443.

> **Encryption protocols scramble data from plain text into cipher text. Nonauthorized users are not able to read the cipher text.**

File Transfer Protocol

File Transfer Protocol (FTP) is used to upload and download files to and from computers on the Internet and within some internal networks. FTP uses TCP for guaranteed delivery of the files.

You can access FTP from the command prompt from many operating systems such as Windows 7. Get commands can download files, and Put commands upload files. Windows Explorer provides some basic FTP functionality including drag-and-drop features. However, there are applications that make the process much simpler. Figure 4.7 shows an FTP application named FileZilla, which is available for free. It's easy to use and can manage the upload and download of multiple files at a time.

> **Many FTP clients are freely available. You can search on the Internet for *download free ftp* to find others.**

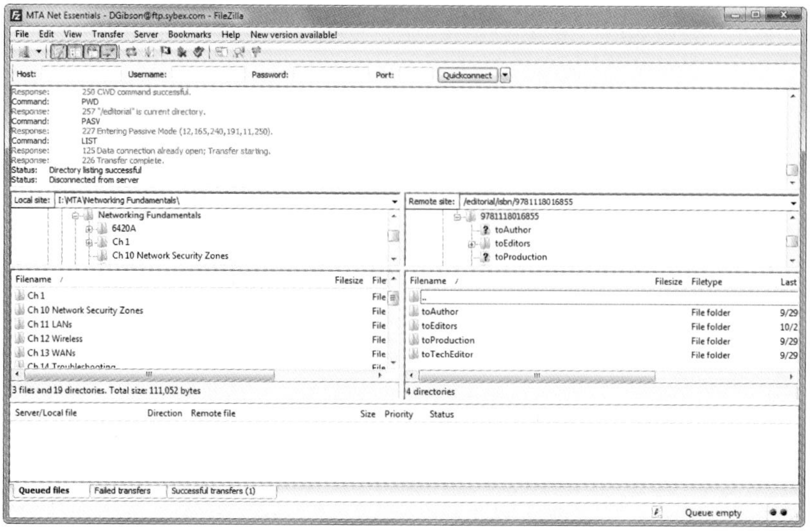

FIGURE 4.7 Using FileZilla to upload and download files

In the figure, a publisher is hosting a website used by authors, editors, and graphics artists to upload and download files to collaborate on a book. The contributors on the book can be located around the world yet share their files as easily as if they worked side by side.

FTP clients such as FileZilla allow you to browse the folders on the destination computer. You can then pick what files you want to upload or download. Most FTP clients allow you to simply right-click a file and select to upload or download depending on what you're trying to do.

Most FTP servers require you to have an account with a password before you can upload files. This prevents malicious users from filling the FTP server with unwanted data. Additionally, FTP sites can limit permissions so that accounts can open and upload files only to certain folders but not others.

However, many FTP servers allow you to download data anonymously. You can use an account name of "anonymous" and then use an email address as a password. The email address is not verified to determine whether it's real, but it is often checked to ensure it's in the format of an email address. For example, d@g.com is a valid format for an email address but it isn't an actual email address. You could use d@g.com as a password for some FTP servers.

Trivial File Transfer Protocol

Trivial File Transfer Protocol (TFTP) is a scaled-down version of FTP. TFTP uses UDP as its transport protocol, which reduces overhead and keeps traffic to a minimum. In contrast, FTP uses TCP, providing guaranteed delivery of the files.

Network administrators often use TFTP when transferring configuration files to network devices such as routers and switches. TFTP should not be used to communicate with FTP servers on the Internet because of its lack of data security features.

Telnet

Telnet is a command-line interface that allows bidirectional communication with network devices and other systems on the network. As a command-line interface, all commands are typed at a command prompt instead of using point-and-click methods within a Windows graphical user interface (GUI).

One of the benefits of Telnet is that it allows terminal emulation. In other words, you can connect to a Telnet server remotely, and it acts as though you are sitting right in front of the server accessing the local terminal. Telnet sessions include a Telnet server, a Telnet client, a Telnet window on the client (usually a command prompt) for issuing commands and viewing data on the server, and the Telnet protocol that transfers the commands between the two.

> Telnet is widely recognized as insecure since it transmits traffic in clear text. Secure Shell (SSH) has replaced Telnet in many applications.
>
> ◀

Remote Desktop Services

Microsoft Windows servers include *Remote Desktop Services* (RDS) as an additional role. An RDS can host applications or entire desktops that are accessible to users on the network.

For example, a client with limited processing power could connect to an RDS server and run Windows 7 from the server. Even though the Windows 7 desktop is running on the server, the end user has full access to all of the Windows 7 capabilities on the older computer.

Similarly, a user running Windows 7 system might need to run a legacy application that is not compatible with Windows 7. The RDS server could host the application, and the user could then run the application from the server without having any compatibility problems.

> ◀
>
> RDS was previously known as Terminal Services. Its name changed to RDS with Windows Server 2008 R2.

RDS uses the *Remote Desktop Protocol*. This is the same protocol used by Windows 7 for Remote Assistance. Remote Assistance allows a help-desk professional to take control of an end user's desktop (with permission) and provide assistance. RDS uses TCP port 3389.

Secure Sockets Layer

SSL is an encryption protocol used for a wide assortment of purposes. As mentioned previously, SSL protects HTTP as HTTPS. SSL provides security in several key areas:

The current version of SSL is 3.0, which was released in 1996.

Confidentiality   Secret data is protected from unauthorized disclosure through encryption. SSL encrypts data into cipher text to ensure that secret data remains secret.

Integrity   Unauthorized users should not modify data. If they do, the data loses integrity and can no longer be trusted as valid. SSL helps ensure integrity by checking the data at different points to ensure it has not been modified.

Authentication   Users and computers need to prove who their identity. Based on their identity, access is granted or denied based on access controls such as permissions. However, the first step is authentication.

SSL uses digital certificates for confidentiality, integrity, and authentication. The digital certificate is a file that includes data used to encrypt the data for confidentiality. It also includes basic information to prove the identity of the certificate holder.

In recent years, many VPNs have emerged using SSL as a tunneling protocol. SSL-based VPNs have the advantage of being able to be used via a web browser rather than requiring a separate VPN client program.

Transport Layer Security

TLS has been upgraded. RFC 5246 defined TLS version 1.2 in August 2008.

Transport Layer Security (TLS) is another security protocol, similar to SSL. It can also provide confidentiality, integrity, and authentication. RFC 2246 defined TLS in 1999, and TLS is designated as a replacement for SSL.

It's interesting to note that even though TLS came out more than 10 years ago as a replacement to SSL, it still hasn't replaced it. SSL is still going strong. Part of the reason for this is that SSL is a strong security protocol.

DIGITAL CERTIFICATES, PKI, AND CAS

In the simplest terms, a digital certificate is just a file stored on a computer. However, this file has a lot of support behind it. Specifically, a Public Key Infrastructure (PKI) includes several elements to support digital certificates.

One of the core elements of a PKI is a certificate authority (CA). A CA is an organization or a service that issues, manages, and validates digital certificates. Many CAs operate on the Internet, and CAs can also operate on internal networks. If an entity (such as a user or computer) needs a certificate, the entity proves their identity to the CA and provides other information (and often money). The CA then issues a certificate.

This certificate helps verify the entity's identity and helps with other uses such as encryption and integrity. When the certificate is presented to a third party, the third party can then query the CA to verify the certificate is valid.

For example, a website can purchase a certificate from a CA. When a user application (such as Internet Explorer) visits the website, the certificate is passed to the application. The application then queries the CA to verify the certificate is still valid. If so, a secure HTTPS session is created using data from the certificate.

Several protocols can use either SSL or TLS for security. For example, the Lightweight Directory Access Protocol (LDAP) can use either TLS or SSL for security.

◄

LDAP is presented later in this chapter.

Secure Shell

Secure Shell (SSH) is an encryption protocol that creates a secure encrypted session that can be used by other protocols. For example, SFTP is FTP encrypted with SSH. SSH has replaced Telnet in many applications. Telnet transfers data in clear text, while SSH encrypts the data. SSH is more secure than Telnet and more suitable for use on the Internet.

PuTTY (pronounced *putty*) is an example application built on SSH. PuTTY is a free terminal emulator program that encrypts traffic with SSH. Many administrators use PuTTY to manage network devices such as routers and switches.

◄

PuTTY isn't an acronym. It's just a way of capitalizing the name that stuck.

Internet Protocol Security

Internet Protocol Security (IPSec) is another encryption protocol used to encrypt traffic traveling over a network. IPSec provides two primary services:

Authentication   IPSec uses an authentication header (AH) to prove the identity of the sender. This provides assurances to the computer receiving the traffic that it was sent by a known computer.

Encryption   IPSec uses Encapsulating Security Protocol (ESP) to encrypt traffic. Only authorized users or computers are able to decrypt and read the traffic.

IPSec also provides integrity. The receiving computer is assured that the data was not changed in transit.

Both IPv4 and IPv6 support IPSec. It uses one of two modes:

Tunnel Mode   IPSec encrypts the entire IP packet (both data and headers). It encapsulates the original encrypted packet within another IP packet and then sends it across the network. Virtual private networks (VPNs) use tunneling to protect the data. The L2TP/IPSec tunneling protocol is one of the popular VPN protocols.

Transport Mode   Only the data is encrypted instead of the entire packet. The source and destination data (such as the IP addresses) within the packet are not encrypted. Transport mode is commonly used to encrypt data within internal networks.

Simple Mail Transfer Protocol

Simple Mail Transfer Protocol (SMTP) is the primary protocol used to deliver email over the Internet and within internal networks. Email servers use SMTP to send and receive email between each other. Additionally, user systems use SMTP to send email to SMTP servers.

Figure 4.8 shows how SMTP is commonly used. You could be using an email application such as Microsoft Outlook. This allows you to connect with an email server to send your email. The email server receives the email and then sends and receives email with other email servers.

Many organizations use Microsoft Exchange Server for email services. Exchange typically runs on a dedicated server.

End User   Email Server   Email Server

F I G U R E 4 . 8 SMTP used to send and receive email

Of course, this brings up a question. If SMTP is used to send email to the server from the end user's computer, how does the end user receive email? Glad you asked.

It depends, but the two common ways that end user's receive email are via a Post Office Protocol (POP) server or an Internet Message Access Protocol (IMAP) server. POP and IMAP are discussed in the next two sections.

Post Office Protocol v3

Post Office Protocol v3 (POP3) is a common protocol used to retrieve email from an email server. The current version is POP3.

As an example, you may use Microsoft Outlook (or another email client) for email at a home computer. You connect to the Internet via an Internet service provider (ISP), and the ISP provides you with email access. When you first configure your email client, you configure it with the name of the POP3 server and the address of an SMTP server. Your computer sends email using the SMTP server, and it receives email using the POP3 server.

The ISP's POP3 server receives email addressed to you and stores it there until you connect to the Internet and contact the server. When you connect to the server, it will then send all your email to your computer. Once your computer receives this email, it's typically removed from the POP3 server.

◀

The POP3 server can be the same server hosting SMTP. They don't have to be separate servers. This is common on smaller networks hosting both SMTP and POP3.

Internet Message Access Protocol

Internet Message Access Protocol (IMAP) is another popular email protocol. It is more commonly used on internal networks rather than on the Internet. The current version is IMAP4.

The primary difference between POP3 and IMAP4 is that messages are not automatically downloaded to the client, and they can be retained on the server with IMAP4. An IMAP4 server allows users to view email message headers individually. They can then choose which email to open. For example, if a user is connected with a slow connection, they can choose to postpone opening an email with a large attachment.

Since messages can be retained on the IMAP server, users can access the server from any computer in the network and still have access to the same email. This is different from a POP3 server that downloads the messages to the user's computer when they connect. With a POP3 server, if they access the server with a different computer, the older messages are no longer on the server.

IMAP is useful for workers who roam the network and don't have a single computer they use all the time. The worker can connect to the IMAP server from any computer and access email on the server.

◀

Messages don't have to be retained on the IMAP server. They can be configured so that email is deleted after it is downloaded.

IMAP also gives users the ability to manage their email in folders. When the email is retained on the IMAP server, users can move email into different folders based on their preferences.

Lightweight Directory Access Protocol

RFC 4510 defines the latest version of LDAP, which is LDAP version 3.

Lightweight Directory Access Protocol (LDAP) is the protocol used to query directories such as Microsoft's Active Directory Domain Services (AD DS). LDAP is derived from the Directory Access Protocol (DAP), which is part of a larger standard known as X.500.

It's easy to confuse the term *directory* since it has two meanings with computers. A directory can be a domain directory in the context of LDAP. A directory can also be a folder on a disk drive, which has nothing to do with LDAP.

Domain Directory   A domain directory is a database of objects such as users, computers, and groups. Administrators use the domain to manage users and computers. Figure 4.9 shows Active Directory Users and Computers (ADUC) for a domain named Wiley.com. The Servers organizational unit is selected, and you can see several servers within the domain. Administrators use ADUC to manage the domain, and ADUC uses LDAP to query the AD DS database.

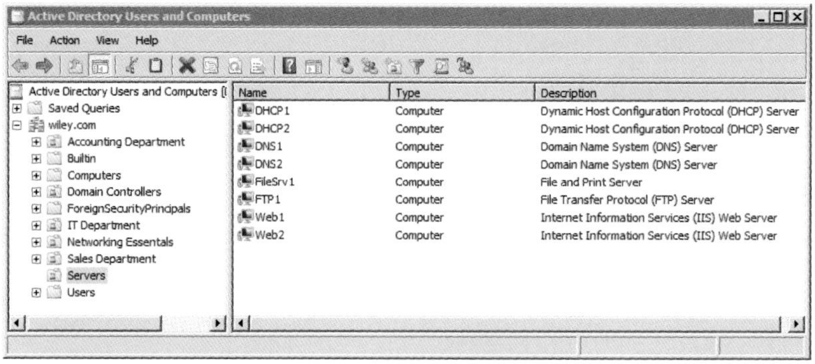

FIGURE 4.9 Active Directory Users and Computers

Disk Drive Folders   You can explore Windows disk drives with Windows Explorer. Drives have folders that are also called *directories*. These folders have nothing to do with LDAP. Instead, these folders or directories are only on disk drives.

Although LDAP is integral to a Microsoft domain, it is also used in other non-Microsoft domains. Its purpose is the same, though. LDAP allows individuals to query the directory to locate and manage resources within the domain.

By default, LDAP transmits data across the network in clear text. Tools such as protocol analyzers or sniffers allow people to capture this data and read it. This is commonly known as *eavesdropping* and is similar to a person listening in on another person's private conversation.

Secure LDAP (SLDAP) uses SSL or TLS to prevent attackers from using sniffers to capture the data. Additionally, secure LDAP uses digital certificates for authentication. This ensures that computers communicating with each other with secure LDAP prove their identity prior to transferring data to each other.

LDAP uses TCP port 389 by default. SLDAP uses TCP port 636.

Kerberos

Kerberos is the primary authentication protocol used within a Microsoft domain and is managed as part of Active Directory. It was developed at the Massachusetts Institute of Technology and is used in other non-Microsoft domains.

The name Kerberos comes from Greek mythology. Kerberos was the three-headed dog that guarded the gates of Hades. Instead of guarding Hades, Kerberos is now helping to guard the secrets within Active Directory.

Kerberos uses a complex process of issuing time-stamped tickets to users after they log on. In simple terms, user accounts present these tickets when they try to access resources such as a file or folder. If the tickets are valid, access to the resource is granted. This is similar to you purchasing a ticket to watch a movie. If you have the ticket, you can get in. If not, access is blocked.

These Kerberos tickets need to be protected so that only specific user accounts can use tickets issued to them. Kerberos uses symmetric cryptography to encrypt the tickets.

Kerberos uses TCP port 88 by default.

◄

Authentication is used to prove identity. For example, a user could provide a username and password to authenticate within a domain.

Point-to-Point Tunneling Protocol

Point-to-Point Tunneling Protocol (PPTP) is a VPN protocol. It provides a secure connection over a public network such as the Internet. PPTP is primarily used in Microsoft networks.

The Point-to-Point Protocol (PPP) is used for dial-up networking. PPTP extended PPP to make it useful for VPNs. The Microsoft Point-to-Point Encryption (MPPE) protocol encrypts the PPTP traffic. PPTP uses port 1723.

Layer 2 Tunneling Protocol

Layer 2 Tunneling Protocol (L2TP) is another tunneling protocol used with VPNs. It's a combination of the Layer 2 Forwarding (L2F) protocol from Cisco and PPTP from Microsoft. However, L2TP is a standard used by more than just Cisco and Microsoft. IPSec is used with L2TP (as L2TP/IPSec) to provide security for the VPN connection.

L2TP uses UDP port 1701 by default.

Simple Network Management Protocol

Simple Network Management Protocol (SNMP) is a management protocol used to manage network devices such as routers and switches. Many different applications are available that use SNMP.

One way this is done is by installing SNMP agents on the network devices. The SNMP agents detect when specific events occur and generates a trap message to report back to a primary server to collect the information. Microsoft's System Center Operations Manager (SCOM) is an example of a server application used to monitor the health of devices on the network.

SNMP uses UDP port 161 by default. Since most of the traffic is diagnostic in nature to check the health of the devices, the guaranteed delivery of TCP is not required.

Internet Group Multicast Protocol

Internet Group Multicast Protocol (IGMP) is used for multicast transmissions. As a reminder, unicast transmissions go from one computer to one other computer. Broadcast transmissions go from one computer in a subnet to all other computers in a subnet. Multicast transmissions go from one computer to a select group of other computers.

If you've ever attended a seminar on the Web, or a *webinar*, then you've probably used IGMP.

▶

There is a specific range of multicast addresses known as Class D addresses. Valid multicast addresses are in the range of 224.0.0.0 through 239.255.255.255. IGMP is used with IPv4. IPv6 uses other methods for group multicasting.

Multicasting is commonly used for audio and video transmissions, including different types of video teleconferencing. One computer creates the multicast session using a valid multicast IP address. Other computers can then join the multicast group.

Internet Control Message Protocol

▶

Chapter 14 covers several troubleshooting tools including Ping, PathPing, TraceRt, and more.

Internet Control Message Protocol (ICMP) is a core protocol used to send error messages. Operating systems use ICMP to communicate the availability or unavailability of services. Additionally, troubleshooting tools such as Ping, PathPing, and TraceRt use ICMP to transfer data. ICMP functions at the Network layer of the OSI model and IP directly.

Understanding Ports

Both TCP and UDP use logical port numbers to identify the contents of a packet. These port numbers help TCP/IP get the packet to the application, service, or protocol that will process the data once it arrives at the computer.

As an example, consider a home user who uses an ISP for access to the Internet including email. The user uses Microsoft Outlook to send and receive email, and Microsoft Outlook has been configured with the IP address of both an SMTP server and a POP3 server, as shown in Figure 4.10.

As a reminder, the IP protocol uses the IP address to get the packet from one computer to another over a network.

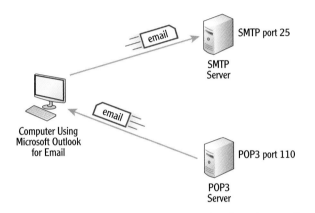

FIGURE 4.10 Using ports to send and receive email

Sending and receiving email are two separate processes. The following steps outline the process for sending SMTP email:

1. The client computer sends the email to the SMTP server with a destination port number of 25.

2. The client computer assigns itself a random unused source port number, such as 49152, and maps it to Microsoft Outlook for SMTP.

3. When the SMTP server receives the data from the client, it recognizes the destination port 25 as SMTP. It then forwards the data to the service handling SMTP.

4. After the email is received, the server sends back an acknowledgment to the computer using port 49152 to confirm the email was received.

5. When the computer receives the packet with port 49152, it sends it to the Microsoft Outlook application. Outlook then moves the email from the Outbox to the Sent folder.

A similar process is used when the computer wants to download email from the POP3 server:

1. The computer sends a request to the POP3 server with a destination port number of 110.

2. The computer assigns itself a random unused source port number, such as 49153, and maps it to Microsoft Outlook for POP3.

3. When the POP3 server receives the request, it recognizes the destination port 110 as POP3. It then forwards the request to the service handling POP3 requests.

4. The POP3 server then sends email to the client using port 49153.

5. When the computer receives the data with port 49153, it sends it to the Microsoft Outlook application. Outlook then moves the email into the Inbox folder.

While the preceding steps showed the process for SMTP and POP3, similar processes are used for many different applications. The IP address gets the packet to the destination computer. The port is then used to get the packet to the correct applications, service, or protocol on the target computer.

There are a total of 65,536 TCP ports and 65,536 UDP ports. *The Internet Assigned Numbers Authority (IANA)* assigns port numbers to protocols. It has divided the ports into different ranges, as shown in Table 4.1. You can view a list of all ports assigned by IANA at **www.iana.org/assignments/port-numbers**.

> ▶
>
> **IANA also oversees the assignment of public IP addresses on the Internet.**

TABLE 4.1 Port ranges for well-known, registered, and dynamic ports

Port names	Port numbers	Comments
Well-known ports	0 through 1023	These ports are associated with specific protocols or applications. Ports and protocols in the well-known port range are registered with IANA.
Registered ports	1024 through 49,151	Some of these ports are registered with IANA for specific protocols, but this is not required. Computers can assign unused ports in this range for applications.
Dynamic ports	49,152 through 65,535	These ports are not registered with IANA and may be used for any purpose.

Controlling Port Traffic with a Firewall

In addition to using ports to get packets to the right protocol, application, or service, ports are also used to control traffic in a network. Firewalls can block traffic based on the TCP or UDP ports they are using.

For example, consider a network that wants to prevent any FTP traffic from being used on the network. FTP uses ports 20 and 21. Figure 4.11 shows how a firewall can block FTP traffic. If the firewall receives any packet with either a source or destination port of 20 or 21, the firewall simply doesn't route the packet.

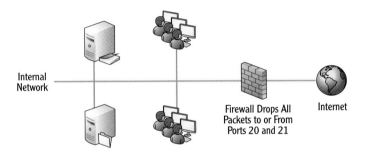

Internal
Network

Firewall Drops All
Packets to or From
Ports 20 and 21

Internet

FIGURE 4.11 Using a firewall to block traffic based on ports

Mapping Internally Used Ports and Protocols

Microsoft networks use several different ports and protocols on internal networks. You should have a good understanding of what these ports and protocols are, as shown in Table 4.2. Most protocols use either TCP or UDP, but some (such as DNS) use both.

◀

Chapter 10 covers DNS along with other name resolution methods. Name resolution resolves computer names to IP addresses.

TABLE 4.2 Commonly used ports

Port	TCP or UDP	Protocol	Comments
20, 21	TCP	FTP	File Transfer Protocol.
22	TCP	SSH	Secure Shell.
23	TCP	Telnet	Can be secured with SSH.
25	TCP	SMTP	Simple Mail Transfer Protocol. Used to send email.
110	TCP	POP3	Post Office Protocol. Used to receive email.

(Continues)

TABLE 4.2 *(Continued)*

Port	TCP or UDP	Protocol	Comments
143	TCP	IMAP4	Internet Message Access Protocol. Used when email stored on server.
80	TCP	HTTP	Hypertext Transfer Protocol. Used for web pages.
443	TCP	HTTPS	Secure HTTPS. Commonly uses SSL for security.
53	TCP/UDP	DNS	Domain Name Service. Used to resolve names to IP addresses.
88	TCP	Kerberos	Primary authentication protocol used by Active Directory.
389	TCP	LDAP	Lightweight Directory Access Protocol (LDAP). Language used to communicate with Active Directory.
636	TCP	SLDAP	Secure LDAP. Uses SSL or TLS to encrypt LDAP communications.
161, 162	UDP	SNMP	Simple Network Management Protocol. Used to manage network devices such as routers and switches.
3389	TCP	Remote Desktop Services	Remote Desktop Services are used for remote assistance and remote desktops in a Microsoft network.
1723	TCP	PPTP	Point-to-Point Tunneling Protocol. Used in VPNs.
1701	UDP	L2TP	Layer 2 Tunneling Protocol. Used in VPNs.

One of the primary reasons you need to know the ports is for configuring firewalls. You can create firewall rules or exceptions to allow or block the traffic based on the port. Firewall administrators have these ports memorized.

THE ESSENTIALS AND BEYOND

TCP and UDP are two primary protocols used to transport data across networks. TCP is connection-oriented and provides guaranteed delivery. UDP is connection-less and uses a best-effort delivery method. Many other application protocols are used within TCP/IP for a wide variety of purposes including email, web pages, encryption, interaction with Active Directory, and more. Application protocols use logical TCP and UDP ports for identification. IANA designates the port numbers for specific applications, and the first 1024 ports are known as well-known ports.

ADDITIONAL EXERCISES

▶ Draw the handshake process used by TCP.

▶ List two protocols used within a Microsoft domain with Active Directory.

▶ View the ARP cache.

▶ List the ports used by the three email protocols.

To compare your answers to the author's, please visit **www.sybex.com/go/ networkingessentials**.

REVIEW QUESTIONS

1. Which of the following protocols is considered connection-oriented?

   A. UDP   **C.** ARP

   B. TCP   **D.** DHCP

2. True or false. UDP traffic accepts the loss of some data.

3. What type of traffic commonly uses UDP? (Choose all that apply.)

   A. Streaming audio   **C.** HTTP traffic

   B. Streaming video   **D.** Voice over IP

4. What is used to resolve an IP address to a MAC address?

   A. DNS   **C.** ARP

   B. TCP   **D.** ICMP

5. List three commonly used protocols for email.

6. L2TP is one of many tunneling protocols used for VPNs. What is used to encrypt L2TP traffic?

(Continues)

THE ESSENTIALS AND BEYOND *(Continued)*

7. The _____ protocol is used to manage multicast transmissions.

8. What port is used by RDS?

   A. 389   C. 1701

   B. 636   D. 3389

9. What port is used by LDAP?

   A. 25   C. 1723

   B. 389   D. 3389

10. What port is used by Kerberos?

    A. 25   C. 88

    B. 80   D. 443

## CHAPTER 5

Exploring IPv4

IPv4 addresses are the most common types of addresses used on the Internet and in internal networks today. It's important to understand the components of an IPv4 address so that you can easily troubleshoot basic problems when a computer has been misconfigured.

Large organizations often divide the network into subnets, and one of the rites of passage for networking is to understand how subnetting works. You don't have to be a master at subnetting, but you should understand the basics.

Most organizations also use the Dynamic Host Configuration Protocol (DHCP) to automatically assign IP addresses and other TCP/IP configuration information. Although this normally works well, it occasionally fails. When a client can't reach a DHCP server, it gives an obvious telltale sign—if you know what to look for.

▶ **Exploring the components of an IPv4 address**

▶ **Exploring an IPv4 address in binary**

▶ **Subnetting IPv4 addresses**

▶ **Comparing manual and automatic assignment of IPv4 addresses**

Exploring the Components of an IPv4 Address

Internet Protocol version 4 (IPv4) has been the standard IP addressing scheme since the 1980s. It's used to get TCP/IP traffic from one computer to another computer over a network. All computers on the Internet have unique IP addresses. As long as the IP addresses are valid, any computer can reach any other computer on the Internet with this IP address.

Similarly, internal networks also use IP addresses. All computers on each internal network have unique addresses within the network, and these IP addresses are used to get traffic from one computer to another.

You can think of an IP address like the street address of a home or business. As long as the full address is valid, you can address a letter, and the post office will deliver it. This also works worldwide. If you have a valid address, your letter will reach its destination. A valid address in the United States has a street address or a post-office box, a city, a state, and a zip code.

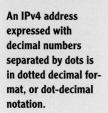

An IPv4 address
expressed with
decimal numbers
separated by dots is
in dotted decimal for-
mat, or dot-decimal
notation.

Valid IP addresses have four decimals separated by three dots. Additionally, the only valid decimal numbers in an IPv4 address are 0 through 255. For example, the following IP addresses are valid:

► 10.80.1.5

► 172.16.5.254

► 192.168.1.4

In comparison, the following are not valid IPv4 addresses:

► 10.80.256.5: No number can be greater than 255.

► 172.16.254: There must be four decimals.

These steps will
work on a variety
of Windows systems
including Windows 7
and Windows
Server 2008.

You can tell what your configured IP address is by using the `ipconfig` command at the command prompt. The following steps show how to do this on a Windows system.

1. Click Start ➢ Run.

2. Type in **cmd** in the Run box, and press Enter.

3. At the command prompt, type **ipconfig**, and press Enter.

The default gateway
is the address of
the near side of a
router. It will typi-
cally provide a path
to the Internet or
other subnets and
is explained further
later in this chapter.

Your display will look similar to Figure 5.1, though you'll probably have different IP addresses displayed. In the figure, both an IPv4 address and an IPv6 address are shown, though you may have only an IPv4 address. Additionally, you can see that the system is using a default gateway of 192.168.1.1.

FIGURE 5.1 Viewing the IP address with `ipconfig`

Ascertaining the Network ID and Host ID of an IP Address

An IP address has two components: a network ID and a host ID. The network ID identifies the subnetwork, or *subnet* where the computer is located. The host ID uniquely identifies the computer within that subnet.

COMPARING A NETWORK ID AND A ZIP CODE

A postal address includes the street address, city, state, and zip code. When the postal service receives a letter, it will get it to the post office in the correct city and state simply by using the zip code. The postal service then uses the street address to get it to the correct home or business.

Similarly, TCP/IP uses the network ID to get a packet to a router in the correct subnet. Once the packet reaches the subnet, it uses the host ID to get the packet to the correct computer on the subnet.

Throughout the United States, zip codes are unique. Each zip code represents a group of addresses relatively close to each other. Similarly, within a network, network IDs are unique. Each network ID represents a group of two or more hosts on a subnet of a network.

Within each zip code, each address is unique. For example, you can't have two addresses of 777 Success Road. If the addresses were the same, mail couldn't be accurately delivered to both addresses. Similarly, within a subnet, computers with the same network ID must have unique host IDs. If two computers have the same host ID and the same network ID (the same IP address), it results in an IP address conflict.

In internal networks, IP addresses are accompanied by a *subnet mask*. The subnet mask identifies the portion of the IP address that is the network ID. The following are common subnet masks:

► 255.0.0.0

► 255.255.0.0

► 255.255.255.0

TCP/IP uses the subnet mask to determine which portion of the IP address is the network ID and which portion is the host ID. More specifically, when the subnet mask is configured at its maximum value (255), that indicates that the corresponding portion of the IP address is part of the network ID. The remaining portion of the IP address is the host ID.

Consider an IP address of 192.168.1.5 with a subnet mask of 255.255.255.0. Figure 5.2 and Table 5.1 show the two parts of this IP address.

Since the first three decimals of the subnet mask are 255, the first three decimals of the IP address make up the network ID. The network ID is always expressed with trailing zeros. In other words, the network ID in this case is

◄

Subnet masks can be more complex, but many internal networks use simple subnet masks with only the numbers 255 or 0 in dotted decimal format.

192.168.1.0. It's incorrect to express it as 192.168.1 without the trailing zeros. The host ID is simply whatever remains after identification of the network ID. In this case, the host ID is the number 5.

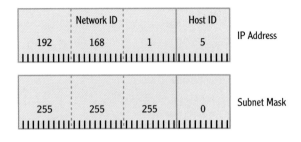

When the subnet mask is maximum (255), that portion of the IP address is the network ID.

Network ID: 192.168.1.0

FIGURE 5.2 An IP address with a subnet mask

TABLE 5.1 The two parts of an IP address

	Network ID			Host ID
IP	192.	168.	1.	5
Subnet mask	255.	255.	255.	0
Network ID	192.	168	1	0
Host ID				5

> **When using advanced subnetting, this rule is worded a little more specifically. Once the first zero *bit* is used, the remaining bits must be zero.**

The subnet mask must have contiguous maximum numbers. In other words, once the first zero is used, the remaining numbers must be zero. A subnet mask of 255.0.255.0 is not valid.

Identifying the network ID and host ID is very important. Every computer on a subnet must have the same network ID as part of their IP address, and each of these computers needs a unique IP address. When IP addresses are manually assigned, a simple typo can result in a computer not communicating at all.

Consider Figure 5.3. You should be able to identify the network ID and the host ID of each of the computers in the two subnets. Additionally, the configuration of two of the computers in subnet A and two of the computers in subnet B are incorrect. The addresses assigned to the router interfaces are correct. Can you identify the errors?

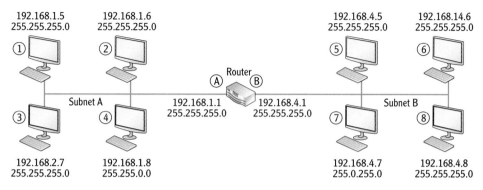

FIGURE 5.3 Identifying the network ID

The answers are given in the following text, but see whether you can figure out the answers on your own before checking your answers.

Notice in the figure that subnet A is on the left and subnet B is on the right. They are separated by a router. The router has two network interface cards (NICs), and each NIC is assigned an IP address. For all computers in subnet A, the NIC labeled A is the default gateway to subnet B. Similarly, for all computers in subnet B, the NIC labeled B is the default gateway to subnet A.

Router Connection A   The network ID is 192.168.1.0, and the host ID is 1. Since this is known to be correct, all computers on this subnet must have the same network ID (192.168.1.0). NIC A on the router is the default gateway for computers on subnet A.

Computer 1   The network ID is 192.168.1.0, and the host ID is 5. This computer is configured correctly.

Computer 2   The network ID is 192.168.1.0, and the host ID is 6. This computer is configured correctly.

Computer 3   The network ID is 192.168.2.0, and the host ID is 7. Notice that the network ID is different from the default gateway. Since the network ID is different from other computers on this subnet and also different from the default gateway, this computer won't be able to communicate on the network.

Computer 4   The network ID is 192.168.0.0, and the host ID is 1.8. Notice that the subnet mask is 255.255.0.0 with only two 255s instead of three. Since the network ID is different from other computers on this subnet and also different from the default gateway, this computer won't be able to communicate on the network.

Router Connection B   The network ID is 192.168.4.0, and the host ID is 1. Since this is known to be correct, all computers on this subnet must have the same

It's common to give a default gateway the first IP address in the subnet such as 192.168.1.1. However, this is not required.

network ID (192.168.4.0). NIC B on the router is the default gateway for computers on subnet B.

Computer 5   The network ID is 192.168.4.0, and the host ID is 5. This computer is configured correctly.

Computer 6   The network ID is 192.168.14.0, and the host ID is 6. Notice that the third number in the IP address is 14 and not 4. Since the network ID is different from other computers on this subnet and also different from the default gateway, this computer won't be able to communicate on the network.

Computer 7   The subnet mask of 255.0.255.0 is invalid. A valid subnet mask can't have numbers greater than zero once the first zero is used. This computer won't be able to communicate on the network.

Computer 8   The network ID is 192.168.4.0, and the host ID is 8. This computer is configured correctly.

Identifying the Default Gateway

The *default gateway* is the IP address of the router on the local subnet. If there's only one router (as shown in Figure 5.3 earlier), it's easy to determine the default gateway. However, if a subnet has more than one router, only one can be the default. The default gateway will usually provide a path to the Internet.

Consider Figure 5.4. It includes three routers with multiple subnets shown. Subnets x, y, and z have computers and IP addresses assigned, but this discussion is focused on subnet A and subnet B. All the IP addresses in subnet A have a network ID of 192.168.1.0, and all the IP addresses in subnet B have a network ID of 192.168.4.0. Notice that both subnet A and subnet B have two routers. However, only one router will provide a path to the Internet.

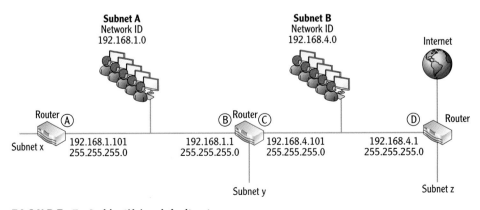

FIGURE 5.4 Identifying default gateways

If this is a typical network, all the computers in subnet A will be configured with a default gateway of 192.168.1.1, and all the computers in subnet B will be configured with a default gateway of 192.168.4.1.

Determining Local and Remote Addresses

The IP protocol looks at the source and destination addresses to determine whether they are both on the same local subnet. If they are on the same subnet, it then uses the Address Resolution Protocol (ARP) to broadcast the IP, learn the physical address, and deliver the packet to the destination computer.

However, if the destination IP address has a different network ID, it is considered to be on a remote subnet. The IP protocol then sends the data to the default gateway.

You should be able to look at two IP addresses and determine whether they are both on the same local subnet or whether the destination IP address is on a remote subnet. You can do this with the following steps:

1. Determine the network ID of the source IP address.

2. Determine the network ID of the destination IP address.

3. Determine whether they are the same:

   ▶ If so, they are local to each other.

   ▶ If not, the destination address is on a remote network and data must be sent through the default gateway.

Give this a try with the following examples. See whether you can determine if the two IP addresses are local (with the same network ID and on the same subnet) or remote (with different network IDs and on different subnets).

Example	Source IP	Destination IP	Local or remote?
1	192.168.1.5	192.168.1.254	
	255.255.255.0	255.255.255.0	
2	10.80.1.23	10.80.2.27	
	255.255.0.0	255.255.0.0	
3	192.168.1.17	192.168.11.23	
	255.255.255.0	255.255.255.0	

The following text provides the answers to this challenge, but see if you can figure them out before checking your answers:

Example 1 The network ID of the source IP address is 192.168.1.0. The network ID of the destination IP address is 192.168.1.0. These are the same, so they are local to each other.

Example 2 The network ID of the source IP address is 10.80.0.0. The network ID of the destination IP address is 10.80.0.0. These are the same, so they are local to each other.

Example 3 The network ID of the source IP address is 192.168.1.0. The network ID of the destination IP address is 192.168.11.0. These are different, so the destination IP address is remote.

Understanding Classful IP Addresses

> You should be able to identify the class of any classful IP address, its subnet mask, and its network ID.

IPv4 is a classful logical addressing scheme using three primary address classes: Class A, Class B, and Class C. The class of the address is determined by the first number in the IP address. Additionally, the subnet mask is predetermined for each class. Table 5.2 shows these three IP ranges with an example IP address in each class.

TABLE 5.2 Classful IP addresses

Class	First number	Range of IP addresses	Subnet mask	Example
Class A	1 to 126	1.0.0.0 to 126.255.255.254	255.0.0.0	10.80.1.15
Class B	128 to 191	128.0.0.0 to 191.255.255.254	255.255.0.0	172.16.32.15
Class C	192 to 223	192.0.0.0 to 223.255.255.254	255.255.255.0	192.168.1.5

Notice that the first example IP address (10.80.1.15) has a 10 as the first number. The number 10 is in the range 1 through 126, making this a Class A address, with a subnet mask of 255.0.0.0 and a network ID of 10.0.0.0. The second example IP address (172.16.32.15) has the number 172 first, making it a Class B address with a subnet mask of 255.255.0.0 and a network ID of 172.16.0.0. The third example (192.168.1.5) has a 192 first, making it a Class C address with a subnet mask of 255.255.255.0 and a network ID of 192.168.1.0.

UNDERSTANDING CLASS D AND CLASS E ADDRESSES

Class D and Class E addresses also exist but aren't as important when understanding classful addressing. Class D is used for multicasting and includes the address range from 224.0.0.0 through 239.255.255.255. Class E is a reserved range from 240.0.0.0 through 255.255.255.255,

Computers are able to determine whether the IP address is a Class A, Class B, or Class C address by looking at only the first two bits in the address. These are the high-order bits with values of 128 and 64, as shown in Table 5.3. Notice that a Class A address has a range of 1 through 126, so the first two bits may be 0 or 0 and 1. Class B has a range 128 through 191, and the highest-order bit is always a 1, and the second bit is always a 0. Class C has a range of 192 to 223, and the two high-order bits are always a 1.

High-order bits are simply the bits with the highest value. In a binary octet, the two high-order bits are on the farthest left with values of 128 and 64.

TABLE 5.3   Identifying the upper-level bits of Classful IP addresses

	2^7	2^6	2^5	2^4	2^3	2^2	2^1	2^0
Decimal value	128	64	32	16	8	4	2	1
Class A	0	0						
Class B	1	0						
Class C	1	1						

Figure 5.5 shows the three classful IP address ranges with their network ID and host IDs separated. It also shows the value of the high-order bits for each of these classes.

One of the benefits of using classful IP addressing is that you can determine the subnet mask by looking only at the IP address. Once you know the subnet mask, you can then determine the network ID. For example, see whether you can determine the network IDs of the following classful IP addresses:

192.168.1.3

172.16.4.7

10.80.20.4

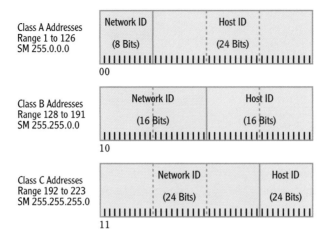

FIGURE 5.5 Classful IP addresses

You need to determine the class of each, identify the subnet mask of the class, and then use that information to determine the network ID. Table 5.4 shows the result for each of these IP addresses.

You can test the TCP/IP stack on a local computer by issuing the `ping 127.0.0.1` **command from the command prompt. It should return four replies.**

TABLE 5.4 Determining network ID of a classful IP address

IP address	Class	Subnet mask	Network ID
192.168.1.3	Class C	255.255.255.0	192.168.1.0
172.16.4.7	Class B	255.255.0.0	172.16.0.0
10.80.20.4	Class A	255.0.0.0	10.0.0.0

Although most of the addresses in the three address ranges can be used, there are some restrictions. For example, you may have noticed that the entire range starting with 127 is missing. This Class A address range is reserved for testing. The address of 127.0.0.1 is known as the *loopback address* and is used to test the installed NIC. There are also several other IP address ranges reserved for use on internal networks only.

A special Automatic Private IP Addressing (APIPA) range is from 169.254.0.1 through 169.254.255.254. APIPA is described later in this chapter.

Identifying Reserved IP Address Ranges

RFC 1918 identifies several IP address ranges for use in private networks only. These addresses aren't assigned to any computers on the Internet but instead are assigned to computers on internal networks. These private IP ranges are as follows:

10.0.0.0 through 10.255.255.255

172.16.0.0 through 172.31.255.255

192.168.1.0 through 192.168.255.255

However, the first and last address in each range is not usable. The only usable addresses in these ranges are:

10.0.0.1 through 10.255.255.254

172.16.0.1 through 172.31.255.254

192.168.1.1 through 192.168.255.254

You may remember that IP addresses on the Internet must be unique. No two computers on the Internet can use the same IP address. However, since private addresses are internal to a company, different companies can use the same IP addresses on their internal networks. In other words, company A can use a range of 192.168.1.1 through 192.168.1.254 for computers in their network, and company B can use the exact same numbers.

Exploring an IPv4 Address in Binary

Although you can usually work with IPv4 addresses using the dotted decimal format, you occasionally need to dig a little deeper. The following section gives some in-depth information on the IPv4 address at the binary level.

Understanding the Bits of an IP Address

People have 10 fingers and generally count using the decimal system with a base of 10. However, computers only understand 1s and 0s and count using the binary system with a base of 2. Each binary number is a bit and can have a value of 1 or 0.

An IPv4 address has 32 bits. You'll commonly see the IP address expressed in dotted decimal format, but it can also be expressed in four groups of eight bits. Each group of eight bits is also known as an *octet* in the IP address. In other words, an IP address has four decimals in dotted decimal format, which can also be expressed as four octets in binary format.

For example, Table 5.5 shows an IP address and subnet mask expressed in both decimal and binary form.

A logical question is "How does 192 in decimal equate to 1100 0000 in binary?" The answer is based on which bits are ones in the binary string. Table 5.6 shows the relative value of the binary bits. The low-order bit (2^0) is 1 since any number raised to the 0 power is 1. 2^1 is 2 since any number raised to the first power is equal to itself. The high-order bit (2^7) has a decimal value of 128.

Octet means eight, and it's accurate to say that an IP address has four octets. Eight bits is also a byte, and the address can be referred to as four bytes.

TABLE 5.5 Comparing dotted decimal and binary

IP decimal	IP binary	Subnet mask decimal	Subnet mask binary
192	1100 0000	255	1111 1111
168	1010 1000	255	1111 1111
1	0000 0001	255	1111 1111
5	0000 0101	0	0000 0000

TABLE 5.6 Binary and decimal values

	2^7	2^6	2^5	2^4	2^3	2^2	2^1	2^0
Decimal value	128	64	32	16	8	4	2	1

> **You should be able to reproduce Table 5.6 from memory so that you can convert binary numbers to decimal and back. Notice that each number doubles from right to left.**

If the first two bits are a 1 (1100 0000), it represents one decimal value of 128 and one decimal value of 64. The sum or 128 + 64 equals 192. These 8 bits can represent any value between 0 and 255. If all eight bits are a 0 (0000 0000), the decimal value is 0. If all eight bits are a 1 (1111 1111), the value is 255.

Look at Table 5.7, and see whether you can determine the decimal values of the different examples. You can calculate the total decimal value by adding the decimal value for each bit that has a binary 1.

TABLE 5.7 Binary values

	2^7	2^6	2^5	2^4	2^3	2^2	2^1	2^0
Decimal value	128	64	32	16	8	4	2	1
Example 1	1	1	0	0	0	0	0	0
Example 2	1	0	1	0	1	0	0	0
Example 3	0	0	0	0	0	0	0	1
Example 4	0	0	0	0	0	1	0	1
Example 5	0	0	0	0	1	0	1	0
Example 6	0	0	0	0	0	0	0	0
Example 7	1	1	1	1	1	1	1	1

Here's the solution to check your answers:

- ► Example 1 = 192 (128 + 64)
- ► Example 2 = 168 (128 + 32 + 8)
- ► Example 3 = 1 (1)
- ► Example 4 = 5 (4 + 1)
- ► Example 5 = 10 (8+ 2)
- ► Example 6 = 0 (none of the bits are a 1)
- ► Example 7 = 255 (128 + 64 + 32 + 16 + 8 + 4 + 2 + 1)

Notice that examples 1 through 4 are the binary values of the IP address 192.168.1.5. In binary form, the full IP address is 1100 0000 . 1010 1000 . 0000 . 0001 . 0000 0101.

DIGIT GROUPING

When using decimal numbers, it's common to group digits in threes separated by a comma for better readability. For example, the number 1,234,567 is easier to read than the number 1234567.

Similarly, binary numbers are grouped with four bits separated by a space. It's easier to read 1100 0000 than it is to read 11000000. When digit grouping is used, it's easy to see that it is two groups of four, but when digit grouping is not used, it's not always apparent how many digits are in the binary string.

The actual value doesn't change when digit grouping is used. The value of 1,234,567 is the same as 1234567, and the value of 1100 0000 is the same as 11000000.

A simpler way of converting binary to decimal and decimal to binary is with the calculator built into the Windows operating system. Figure 5.6 shows the Windows 7 calculator in the Programmer View (from the View drop-down menu). Other operating systems provide the same capability in the Scientific View.

After selecting the proper view in the calculator, enter the decimal number, and then click Bin to convert it to binary. If you want to convert it back to decimal, simply click Dec. You can also convert numbers to base 16 hexadecimal numbers (Hex) or base 8 octal numbers (Oct).

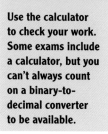

FIGURE 5.6 Converting decimal to binary

Understanding CIDR Notation

The subnet mask is sometimes referenced in a type of shorthand called *Classless Inter-Domain Routing (CIDR)* notation based on the number of bits. For example, if the subnet mask is 255.0.0.0, it has 8 bits in use and can be referenced as /8. If the subnet mask is 255.255.0.0, it has 16 bits in use and can be referenced as /16. If the subnet mask is 255.255.255.0, it has 24 bits in use and can be referenced as /24.

Table 5.8 shows some example IP addresses expressed with CIDR notation.

TABLE 5.8 Examples of CIDR notation

IP address	Subnet mask	CIDR notation
192.168.1.5	255.255.255.0	192.168.1.5 /24
172.17.34.5	255.255.0.0	172.17.34.5 /16
10.80.4.7	255.0.0.0	10.80.4.7 /8

Masking the IP Address

An important point of this chapter is understanding that an IPv4 address includes two components: a network ID and a host ID. The subnet mask identifies which is which by masking out the network ID. This was shown earlier with decimal numbers. When the subnet mask is configured at its maximum value (255), that portion of the IP address is the network ID.

The same point is true when using binary numbers. Consider an IP address of 192.168.1.5 with a subnet mask of 255.255.255.0, as shown in Table 5.9. When the subnet mask is configured at its maximum (1 in binary), that portion of the IP address is the network ID.

TABLE 5.9 Masking an IP address

	Fist octet	**Second octet**	**Third octet**	**Fourth octet**
192.168.1.5	1100 0000	1010 1000	0000 0001	0000 0101
255.255.255.0	1111 1111	1111 1111	1111 1111	0000 0000
Network ID	1100 0000	1010 1000	0000 0001	0000 0000

The computer looks at the first bit in the IP address (in this case it is set to 1) and the first bit in the subnet mask (also set to 1), and then ANDs them together, which yields a 1 as the first bit in the network ID. It then looks at the second bit in the IP address (1) and the second bit in the subnet mask (also set to 1) and is set to a 1 as the second bit in the network ID. It does this with each of the bits to determine the network ID.

You can do it bit by bit, but it is simpler to just look at which bits are 1s in the subnet mask and recognize that the corresponding bits in the IP address make up the network ID.

BOOLEAN AND LOGIC

Within the computer, the "masking" is done by using Boolean AND logic. Boolean AND logic compares two bits and provides a single bit as the output. If both bits are a 1, the output is a 1. However, if either of the bits is a 0 or both bits are a 0, the output is a 0.

The following list shows the four possibilities when ANDing two bits:

▶ 0 AND 0 = 0

▶ 0 AND 1 = 0

▶ 1 AND 0 = 0

▶ 1 AND 1 = 1

Using Classless IP Addresses

Classful IP addresses include Class A, Class B, and Class C addresses as described earlier. Remember that when a classful IP address is used, the subnet mask is implied and doesn't need to be included. Classless IP addressing can also be used.

When a classless IP address is used, you must have both the IP address and the subnet mask to determine the network ID. As an example, an address of 10.80.1.5 is a classful IP address with a subnet mask of 255.0.0.0 and a network ID of 10.0.0.0. However, Table 5.10 shows how the same IP address can be used as a classless IP address with different subnet masks, resulting in different network IDs.

TABLE 5.10   Examples of classless IP address

IP address	Subnet mask	Network ID
10.80.1.5	255.255.0.0	10.80.0.0
10.80.1.5	255.255.255.0	10.80.1.0

Subnetting IPv4 Addresses

Classful IPv4 address ranges can be divided into smaller groups of addresses, therefore creating subnets. Smaller organizations rarely need to do this, but large organizations frequently subnet the network instead of using the typical classful IP address ranges.

Administrators and IT support personnel need to understand subnetting to ensure that systems have the correct IP addresses assigned. Earlier in this chapter you had the opportunity to compare different IP addresses and subnet masks for computers on a subnet to determine whether they were correct. This section has the same goal but with advanced subnetting techniques.

Consider a single class C network of 192.168.1.0 /24, as shown in Figure 5.7. It can host 254 computers on the same subnet.

Imagine that users on this network are in four primary groups as follows:

▶ One group is regularly streaming video from a server.

▶ Another group is regularly uploading and downloading large graphics files.

▶ A third group is downloading large volumes of data from the Internet.

▶ The last group is just a regular group of users with occasional server and Internet access.

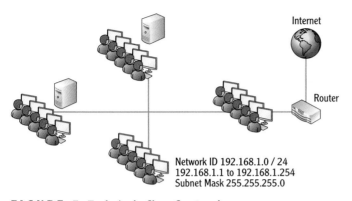

Network ID 192.168.1.0 / 24
192.168.1.1 to 192.168.1.254
Subnet Mask 255.255.255.0

FIGURE 5.7 A single Class C network

If all four groups of users are on the same subnet, their traffic will compete with each other for network bandwidth. The overall performance of the subnet may be slow. However, if the four groups are divided into different subnets, each subnet will enjoy better performance.

Determining the Number of Subnet Bits

In the example shown previously in Figure 5.7, it makes sense to create four separate subnets. This is done by borrowing bits from the host ID portion of the IP address and adding them to the network ID. They create a new portion of the network ID referred to as the subnet ID. If you borrow one bit, you can create two subnets. A single bit has two states, either a 1 or a 0, but you need four subnets, not two. If you borrow two bits, you can create four subnets.

Figure 5.8 shows how the single Class C address is subdivided by borrowing the two high-order bits from the host ID portion of the address. The Class C address has a subnet mask of 255.255.255.0, with 24 bits in the network ID portion of the IP address and 8 bits in the host ID portion.

If you borrow two bits from the original eight bits in the host ID portion, you now have six bits left for the host ID. The 24 bits of the original network ID and the two bits of the subnet ID are combined to give a total of 26 bits for the network ID.

It's important to realize that the two borrowed bits are the high-order bits in host ID. They have the values of 128 and 64. These two bits have four possible combinations of 0 0, 0 1, 1 0, and 11, which will be used within the host ID to create four separate subnets. Table 5.11 shows these combinations and their values.

Figure 5.7 shown earlier was a single large subnet of 254 hosts. By subnetting the Class C address, you can get the four subnets shown in Figure 5.9.

This gives a new subnet mask of 255.255.255.192 must be used.

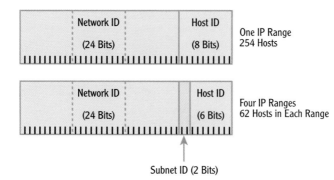

FIGURE 5.8 Creating subnets

TABLE 5.11 Subnetting with the two high-order bits

2^7 (Decimal 128)	2^6 (Decimal 64)	Decimal value
0	0	0
0	1	64
1	0	128
1	1	192

Notice that each subnet has a specific nonoverlapping range of IP addresses. This is an extremely important point. If you assigned an IP address of 192.168.1.200 to a computer in subnet A, it wouldn't be able to communicate with any other computer since it has an incorrect network ID for the subnet.

If you wanted to create more subnets, you'd need to borrow more bits. You can use the following formula to determine how many subnets you can create based on how many bits you borrow: 2^n, where n is the number of bits you borrow.

For example, if you borrow two bits (2^2), you can create four subnets. If you borrow three bits (2^3), you can create eight subnets. Of course, the more bits you borrow from the host ID, the fewer hosts that you can create in a network.

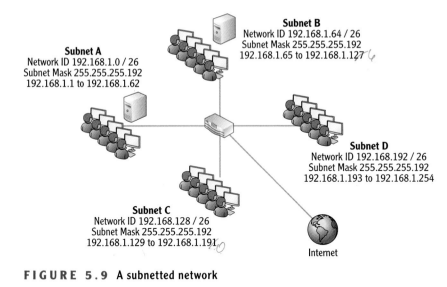

Subnet A
Network ID 192.168.1.0 / 26
Subnet Mask 255.255.255.192
192.168.1.1 to 192.168.1.62

Subnet B
Network ID 192.168.1.64 / 26
Subnet Mask 255.255.255.192
192.168.1.65 to 192.168.1.127

Subnet D
Network ID 192.168.192 / 26
Subnet Mask 255.255.255.192
192.168.1.193 to 192.168.1.254

Subnet C
Network ID 192.168.128 / 26
Subnet Mask 255.255.255.192
192.168.1.129 to 192.168.1.191

Internet

FIGURE 5.9 A subnetted network

Determining the Number of Hosts in a Network

Valid IP addresses cannot have all 0s in the host ID because that represents the network ID. Also, they can't have all 1s in the host ID because that represents a broadcast address within the subnet. This eliminates two possible IP addresses in the range of IP addresses for any subnet.

For example, if you use a typical Class C network of 192.168.10 with a subnet mask of 255.255.255.0, you can't have the following two IP addresses:

- ▶ 192.168.1.0 (since this is the network ID)

- ▶ 192.168.1.255 (since this is the broadcast address for the network ID)

This gives a valid range of 192.168.1.1 through 192.168.1.254 for a total of 254 possible hosts. You can determine how many hosts are supported in any subnet based on the following formula: $2^h - 2$, where h is the number bits in the host ID.

A Class C address uses 24 bits in the network ID and 8 bits in the host ID, so the formula is $2^8 - 2$. This gives a value of 254 (2^8 is 256 and $256 - 2 = 254$). Table 5.12 shows the number of hosts from a subnetted Class C address.

Although the discussion so far has been focused on subnetting a Class C network, the same concepts can be applied to subnet a Class B or Class A network. Remember, a Class B network starts with 16 bits for the network ID and 16 bits for the host ID. Table 5.13 shows the number of subnets and the number of hosts a subnetted Class B network will support.

TABLE 5.12   Determining the number of subnets and hosts in a Class C network

Borrowed bits from a Class C address	Subnet mask value	Number of subnets (2^n)	Number of hosts ($2^h - 2$)
1 0	192.168.1.128	2 (2^1)	126 ($2^7 - 2$)
2 0 0	192.168.1.192	4 (2^2)	62 ($2^6 - 2$)
3 0 0 0	192.168.1.224	8 (2^3)	30 ($2^5 - 2$)
4 0 0 0 0	192.168.1.240	16 (2^4)	14 ($2^4 - 2$)
5 0 0 0 0 0	192.168.1.248	32 (2^5)	6 ($2^3 - 2$)
6 0 0 0 0 0 0	192.168.1.252	64 (2^6)	2 ($2^2 - 2$)
7 Not valid since zero hosts are supported	192.168.1.254	126 (2^7)	0 ($2^2 - 2$)

TABLE 5.13   Determining the number of subnets and hosts in a Class B network

Borrowed bits from a Class B address	Subnet mask value	Number of subnets (2^n)	Number of hosts ($2^h - 2$)
1 0	172.16.1.128	2 (2^1)	32,766 ($2^{15} - 2$)
2 0 0	172.16.1.192	4 (2^2)	16,384 ($2^{14} - 2$)
3 0 0 0	172.16.1.224	8 (2^3)	8,190 ($2^{13} - 2$)
4 0 0 0 0	172.16.1.240	16 (2^4)	4094 ($2^{12} - 2$)
5 0 0 0 0 0	172.16.1.248	32 (2^5)	2046 ($2^{11} - 2$)
6 0 0 0 0 0 0	172.16.1.252	64 (2^6)	1022 ($2^{10} - 2$)
7 0 0 0 0 0 0 0	172.16.1.254	126 (2^7)	510 ($2^9 - 2$)

A Class A network starts with 8 bits for the network ID and 24 bits for the host ID. Table 5.14 shows the number of subnets and the number of hosts a subnetted Class A network will support.

TABLE 5.14 Determining the number of subnets and hosts in a Class A network

Borrowed bits from a Class A address		Subnet mask value	Number of subnets (2^n)	Number of hosts ($2^h - 2$)
1	0	192.168.1.128	2 (2^1)	8,388,606 ($2^{23} - 2$)
2	0 0	192.168.1.192	4 (2^2)	4,194,302 ($2^{22} - 2$)
3	0 0 0	192.168.1.224	8 (2^3)	2,097,150 ($2^{21} - 2$)
4	0 0 0 0	192.168.1.240	16 (2^4)	1,048,574 ($2^{20} - 2$)
5	0 0 0 0 0	192.168.1.248	32 (2^5)	524,286 ($2^{19} - 2$)
6	0 0 0 0 0 0	192.168.1.252	64 (2^6)	262,142 ($2^{18} - 2$)
7	0 0 0 0 0 0 0	192.168.1.254	126 (2^7)	131,070 ($2^{17} - 2$)

WHAT IS SUPERNETTING?

You may run across the term *supernetting* in your studies. Although the process is more advanced than you'll need to learn at this point, it is worthwhile understanding the big picture of supernetting. In short, supernetting is the opposite of subnetting.

You've learned that subnetting divides a larger network into multiple smaller networks by taking bits from the host ID. Supernetting combines multiple smaller networks into a single larger network by taking bits from the network ID. This is a useful function when optimizing routing devices on a network.

Identifying Local and Remote Addresses

Earlier in this chapter, you had the opportunity to determine whether simple IP address and subnet mask combinations were on the same subnet (local to each other) or whether the destination IP address was on a remote subnet. You should be able to make the same determination even when advanced subnetting techniques are used on your network.

As a reminder, the following steps are used to determine whether an address is local or remote.

1. Determine the network ID of the source IP address.

2. Determine the network ID of the destination IP address.

3. Determine whether they are the same:

   ▶ If so, they are local to each other.

   ▶ If not, the destination address is on a remote network and must be sent through the default gateway.

However, when advanced subnetting is used, it's a little harder to determine the network ID. For example, it's not readily apparent what the network ID is of the following IP and subnet mask combinations:

▶ Source IP: 192.168.1.61, 255.255.255.192

▶ Destination IP: 192.168.1.65, 255.255.255.192

You can simplify the process of determining the network ID with the following five steps:

1. Convert the IP address to binary. You can use a calculator to do this.

2. Convert the subnet mask to binary.

3. Draw a vertical line after the last one in the subnet mask:

   ▶ Everything to the left of the line is the network ID.

   ▶ Everything to the right of the line is the host ID.

4. Determine the network ID in binary. This is as simple as copying the IP address in binary to the left of the line and writing 0s to the right of the line.

5. Convert the network ID to decimal.

Figure 5.10 shows the steps for the 192.168.1.61 IP address, and Figure 5.11 shows the steps for 192.168.1.65.

Once you complete these steps, you can determine that the network ID of the source IP address is 192.168.1.0 and the network ID of the destination IP address is 192.168.1.64. These network IDs are not the same, so the destination IP address is remote.

▶

Really, draw the line. It's a simple step and provides an easy way to visually separate the network ID and the host ID.

Applying Subnetting Knowledge

On the job, subnetting knowledge is important because a misconfigured computer won't communicate with other systems. You should be able to look at the IP address and determine whether it is correct.

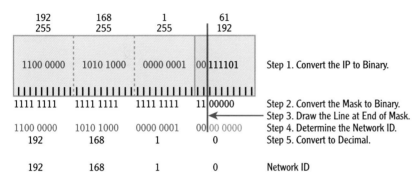

FIGURE 5.10 Determining the network ID of 192.168.1.61

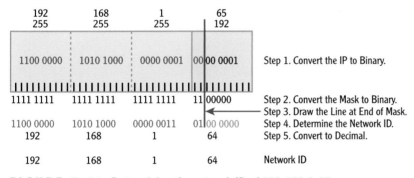

FIGURE 5.11 Determining the network ID of 192.168.1.65

At the beginning of this chapter, you had the opportunity to do some basic troubleshooting with Figure 5.3. It showed you the IP address and subnet mask of several computers with some computers configured incorrectly. However, those examples used subnet masks of 255.255.255.0 and 255.255.0.0 only. An actual network may have advanced subnet masks.

Take a look at Figure 5.12. The default gateways are configured correctly. The configured IP address, subnet mask, and default gateway are shown for each of these computers, but they aren't necessarily configured correctly. Instead, they show common typo errors that occur when a system is configured manually.

Can you determine what computers are configured correctly and what the errors are for the other computers?

Remember, all computers on the same subnet must have the same network ID, and they must be configured with the correct IP address of the default gateway. Use the steps shown earlier to calculate the network ID of the default gateways and each of the computers on the subnets.

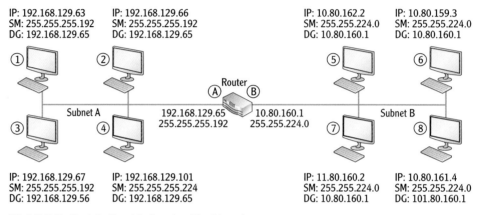

IP: 192.168.129.63
SM: 255.255.255.192
DG: 192.168.129.65

IP: 192.168.129.66
SM: 255.255.255.192
DG: 192.168.129.65

IP: 10.80.162.2
SM: 255.255.224.0
DG: 10.80.160.1

IP: 10.80.159.3
SM: 255.255.224.0
DG: 10.80.160.1

Router
A   B

Subnet A   192.168.129.65   10.80.160.1   Subnet B
                  255.255.255.192   255.255.224.0

IP: 192.168.129.67
SM: 255.255.255.192
DG: 192.168.129.56

IP: 192.168.129.101
SM: 255.255.255.224
DG: 192.168.129.65

IP: 11.80.160.2
SM: 255.255.224.0
DG: 10.80.160.1

IP: 10.80.161.4
SM: 255.255.224.0
DG: 101.80.160.1

FIGURE 5.12 Troubleshooting IP addressing

> **Hint: Two of the computers are configured correctly. The remaining computers have errors.**

The following text provides the solution to the challenge in Figure 5.12. After identifying all the errors you can find, check out these solutions.

Computer 1   The network ID of the computer is 192.168.129.0. However, the network ID of the default gateway is 192.168.129.64. Since the network IDs are different and the default gateway is known to be correct, the computer is configured with an incorrect IP address.

Computer 2   The network ID is 192.168.129.64, which is the same as the default gateway. This computer is configured correctly.

Computer 3   The network ID is 192.168.129.64, which is the same as the default gateway. However, the default gateway is configured incorrectly as 192.168.129.56 instead of 192.168.129.65.

Computer 4   The subnet mask is incorrect on this computer. All of the computers on the same subnet must have the same subnet mask. The network ID is 192.168.129.100, which is different from the network ID of the default gateway (192.168.129.64).

Computer 5   The network ID of the computer is 10.80.160.0, which is the same as the network ID of the default gateway. This computer is configured correctly.

Computer 6 The network ID of the computer is 10.80.128.0, which is different from the network ID of the default gateway (10.80.160.0). This computer is not configured correctly.

Computer 7 The network ID of the computer is 11.80.128.0 (notice the first octet is 11 instead of 10), which is different from the network ID of the default gateway (10.80.160.0). This computer is not configured correctly.

Computer 8 The network ID of the computer is 10.80.160.0, which is the same as the network ID of the default gateway. However, the default gateway is configured with an incorrect IP address. It should be 10.80.160.1 instead of 101.80.160.1.

As a final exercise with subnetting, consider a single Class C network with a network ID of 192.168.20.0 and a subnet mask of 255.255.255.0. You are tasked with dividing this network into two separate subnets.

See if you can answer the following questions:

> What is the network ID of each subnet?
>
> What is the subnet mask of each subnet?
>
> What is the first IP address of each subnet?
>
> What is the last IP address of each subnet?

The graphic at the end of the Understanding APIPA section in this chapter shows one possible solution for this challenge.

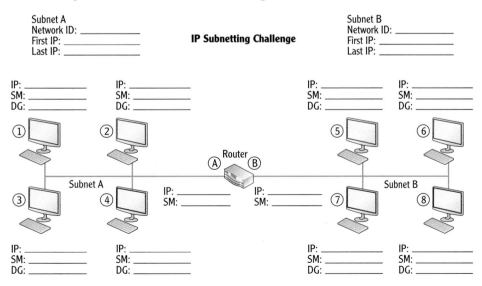

Comparing Manual and Automatic Assignment of IPv4 Addresses

IPv4 information can be assigned either manually or automatically. Manually means that you actually type in the IP address, subnet mask, default gateway, and other TCP/IP information such as the address of the DNS server into the configuration screens on each computer. Automatic assignment uses *Dynamic Host Configuration Protocol (DHCP)* server to assign the information to the computers without user intervention.

In most networks, it is much easier to use DHCP. The majority of the clients automatically get their TCP/IP configuration from a DHCP server. However, some clients may need to have a manually configured IP address. For example, the DHCP server must be assigned an address manually. Additionally, some clients don't support DHCP, and devices such as routers need to be manually assigned.

Manually Configuring IPv4

You can use the following steps to manually view or configure the IPv4 information on a Windows Server 2008 server or Windows 7 system.

You can also just view the information here without changing it. If you are using a DHCP server, it will be set to Obtain An IP Address Automatically.

1. Click Start ➢ Control Panel.

2. Type **Network** in the Control Panel Search box. Select Network And Sharing Center.

3. Click Manage Network Connections in the Tasks pane on the left.

4. Right-click Local Area Connection, and select Properties.

5. Select Internet Protocol Version 4 (TCP/IPv4), and click Properties. Your display will look similar to Figure 5.13.

6. Enter the appropriate IP address, subnet mask, default gateway, and address of a DNS server.

Using DHCP

If your system is configured to obtain an IP address automatically, a server on your network will be running DHCP. Windows Server 2008 servers include the DHCP role and can be configured to run DHCP.

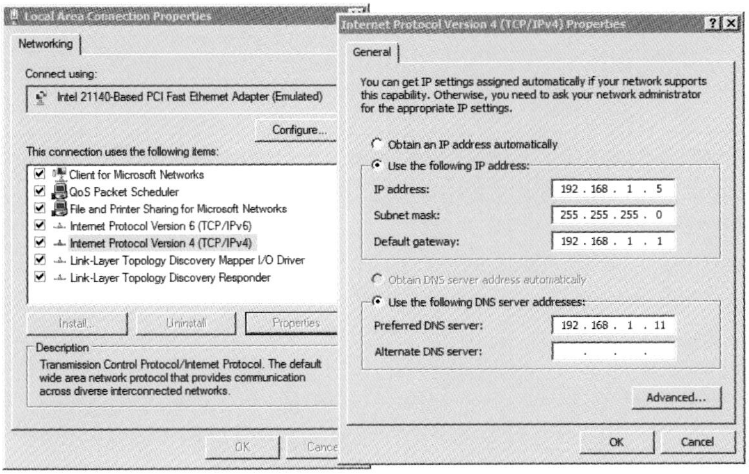

FIGURE 5.13 Viewing the IPv4 configuration of the NIC

Figure 5.14 shows the process a DHCP client uses to obtain an IP address and other IP information from a DHCP server. This process is commonly called the *DORA process*, referring to the first letter in each of the packets (Discover, Offer, Request, and Acknowledge).

1. When the DHCP client turns on, it sends a broadcast looking for a DHCP server. This is the Discover packet.

2. The DHCP server answers with an Offer packet. The offer includes an IP address, subnet mask, and other information such as the address of a DNS server. This offer is also referred to as a *lease offer*.

3. The DHCP client replies with a Request packet to request the lease. If the DHCP client receives offers from multiple DHCP servers, it requests a lease only from the first DHCP that offers a lease.

4. The DHCP server responds with an Acknowledge packet. The DHCP server assigns this IP address to this client and removes the IP address from the list of available IP addresses to lease to other clients.

◄

The default lease length on a Windows Server 2008 DHCP server is eight days. Clients try to renew their lease after four days.

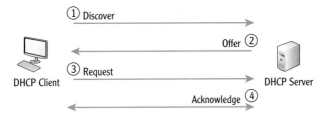

FIGURE 5.14 DHCP DORA process

▶

Routers that can pass these bootp broadcasts on UDP ports 67 and 68 are RFC 1542 compatible.

The DHCP broadcast packets are special bootp broadcast messages defined in RFC 1542. A regular broadcast message would not pass through a router, but a bootp broadcast uses UDP ports 67 and 68. Routers on the network can be configured to pass these bootp broadcasts. Without bootp broadcasts, you'd have to place a DHCP server on each subnet, or utilize a DHCP Proxy service to act as a liaison between the DHCP client and server.

Understanding APIPA

If a DHCP client is unable to reach a DHCP server, it will automatically assign itself an IP address using *Automatic Private Internet Protocol Addressing (APIPA)*. The APIPA address always starts with 169.254 in the IP address and always has a subnet mask of 255.255.0.0. The host ID is randomly generated by the client computer and then broadcast on the network to check for IP address conflicts. If no conflicts are found the client will assume the generated IP address.

The APIPA address provides limited connectivity for clients on the network. If other clients also have an APIPA address, then they have a network ID of 169.254.0.0, and they can communicate with each other. However, APIPA doesn't provide a default gateway, so clients will not be able to access any resources outside of the subnet, including the Internet.

You can tell whether a client has been assigned an IPv4 address by typing **ipconfig /all** at the command prompt. Listing 5.1 shows the results.

Listing 5.1: `ipconfig /all` **output**

```
C:\>ipconfig /all

Windows IP Configuration

        Host Name . . . . . . . . . . . . : FS1
        Primary Dns Suffix  . . . . . . . : wiley.com
        Node Type . . . . . . . . . . . . : Hybrid
        IP Routing Enabled. . . . . . . . : No
        WINS Proxy Enabled. . . . . . . . : No
        DNS Suffix Search List. . . . . . : wiley.com

Ethernet adapter Local Area Connection:

        Connection-specific DNS Suffix  . :
        Description . . . . . . . . . . . :
            Intel 21140-Based PCI Fast Ethernet Adapter
        Physical Address. . . . . . . . . : 00-03-FF-5A-02-00
        DHCP Enabled. . . . . . . . . . . : Yes
```

```
        Autoconfiguration Enabled . . . . : Yes
        Link-local IPv6 Address . . . . . : fe80::184:e9f8:a71b:304%10
    (Preferred)
        Autoconfiguration IPv4 Address. . : 169.254.3.4(Preferred)
        Subnet Mask . . . . . . . . . . . : 255.255.0.0
        Default Gateway . . . . . . . . . :
        DNS Servers . . . . . . . . . . . :
        NetBIOS over Tcpip. . . . . . . . : Enabled
```

In the code listing, three lines are in bold:

DHCP Enabled   When set to Yes, it shows this system is a DHCP client.

Autoconfiguration Enabled   When set to Yes, this indicates that APIPA is enabled and an APIPA address will be assigned if a DHCP server can't be reached.

Autoconfiguration IPv4 Address   An address starting with 169.254 shows this is an APIPA address. More, this shows that the DHCP client could not receive an address from a DHCP server.

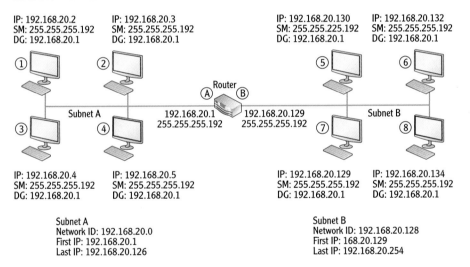

IP: 192.168.20.2
SM: 255.255.255.192
DG: 192.168.20.1

IP: 192.168.20.3
SM: 255.255.255.192
DG: 192.168.20.1

IP: 192.168.20.130
SM: 255.255.225.192
DG: 192.168.20.1

IP: 192.168.20.132
SM: 255.255.255.192
DG: 192.168.20.1

IP: 192.168.20.4
SM: 255.255.255.192
DG: 192.168.20.1

IP: 192.168.20.5
SM: 255.255.255.192
DG: 192.168.20.1

IP: 192.168.20.129
SM: 255.255.255.192
DG: 192.168.20.1

IP: 192.168.20.134
SM: 255.255.255.192
DG: 192.168.20.1

Subnet A
Network ID: 192.168.20.0
First IP: 192.168.20.1
Last IP: 192.168.20.126

Subnet B
Network ID: 192.168.20.128
First IP: 168.20.129
Last IP: 192.168.20.254

THE ESSENTIALS AND BEYOND

In this chapter, you learned about the two primary components of an IPv4 address: the network ID and the host ID. All computers on the same subnet must have the same network ID, and all these computers must have unique host IDs. IP addresses can be expressed in dotted decimal format or using binary. Classful IP addresses are identified by the value in the first octet of the IP address and have known subnet masks. Classless IP addresses are accompanied

(Continues)

THE ESSENTIALS AND BEYOND *(Continued)*

by a subnet mask, which is used to determine the network ID. Classful IP addresses can be subnetted to create multiple subnetworks, or subnets. IP addresses and other TCP/IP configuration can be assigned manually or automatically using a DHCP server.

ADDITIONAL EXERCISES

▶ Identify your IPv4 address.

▶ Identify whether your computer has a public IP address or a private IP address.

▶ Determine the network ID of the following classful IP addresses:

　　▶ 192.168.20.5

　　▶ 172.16.178.17

　　▶ 10.80.3.18

▶ Determine the subnet mask and network ID of the following classless IP addresses:

　　▶ 192.168.232.222 /26

　　▶ 172.16.129.25 /20

　　▶ 10.178.215.111 /11

To compare your answers to the author's, please visit **www.sybex.com/go/ networkingessentials**.

REVIEW QUESTIONS

1.　Which of the following addresses is a valid IPv4 address?

　　A.　192.168.1.256　　**C.**　2001:0000:4137:9e76:3c2b:05ad:3f57:fe98

　　B.　10.1.25.2　　　　**D.**　2001:0000:4137:9g76:3c2b:05zd:3x57:gh98

2.　What class is the following IP address: 192.168.1.5?

　　A.　Class A　　**C.**　Class C

　　B.　Class B　　**D.**　Class D

3.　True or false. The following two classful IP addresses have the same network ID: 192.168.1.5 and 192.168.2.6

4.　True or false. The following two classful IP addresses have the same network ID: 10.80.4.2 and 10.81.15.2

(Continues)

THE ESSENTIALS AND BEYOND (Continued)

5. Look at the following graphic. Which letter or number would represent the default gateway for subnet B?

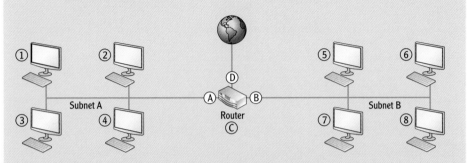

6. What is the subnet mask for the following IP address: 192.168.1.5 /26?

  A. 192.168.1.5   **C.** 255.255.255.192

  B. 255.255.255.0   **D.** 255.255.255.240

7. Which of the following IP addresses is in one of the reserved IP address ranges defined by RFC 1918?

  A. 10.80.256.1   **C.** 192.169.4.5

  B. 172.17.34.14   **D.** 224.17.2.5

8. How many hosts are supported in subnet with a network ID of 192.168.1.128/26?

  A. 30   **C.** 62

  B. 32   **D.** 64

9. True or false. The following two classless IP addresses have the same network ID: 192.168.1.105 /26 and 192.168.1.136 /26.

10. A computer is unable to communicate with other computers on the network. You use `ipconfig` and see the following information:

  IP address: 169.254.5.7

  Subnet mask: 255.255.0.0

  Default gateway: blank

  DNS server: blank

  A. A DHCP server can't be reached.

  B. The default gateway needs to be manually configured.

  C. The DNS server IP address needs to be manually configured.

  D. None of the above.

## CHAPTER 6

Exploring IPv6

Although IPv4 has been the primary IP addressing scheme used on the Internet and within internal networks for many years, IPv6 is also being used today. The differences are significant, and even technicians who have mastered IPv4 have a lot to learn to master IPv6. This includes the basics of an IPv6 address, its different components, how IPv4 and IPv6 coexist, and how you can assign IPv6 addresses.

▶ **Understanding IPv6 addresses**

▶ **Exploring the components of an IPv6 address**

▶ **Understanding the dual IP stack**

▶ **Comparing manual and automatic assignment of IPv6**

Exploring IPv6 Addresses

IPv4 uses 32 bits and can address about 4 billion addresses. When the Internet was in its infancy, 4 billion addresses seemed like they would last forever—they didn't. The astronomical growth of the Internet resulted in the concern that we may run out of IPv4 addresses, so IPv6 was created.

> ▶
>
> **IPv5 used 64 bits. It was never adopted since designers realized the Internet would quickly run out of IP addresses again if it was adopted.**

IPv6 uses 128 bits and can address more than 340 undecillion IP addresses. That's more than 340,000,000,000,000,000,000,000,000,000,000,000,000 addresses, or more than 340 trillion, trillion, trillion addresses. This will be enough addresses to last quite a while. IPv4 lasted a few decades before needing an upgrade. Perhaps in the year 2040 a newer version of IP will come out to give us some more addresses.

IPv6 is slowly replacing IPv4 on the Internet and on internal networks. In addition to adding more IP addresses, it includes many new capabilities that simply aren't available in IPv4.

You'll easily be able to tell the difference between an IPv4 address and an IPv6 address just by looking at it. IPv6 addresses are displayed as hexadecimal characters instead of the dotted decimal format of IPv4.

> **The IPv6 address starts with fe80, indicating it is a link-local address. Other types include global and unique local addresses.**

As an example, Figure 6.1 shows the IPv4 and IPv6 addresses of a Windows Server 2008 server. The IPv6 address is fe80::184:e9f8:a71b:304. The %10 at the end of the IPv6 address is a zone index and identifies the network interface card.

```
Administrator: Command Prompt

Microsoft Windows [Version 6.0.6001]
Copyright (c) 2006 Microsoft Corporation. All rights reserved.

C:\Users\Administrator>ipconfig

Windows IP Configuration

Ethernet adapter Local Area Connection:

   Connection-specific DNS Suffix  . :
   Link-local IPv6 Address . . . . . : fe80::184:e9f8:a71b:304%10
   IPv4 Address. . . . . . . . . . . : 192.168.1.10
   Subnet Mask . . . . . . . . . . . : 255.255.255.0
   Default Gateway . . . . . . . . . : 192.168.1.1
```

F I G U R E   6.1   Viewing IPv4 and IPv6 addresses

Comparing IPv4 Classes and IPv6 Prefixes

Chapter 5 presented IPv4 classful addresses (Class A, Class B, and Class C). A classful IP address is identified by the first decimal in the IP address. For example, an IP address of 10.80.1.1 has 10 as the first decimal, which is in the Class A range of 1 to 126.

> **The IPv6 prefix notation is similar to CIDR notation in IPv4. It indicates how many bits are a 1 in the subnet mask.**

Similarly, an *IPv6 prefix* identifies the type of IPv6 address. As an example, Figure 6.1 showed an IP address starting with fe80, which is a link-local address. You'll see many other prefixes in this chapter that identify specific types of IPv6 addresses.

Prefixes often are accompanied by a prefix notation similar to /3 or /32. This indicates how many bits are in the prefix. For example, 2001 /3 indicates only the first three bits are in the prefix, but 2001:0000 /32 indicates the first 32 bits are in the prefix.

As an introduction, Table 6.1 summarizes the prefixes covered in this chapter.

T A B L E   6.1   Common IPv6 prefixes

IPv6 prefix	Description
2 /3	Global unicast addresses.
	These commonly start with 2001:, but other prefixes starting with 2 are possible.
2001:0000 /32	Teredo tunneling protocol address.
	This is used for IPv4 and IPv6 compatibility.

(Continues)

TABLE 6.1   *(Continued)*

IPv6 prefix	Description
fe80 /10	Link-local addresses.
	These are similar to IPv4 APIPA addresses.
fc /7 (fd /8)	Unique local unicast addresses.
	These are IPv6 addresses assigned in an internal network similar to IPv4 private addresses. The prefix is only 7 bits, which is literally identified as fc in hexadecimal, but the 8th bit is always a 1, so this is always seen as fd in an IPv6 address.
::1	Loopback address.
	A prefix of 127 zeros followed by a single 1 as the 128th bit is the loopback address. This is similar to the IPv4 loopback address of 127.0.0.1.

Understanding Hexadecimal

IPv6 addresses are displayed in hexadecimal, so it's important to understand hexadecimal numbers. Chapter 5 introduced binary and compared it to decimal. As a reminder, decimal uses a base of 10 with numbers from 0 through 9, and binary uses a base of 2 with 0 and 1 as the only two values.

Hexadecimal uses a base of 16 with the numbers 0 through 9 followed by *a* through *f*. Each hexadecimal number can be represented using four binary bits. Table 6.2 shows how to count from 0 through F in hexadecimal and includes both the binary and decimal values for each number.

◄

Hexadecimal values can be either uppercase or lowercase. For example, f is the same as F. IPv6 addresses are commonly displayed in lowercase.

TABLE 6.2   Hexadecimal values

Hexadecimal number	Binary value 2^3 8	2^2 4	2^1 2	2^0 1	Decimal value
0	0	0	0	0	0
1	0	0	0	1	1
2	0	0	1	0	2
3	0	0	1	1	3

(Continues)

TABLE 6.2 *(Continued)*

Hexadecimal number	Binary value				Decimal value
	2^3	2^2	2^1	2^0	
	8	4	2	1	
4	0	1	0	0	4
5	0	1	0	1	5
6	0	1	1	0	6
7	0	1	1	1	7
8	1	0	0	0	8
9	1	0	0	1	9
a	1	0	1	0	10
b	1	0	1	1	11
c	1	1	0	0	12
d	1	1	0	1	13
e	1	1	1	0	14
f	1	1	1	1	15

Displaying IPv6 Addresses

When a full IPv6 address is displayed, it will include eight groups of four hexadecimal numbers, separated by colons similar to this:

fe80:0000:0000:0000:0184:e9f8:a71b:0304

However, you can shorten the IPv6 address using two techniques. First, you can use zero compression to identify a contiguous group of zeros. Zero compression replaces a group of zeros with two colons. Second, you can drop leading zeros in any hexadecimal grouping. Table 6.3 shows the three ways you can display the same IPv6 address.

TABLE 6.3   Displaying an IPv6 address

Example	Description
fe80:0000:0000:0000:0184:e9f8:a71b:0304	Full IPv6 address
fe80::0184:e9f8:a71b:0304	IPv6 address using zero compression
fe80::184:e9f8:a71b:304	IPv6 address using zero compression and dropping leading zeros

It's important to note that you can use only one set of double colons. In the example (fe80::0184:e9f8:a71b:0304), five groups of hex numbers are displayed. Since an IPv6 address has eight groups of hex numbers, the double colon (::) takes the place of three groups of zeros (0000:0000:0000).

However, if a number had two groups of double colons (for example fe80::0184:e9f8::0304), there would be no way to determine how many groups of zeros each double colon represents. In other words, you can have only one set of double colons in an IPv6 address. Two sets of double colons are not valid in an IPv6 address.

Comparing IPv6 Transmission Types

Chapter 2 introduced the three methods of transmission for IPv4 as unicast, multicast, and broadcast. As a reminder, these transmissions are as follows:

Unicast   Traffic sent from one computer to one other computer

Broadcast   Traffic sent from one computer to all other computers on the same subnet

Multicast   Traffic sent from one computer to multiple other computers using the IGMP protocol

IPv6 uses three types of transmission known as unicast, multicast, and anycast. These have some similarities to IPv4.

Unicast   An IPv6 unicast transmission is traffic sent from one computer to one other computer, just as it works in IPv4.

Multicast   An IPv6 multicast transmission is traffic sent from one computer to multiple other computers, similar to multicast in IPv4. IPv6 provides some improvements in multicasting.

Anycast   An IPv6 anycast transmission is traffic sent from one host to one other host from a list of multiple hosts. It is typically used to locate the nearest router or to locate services on the network.

▶

Anycast is some-
times called one-to-
one-of-many.

Understanding the Need for IPv6

▶

Chapter 11 explains
NAT in more depth.

The primary driving force of IPv6 was to provide more IP addresses. If only IPv4 addresses were used, experts predicted that the Internet would run out of IPv4 addresses sometime in 2011. Earlier predictions indicated the Internet was on track to run out of addresses during 1990s or 2000s, but steps were taken to extend its lifetime. For example, Network Address Translation (NAT) helped reduce the number of public IP addresses needed.

As mentioned previously, IPv4 uses 32 bits in the IP address. The math shows that 2 raised to the 32nd power (2^{32}), or 2 times itself 32 times, equals 4,294,967,296, which is more than 4 billion addresses. However, because of how IPv4 reserved so many different IP address ranges, there are only about 3.7 billion IP addresses available on the Internet. No one wants to see the growth of the Internet stop, and with the 128 bits in an IPv6 address, it has plenty of room for growth.

In addition to providing trillions of trillions more IP addresses, IPv6 also provides several improvements:

Native Support for IPSec   IPv6 supports Internet Protocol Security (IPSec) without any additions. This allows clients to easily encrypt IPv6 data. IPv4 can use IPSec, but it takes extra effort to make it work.

More Efficient Routing   IPv6 uses global addresses on the Internet. These are designed for worldwide delivery and reduce the number of routes that Internet routers need to remember. In contrast, many Internet backbone routers maintain routing lists of more than 85,000 IPv4 routes.

Easy Host Configuration   IPv6 routers can automatically configure internal computers. You can also use Dynamic Host Configuration Protocol version 6 (DHCPv6) servers to provide IPv6 information. However, even if an IPv6 router or DHCPv6 server isn't available, systems can configure themselves with internal IPv6 addresses.

Understanding Neighbor Discovery

Neighbor Discovery (ND) is an IPv6 protocol that uses Internet Control Message Protocol version 6 (ICMPv6) messages to discover details about the network.

It performs several key functions:

Discovers Routers   ND identifies routers on the local subnet. These routers can then be queried for IPv6 configuration.

Discovers Prefixes   The prefix is used in IPv6 similar to how the subnet mask is used in IPv4. ND identifies the prefix used by other hosts on the subnet.

Discovers Parameters   ND messages tell the computer what IPv6 parameters are being used by other hosts on the subnet.

Address Autoconfiguration   This determines whether the host can obtain an IP address from a router or a DHCPv6 server. If not, it assigns itself a link-local address, which is similar to IPv4's APIPA addressing.

Detects Duplicate Addresses   This prevents the computer from using an IPv6 link-local address that is already in use.

Resolves Addresses   ND can resolve a neighbor's IPv6 address to its link-layer address. This is similar to how the Address Resolution Protocol (ARP) resolves IP addresses to MAC addresses in IPv4.

Exploring the Components of an IPv6 Address

An IPv4 address has a network ID component and a host ID component. Similarly, an IPv6 address has a network identifier and interface identifier components.

Figure 6.2 shows the two basic components of the IPv6 address used on a Windows Server 2008 server. In IPv6, the first 64 bits are typically the network ID, and the last 64 bits are typically the interface identifier, though there are exceptions.

IPv4-mapped IPv6 addresses and Teredo addresses differ from this basic format, but they still have 128 bits.

Network Identifier	Extended Unique Identifier (EUI)
64 Bits	64 Bits

FIGURE 6.2 The components of an IPv6 address

The interface identifier is similar to the Media Access Control (MAC) address, or physical address used in IPv4. You may remember that the MAC is a group of 48 bits expressed as 12 hexadecimal numbers similar to this: 12:34:56:78:9A:BC.

The first six hex numbers are the organizational unique identifier (OUI) identifying the manufacturer, and the last six are unique on the network interface card.

In an IPv6 address, the interface identifier (the last 64 bits) is used in place of the MAC address. Windows Server 2008 uses an EUI 64-bit address (EUI-64) defined as part of IPv6. Gigabit network interface cards are configured with EUI-64 addresses. IPv6 uses the 48-bit MAC addresses on older cards and adds 16 extra bits to reach 64 bits.

The interface identifier can also be created using other methods:

▶ A randomly generated temporary identifier

▶ A randomly generated permanent identifier

▶ A manually assigned identifier

> **EUI-48, EUI-60, and other alternatives are also available. However, Windows Server 2008 uses EUI-64.**

These alternative interface identifiers provide a level of privacy in network communication by hiding the actual identifier of the host.

Understanding Global Unicast Addresses

Global unicast addresses are used on the Internet. You can compare them to IPv4 public IP addresses. However, global unicast addresses are designed for hierarchical routing, which makes them easier to route throughout the Internet.

Figure 6.3 shows the components of a global unicast address. Notice that the first three bits are 001. If the first number of the address is a 2, you know that it is a global unicast address used on the Internet.

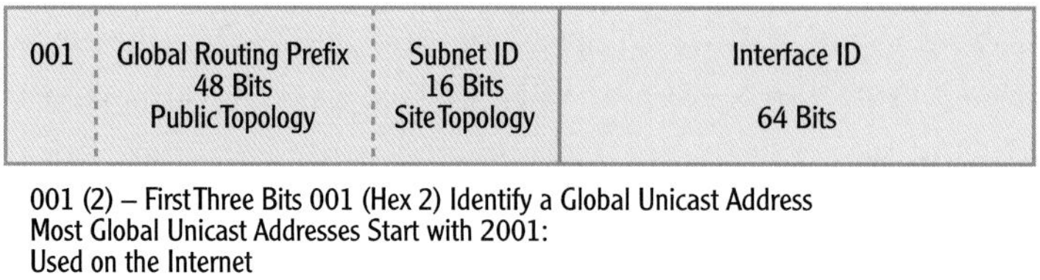

001	Global Routing Prefix 48 Bits Public Topology	Subnet ID 16 Bits Site Topology	Interface ID 64 Bits

001 (2) – First Three Bits 001 (Hex 2) Identify a Global Unicast Address
Most Global Unicast Addresses Start with 2001:
Used on the Internet

FIGURE 6.3 IPv6 global unicast address

The formal definition for global unicast addresses says that only the first three digits are specified as 001, meaning that it could be 0010 (hex 2) or 0011 (hex 3). However, 0011 is reserved and can't be used. In other words, the first number will always be a 2.

Although a wide range of global unicast addresses are possible, the most common one used is 2001. IPv6 global unicast addresses are assigned by the Internet

Assignment Numbers Authority (IANA). They have assigned several banks of IPv6 addresses starting with 2001 (such as 2001:0000, 2001:0200, 2001: 0400, and so on). They have also assigned some addresses starting with 2400, 2600, and more, but 2001 remains the most popular.

The first 48 bits of the global unicast address make up the public topology, and the next 16 bits make up the site topology. Addresses in public topology are assigned to Internet service providers (ISPs). ISPs can then use the 16 bits in the site topology to create as many as 65,536 subnets, with each subnet having more than 18 quintillion addresses each.

You can read more about global unicast addresses in the document "IPv6 Global Unicast Address Format" at **www.ietf.org/rfc/rfc3587.txt**.

> ◀
> **You probably know thousands, millions, and billions. What's next? Trillions, quadrillions, quintillions, sextillions, and more.**

Understanding Link-Local Addresses

In Chapter 5, you learned about Automatic Private Internet Protocol Addressing (APIPA) addresses. When a DHCP client is unable to reach a DHCP server, it assigns itself an IP address in the 169.254.x.y range.

Link-local addresses are similar to APIPA addresses. If a DHCPv6 server or an IPv6 router isn't available to assign an IPv6 address, an IPv6 client can assign itself a link-local address to communicate with other hosts on the same network. Just as APIPA limits communication to the local subnet, a link-local address limits a client to communication only on the local subnet. This is because link-local addresses are not routable.

However, IPv6 clients can also have another IPv6 address in addition to the link-local address. For public systems, they can also have a global unicast address. For private systems, they can also have a unique local address. The link-local address is used to communicate with local nodes, and the other address is used to communicate with clients past the router.

In contrast, IPv4 uses APIPA as a fallback when a DHCP client doesn't receive a DHCP address. In IPv4, you'll have only one address assigned.

Figure 6.4 shows the format of a link-local address. Notice that the first 10 bits are always 1111 1110 10. This equates to fe80 in hexadecimal.

> ◀
> **Link-local IPv6 addresses always start with fe80.**

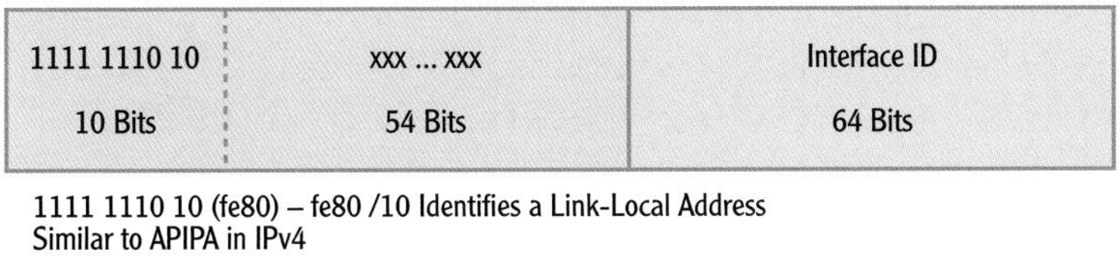

1111 1110 10	xxx ... xxx	Interface ID
10 Bits	54 Bits	64 Bits

1111 1110 10 (fe80) – fe80 /10 Identifies a Link-Local Address
Similar to APIPA in IPv4

FIGURE 6.4 IPv6 link-local address

▶

Microsoft recommends leaving IPv6 enabled on all systems.

If IPv6 is installed on a system, a link-local address will always be configured. Microsoft systems use the link-local address for Neighbor Discovery processes, and these processes won't work if IPv6 is not enabled on the system.

Autoconfiguration of IPv6 addresses is either stateless or stateful.

Stateless   The configuration is performed based on router advertisements. The system will start with a self-assigned fe80 address and then go through a process to verify it and learn about the network by communicating with local routers.

Stateful   The configuration is performed by a DHCPv6 server. The "Using DHCP" section later in this chapter presents the process used by a DHCPv6 client and a DHCPv6 server.

Early documentation specified the use of site-local addresses starting with a prefix of fec0:: /10. You may still see this in some documentation; however, the use of site-local addresses has been deprecated and is not recommended.

You can read more about unique local addresses in the paper "IPv6 Stateless Address Autoconfiguration" at **http://tools.ietf.org/html/rfc4862**.

Understanding Unique Local Addresses

Unique local addresses are IPv6 addresses used in an internal network. They are similar to IPv4 private IP addresses in that you assign them to computers on your internal network.

▶

Unique local IPv6 addresses always start with an IP prefix of fd.

Figure 6.5 shows the format of unique local addresses. Unique local addresses are identified by the first seven bits as 1111 110. Additionally, the 8th bit is always a 1.

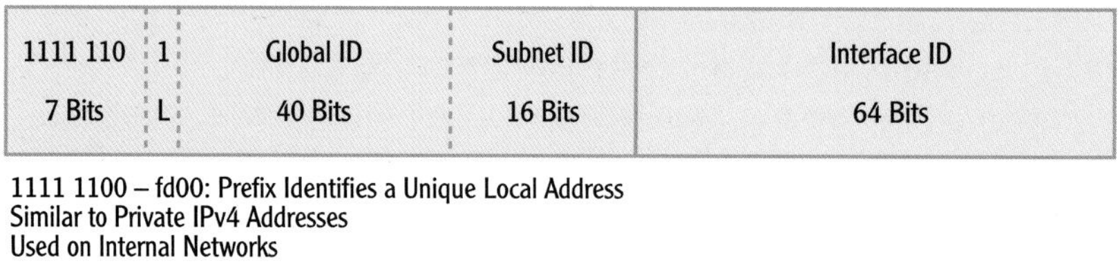

1111 110	1	Global ID	Subnet ID	Interface ID
7 Bits	L	40 Bits	16 Bits	64 Bits

1111 1100 – fd00: Prefix Identifies a Unique Local Address
Similar to Private IPv4 Addresses
Used on Internal Networks

FIGURE 6.5 IPv6 unique local unicast addresses

You can dig into the details of unique local addresses in the paper "Unique Local IPv6 Unicast Addresses" at **http://tools.ietf.org/html/rfc4193**.

FC or FD for Unique Local Addresses?

Some documentation indicates that a unique local address has the first seven bits to 1111 110, giving it a 7-bit prefix of fc hexadecimal. Other documentation indicates that all unique local IPv6 addresses start with a prefix of fd hexadecimal. Which one is correct? Actually both.

RFC 4193 defines unique local addresses and specifies the eighth bit should be a 1. This "L" bit indicates the address is locally assigned. RFC 4193 states that the value of 0 for the "L" bit may be defined in the future, but for now it's always a 1.

If only the first seven bits are counted (1111 110), then the eighth bit is implied as a zero. This gives a value of binary value 1111 1100, or fc in hex. However, if the eighth bit is a 1 in the actual IPv6 address, then the first eight bits are 1111 1101, which equates to fd.

In other words, if you see the full IPv6 address, the prefix is fd in hex. If only the first seven bits are represented, the value is fc in hex.

Understanding the Dual IP Stack

In a perfect world, every computer on the Internet could switch from IPv4 to IPv6 on a specific day. For example, November 9, 2010, could have been designated international IPv6 day, and everyone in the world could have magically switch each computer's configuration at midnight Greenwich mean time. No one realistically envisions such as a perfect world, though.

Instead, IPv4 and IPv6 must be able to interoperate side by side. IPv6 is currently working on the Internet and will gradually replace IPv4. In the meantime, operating systems and routers support IPv4-mapped IPv6 addresses and Teredo tunneling.

Using IPv4-Mapped IPv6 Addresses

One way that the IPv4/IPv6 dual IP stack works is by supporting IPv4-mapped IPv6 addresses. Figure 6.6 shows an IPv4-mapped IPv6 address. The first 80 bits are set to 0, the next 16 bits are set to 1, and the last 32 bits hold the IPv4 address.

000 ... 000	111 ... 111	IPv4 Address
First 80 Bits Set to Zero	16 Bits	32 Bits

::ffff:192.168.1.5

FIGURE 6.6 IPv4-mapped IPv6 address

The IPv4-mapped IPv6 address is expressed with the leading zeros omitted with zero compression (using a double colon, ::), the 16 ones expressed as ffff, and the IPv4 address in traditional dotted decimal format.

Understanding IPv4 to IPv6 Tunneling Protocols

Some devices accessible from the Internet aren't yet IPv6 enabled. If only IPv6 was used, data couldn't transit through these devices. *Teredo* is a tunneling protocol that encapsulates IPv6 packets within IPv4 datagrams. This allows the IPv6 packets to transit through these devices.

Teredo is needed for NAT devices that translate private IPv4 addresses to public IPv4 addresses and translate public IPv4 addresses back to private IPv4 addresses. Once IPv6 is fully implemented, Teredo won't be needed anymore.

If Teredo traffic needs to pass through a firewall, the firewall must be configured to allow the Teredo traffic to pass through. By default, a firewall will block traffic using a Teredo tunnel.

Figure 6.7 shows the mapping of a Teredo IPv6 address.

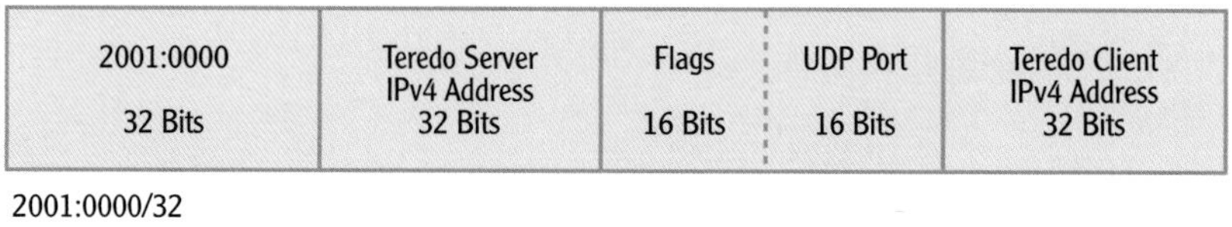

Teredo clients have an IPv6 address that starts with 2001:0000/32. This is known as the Teredo prefix.

2001:0000	Teredo Server IPv4 Address	Flags	UDP Port	Teredo Client IPv4 Address
32 Bits	32 Bits	16 Bits	16 Bits	32 Bits

2001:0000/32

FIGURE 6.7 Teredo IPv6 address

You can tell whether your system is using Teredo by entering **ipconfig /all** at the command prompt. Listing 6.1 shows a partial output from a system that has a Teredo address assigned. Notice the prefix is 2001:0.

Listing 6.1 Partial result of ipconfig /all

```
Tunnel adapter Local Area Connection* 18:
```

```
    Connection-specific DNS Suffix  . :
    Description . . . . . . . . . . . : Teredo Tunneling Pseudo-
Interface
    Physical Address. . . . . . . . . : 00-00-00-00-00-00-00-E0
    DHCP Enabled. . . . . . . . . . . : No
    Autoconfiguration Enabled . . . . : Yes
    IPv6 Address. . . . . . . . . . . :
2001:0:4137:9e76:4c9:399b:3f57:fe98(Preferred)
    Link-local IPv6 Address . . . . . :
fe80::4c9:399b:3f57:fe98%39(Preferred)
    Default Gateway . . . . . . . . . : ::
    NetBIOS over Tcpip. . . . . . . . : Disabled
```

6to4 is another method that used to help the migration between IPv4 and IPv6. It allows IPv6 traffic to be transmitted over an IPv4 network and is popular with routers used in small offices and home offices (SOHOs).

Comparing Manual and Automatic Assignment of IPv6

Just as you can assign IPv4 addresses manually or via DHCP, you can also assign IPv6 manually or with DHCPv6. Both processes are very similar in IPv4 and IPv6.

Manually Configuring IPv6

You can use the following steps to manually view or configure the IPv6 information on a Windows Server 2008 server:

1. Click Start ➢ Control Panel.

2. Type **Network** in the Control Panel Search box.

3. Select Network And Sharing Center.

4. Click Manage Network Connections in the Tasks pane on the left.

5. Right-click Local Area Connection, and select Properties.

6. Select Internet Protocol Version 6 (TCP/IPv6), and click Properties. Your display will look similar to Figure 6.8.

7. Enter the appropriate IP address, subnet mask, default gateway, and address of a DNS server. In the figure, the server is also the DNS server, so the DNS server is set to the IPv6 loopback address of ::1.

Although these steps work on Windows Server 2008, you can also use them on a Windows 7 system.

◄

You can view the information without changing it. If you are using link-local addresses or a DHCPv6 server, it will be set to Obtain An IP Address Automatically.

◄

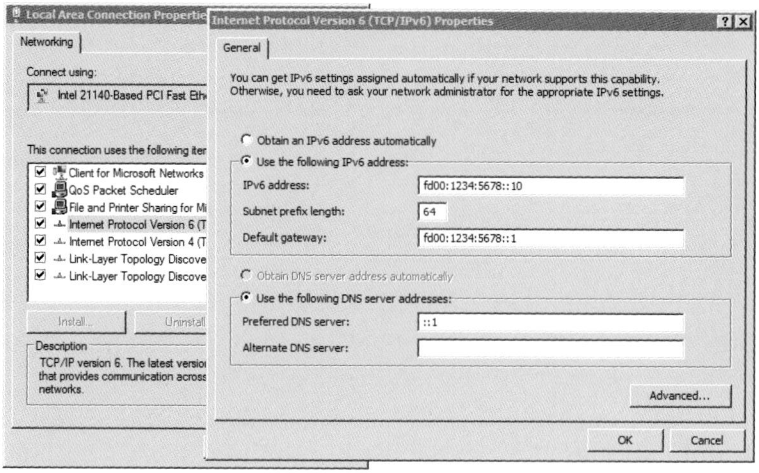

FIGURE 6.8 Viewing the IPv6 configuration of the NIC

Using DHCPv6

Just as you can use DHCP to assign TCP/IP information for IPv4 clients, you can also use DHCPv6 to assign TCP/IP information for IPv6 clients. The process is similar. The benefit is that you can assign all the TCP/IP information including the IP addresses of DNS servers, default gateways, and more. The system can configure itself with link-local addresses, but link-local addresses won't provide access outside the subnet since they are not routable and won't include addresses of DNS servers.

Figure 6.9 shows the process of a DHCPv6 client receiving an IPv6 address from a DHCPv6 server.

1. When the DHCPv6 client turns on, it sends a solicit message looking for a DHCPv6 server.

2. The DHCPv6 server answers with an Advertise message. This lets the client know that the server can offer IPv6 configuration information.

3. The DHCPv6 client replies with a Request message formally requesting the IPv6 information.

4. The DHCPv6 server responds with a Reply message. This message includes IPv6 information such as the IPv6 address, the default gateway, and the address of a DNS server.

DHCPv6 servers aren't required on each subnet. If your network includes multiple subnets, you can place DHCPv6 relay agents on each subnet to listen for the DHCPv6 solicit messages and then forward them to the DHCPv6 server. The relay agent then acts as the intermediary, or the proxy, for the four messages going back and forth between the DHCPv6 server and the DHCPv6 client.

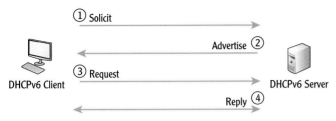

FIGURE 6.9 DHCPv6 process

THE ESSENTIALS AND BEYOND

In this chapter, you learned about IPv6 addresses. IPv6 is slowly replacing IPv4, and it uses 128 bits instead of the 32 bits used in IPv4. IPv6 addresses are displayed in hexadecimal, and the type of IPv6 address is identified by the prefix. Global unicast addresses start with a prefix of 2 /3. Teredo tunneling protocol addresses (used for IPv4 to IPv6) start with a prefix of 2001:0000 /32. Link-local addresses (automatically assigned) start with fe80 /10. Unique local addresses (private IPv6 addresses) start with fd and are sometimes referenced as fc /7.

ADDITIONAL EXERCISES

► Identify whether your computer has an IPv6 address. If so, determine the type of address based on the prefix.

► Ping the IPv6 loopback address. This is possible only if your computer has an IPv6 address. If your computer doesn't have an IPv6 address, identify the IPv6 loopback address.

► Use the `ipconfig /all` command to determine whether you have a Teredo address assigned.

► View the current IPv6 configuration of the network interface card. Document the current settings of the IP address, prefix, default gateway, and DNS server.

To compare your answers to the author's, please visit **www.sybex.com/go/ networkingessentials**.

REVIEW QUESTIONS

1. Which of the following addresses is a valid IPv6 address?

    A. 192.168.1.256

    B. 10.1.25.2

    C. 2001:0000:4137:9e76:3c2b:05ad:3f57:fe98

    D. 2001:0000:4137:9g76:3c2b:05zd:3x57:gh98

(Continues)

THE ESSENTIALS AND BEYOND *(Continued)*

2. You need to manually assign an IPv6 address to a client computer for use within a private network. Which one of the following addresses should you use?

   A. 0000::a123:4567:89ab:cdef

   B. 2001:0001::fcde:ba98:7654

   C. 2001:0000: fcde:ba98:7654

   D. fe80:: a123:4567:89ab:cdef

   E. fd00:: a123:4567:89ab:cdef

3. Which of the following features is built into IPv6 to provide extra security?

   A. Teredo tunneling

   B. Global addresses

   C. Unique local addresses

   D. IPSec

4. True or false. An IPv6 address with a prefix of fd is a link-local address.

5. What IPv6 to IPv4 technology uses tunneling to encapsulate an IPv6 packet within an IPv4 packet?

6. You need to assign IPv6 addresses to hosts on a private network. You should use _____ addresses.

7. What IPv6 protocol is used to identify routers on the same network?

   A. Network Discovery

   B. Teredo

   C. IGMP

   D. Anycast

8. IPv4 addresses use public address on the Internet. IPv6 uses _____ addresses on the Internet.

## CHAPTER 7

Connecting Computers to a Network

Although the process of connecting a computer to a network is often as simple as plugging it in, there is a lot to consider. Many problems can interfere with the transmission of data. Some transmission media (such as fiber-optic cable) is immune to many of the problems, but it also adds significant costs to a network.

In this chapter, you'll learn about many of the potential problems with transmission media. In addition, you'll learn about many of the common transmission methods and how they can be affected by these problems.

▶ **Identifying potential problems with connectivity**

▶ **Exploring cable types and their characteristics**

Identifying Potential Problems with Connectivity

Several potential problems exist that you should know about with network connectivity. Although many technologies exist to minimize these problems, you still need to be aware of them. Common problems explored in this section include the following:

- ▶ Electromagnetic interference
- ▶ Radio frequency interference
- ▶ Power spikes
- ▶ Interception of signals
- ▶ Fire hazards
- ▶ Cross talk

Each of these problems can affect the quality, reliability, and security of networks. For example, different types of interference can corrupt transmissions or reduce the distance they can travel. Power spikes can damage equipment if steps aren't taken to protect them. If the wrong cable is used in certain areas of a building, a fire can result in toxic fumes spreading throughout spaces where people are working. Once you understand the problems, it's easier to understand the purpose of the solutions.

Understanding EMI

Electromagnetic interference (EMI) is interference caused by machinery or electrical devices or natural phenomena such as electrically charged raindrops. When the EMI reaches a computer or network, it has the potential to interfere and degrade signals. When the interference is significant, data transmissions are blocked.

▶
Common categories of cables (including Category 7) are discussed later in this chapter.

A common source of EMI is devices with motors. For example, manufacturing environments often include a lot of equipment. When computers and networks are used in manufacturing environments, they often need additional protection against EMI. For example, a special type of cable called Category 7 has special shielding for use in manufacturing environments.

Other sources of EMI include electronic devices such as laser printers, microwave ovens, and even older fluorescent lights. These devices aren't intended to transmit signals, but while they operate, they do emit signals. These signals can interfere with nearby electronic equipment.

Understanding RFI

▶
Both EMI and RFI can interfere and degrade signals.

Radio frequency interference (RFI) is interference from broadcasted radio signals. When a transmitter is close enough and/or transmits the signals at a high enough amplitude (or volume), unintended systems can pick it up. When RFI enters a computer system, it may corrupt the data intended for the computer.

As an example, consider a wireless network. It broadcasts data signals using specific frequencies. When two wireless networks are broadcasting close to each other, they can interfere with other. The signals from one network can bleed over into the other network.

Some other sources of RFI include cordless phones and Bluetooth devices. For example, cordless phones transmit data using specific frequencies. These signals can sometimes be picked up by wireless systems and interfere with the signals.

Avoiding Power Spikes

Computers and network devices receive alternating current (AC) power, which is usually provided by commercial power companies. These devices have internal direct current (DC) power supplies that convert the AC power to DC power required by the device.

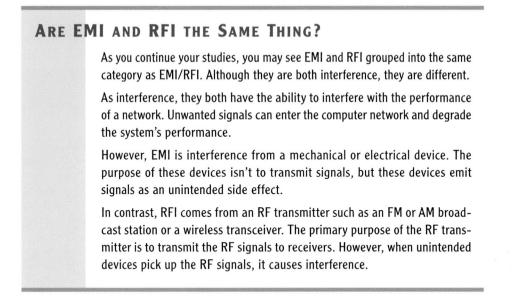

ARE EMI AND RFI THE SAME THING?

As you continue your studies, you may see EMI and RFI grouped into the same category as EMI/RFI. Although they are both interference, they are different.

As interference, they both have the ability to interfere with the performance of a network. Unwanted signals can enter the computer network and degrade the system's performance.

However, EMI is interference from a mechanical or electrical device. The purpose of these devices isn't to transmit signals, but these devices emit signals as an unintended side effect.

In contrast, RFI comes from an RF transmitter such as an FM or AM broadcast station or a wireless transceiver. The primary purpose of the RF transmitter is to transmit the RF signals to receivers. However, when unintended devices pick up the RF signals, it causes interference.

Ideally, the AC power supplied by the commercial power company will be a perfect sine wave similar to Figure 7.1. This sine wave cycles at a rate of 60 Hertz (Hz), or one cycle per second. Unfortunately, it's not always a perfect sine wave.

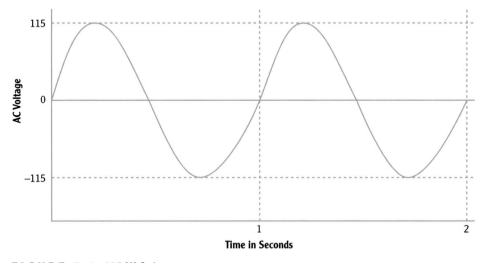

A sine wave cycle is one full 360-degree iteration of the signal. In other words, it starts at zero, goes up, goes back down through zero, and then returns to zero for one cycle.

FIGURE 7.1 115 VAC sine wave

A power spike is a short duration increase in voltage. Although it's quick, it can cause damage to electrical equipment. The most common source of power spikes is a lightning strike. Figure 7.2 shows how spikes may look on an AC sine wave.

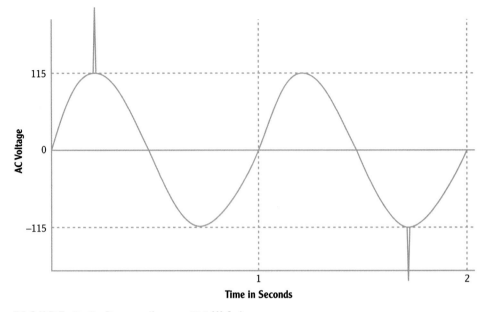

FIGURE 7.2 Power spike on a 115 VAC sine wave

Electrical components are protected from power spikes with surge protectors.

Consider lights in your home. They require 115 VAC, but if there's an increase or decrease in voltage, you'll see them flicker. If the voltage increases too high or stays high for too long, they'll probably burn out. However, lights don't respond to changes in voltage as quickly as electrical components do. A short spike may not even be noticeable in the light. However, if the same spikes reach electronic components, they will often fail.

Other anomalies with AC voltage include the following:

Power Surge   A power surge lasts longer than a power spike and is usually less of an increase in voltage. For example, a power spike from lightening can be thousands of volts for only a few milliseconds. However, a power surge may be only about 20 percent above normal but may last as long as a minute or so.

Power Sag   A power sag occurs when the AC voltage falls below normal for a period of time. When a DC power supply doesn't receive enough AC power, it can't provide enough DC power to the internal system. Power sags often result in the system turning off.

You can protect computer and networking equipment from power anomalies using different types of equipment:

Surge Protector   A surge protector protects against both power spikes and power surges. If excessive voltage reaches the surge protector, a built-in circuit breaker pops and prevents the voltage from reaching the equipment. Most (but not all) power strips include surge protectors. Surge protectors have different rating levels based on their response time and power threshold sensitivity.

Uninterruptible Power Supply (UPS)   A UPS provides continuous power to a system even if a power sag occurs or if power is lost for a short period. The primary purpose of a UPS is to provide power to a system by battery long enough to complete a logical shutdown or for generators to come online and stabilize. A UPS is not intended as a long-term power source.

Power Filters   Power filters can filter out dirty power. Dirty power occurs when random noise enters the power line and is carried on the sine wave. Instead of a clean sine wave (as shown in Figure 7.1), the signal includes dozens to hundreds of small spikes along the line, as shown in Figure 7.3. This noise can cause damage to power supplies, but a power filter filters out the noise producing a clean sine wave. Power filters also include a surge protector.

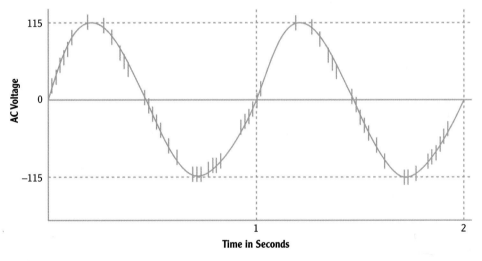

FIGURE 7.3 Dirty power

Generators   Generators provide long-term power when the commercial power source fails or is unavailable. Most generators use diesel fuel, though some use natural gas, propane, and even gasoline. Typically, only critical systems require generator power.

Avoiding Interception

Another potential problem with connecting computers on a network is the risk of interception of data as it crosses the network. Just as people can eavesdrop by listening in on conversations, attackers can use tools to eavesdrop on network conversations.

> **Protocol analyzers are also called packet analyzers, network analyzers, and sniffers.**

Protocol analyzers can capture traffic going across a network. Although some are hardware devices, most protocol analyzers are simply software programs you can run on any personal computer. They capture the individual packets or frames that cross a network and then allow you to dissect the data. Microsoft provides a free protocol analyzer called Network Monitor.

Figure 7.4 shows *Network Monitor*. While this was running and capturing data, I opened a file named `Passwords.txt` from a network drive named MYBOOKWORLD. Network Monitor captured the entire process including the contents of the opened file.

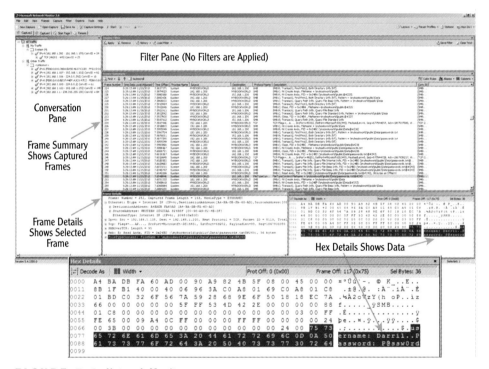

FIGURE 7.4 Network Monitor

Notice that the contents of the `Passwords.txt` file (`username: Darril..` `Password: P@ssw0rd`) are displayed in readable form in the Hex Details section. (The Hex Details section is shown larger by itself so you can read it easier.)

If someone has this tool, a little bit of knowledge, and some patience, they can intercept data on your network and learn its secrets. Because of this, it's important to protect your network from interception tactics. Here are some basics:

Use Switches Instead of Hubs   Hubs pass all traffic to all ports. A network monitor connected to a hub will capture all traffic going through the hub. In contrast, switches internally switch traffic so that only the traffic that is addressed to a host is sent to the host's port. In other words, each port is limited in the traffic that it can capture.

Protect Network Devices   Most routers and switches have maintenance ports that can capture all traffic going to and from the device. If someone has physical access to the devices, they can connect listening devices to these ports and capture all the traffic. Most organizations use physical security to protect network devices such as routers and switches.

◄

Many organizations prohibit the use of hubs in the network to prevent risks of interception.

◄

Most organizations protect routers and switches in locked wiring closets or server rooms.

NONPROMISCUOUS MODE VS. PROMISCUOUS MODE

Sniffers run in one of two modes: *nonpromiscuous mode* or *promiscuous mode*.

In nonpromiscuous mode, the sniffer will only capture data sent directly to or from the system capturing the traffic. Each frame includes the source and destination IP address, and if the neither of these matches the IP address of capturing computer, the frame isn't captured. In other words, the sniffer will not capture unicast traffic sent to and from other systems. Microsoft's Network Monitor runs in this mode by default but can be switched to promiscuous mode.

In promiscuous mode, the sniffer will capture any traffic that reaches the interface card of the system capturing the traffic. Most sniffers can operate in promiscuous mode. Although older free versions of Microsoft's Network Monitor would not operate in promiscuous mode, the current version can.

You can enter systeminfo at the command prompt to get details on your system. The System Type identifies whether it is x64- or x32-based architecture.

◄

Network Monitor comes in three versions, based on the architecture of the system:

- ► x86 for 32-bit systems
- ► x64 for 64-bit systems (including both Intel and AMD 64-bit systems)
- ► ia64 for high-end Itanium servers

If you try to install the wrong version on a computer, such as installing a 64-bit version on a 32-bit system, the installation program will stop and prompt you to use the correct version.

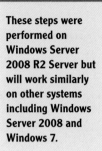

These steps were performed on Windows Server 2008 R2 Server but will work similarly on other systems including Windows Server 2008 and Windows 7.

You can use the following steps to download and install Network Monitor:

1. Go to Microsoft's download site (**www.microsoft.com/downloads**).

2. Type **Network Monitor** in the Search All Download Center text box, and press Enter.

3. Select Microsoft Network Monitor from the list. At this writing, the current version is 3.4.

4. Identify the version you need (such as the 32-bit version or the 64-bit version), and click the download button for that version.

5. Click Save, and browse to a location on your computer to save it. Once the download is complete, you're ready to install it.

6. Click Start ➢ Computer. Browse to the location where you saved the Network Monitor download, and double-click it.

7. Review the information in the dialog box, and click Yes to continue.

8. Review the information on the Welcome page, and click Next.

9. Review the End-User License Agreement, select I Accept The Terms In The License Agreement, and click Next.

This page may not appear on some systems if Windows Update has already been configured.

10. If the Microsoft Update page appears, accept the defaults, and click Next.

11. Click the Typical button on the Choose Setup Type page. Click Install.

12. After a moment, the installation of Network Monitor will complete. Click Finish. The installation of additional components will then begin and may require several minutes to finish. When it completes, it will automatically close.

After you've downloaded and installed Network Monitor, you can use it to capture and review traffic. The following steps assume you have downloaded and installed Network Monitor on a system:

These steps were performed on Windows Server 2008 R2 Server but will work similarly on other systems including Windows Server 2008 and Windows 7.

1. Click Start, and enter **Network Monitor** in the Search Programs And Files text box.

2. Right-click Microsoft Network Monitor, and select Run As Administrator. If the Microsoft Update Opt-In dialog box appears, choose Yes or No depending on whether you want to check for updates.

3. On the Start Page, locate the Select Networks pane at the bottom left. Ensure your network interface card is selected, as shown in Figure 7.5. If desired, you can select all networks.

Network Monitor works in nonpromiscuous mode by default. You can configure it to work in promiscuous mode by clicking the P-Mode button in the Select Networks pane.

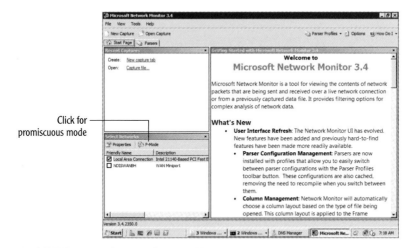

Click for promiscuous mode

FIGURE 7.5 Starting Network Monitor

4. Click New Capture on the toolbar.

5. Click Start page to begin capturing traffic.

6. Open a command prompt, and ping the IP address of one or more systems on your network such as the default gateway or other computers.

You can use `ipconfig /all` to determine the IP address of your default gateway.

7. When the ping completes, return to Network Monitor, and click Stop.

8. Click All Traffic in the Network Conversations pane. This shows all the traffic that your computer captured during this short time.

9. Click My Traffic. This shows traffic with your computer's IP address in the Source or Destination column. Enter **icmp** in the Display Filter pane, and click Apply. Your display will look similar to Figure 7.6. Only ICMP traffic from your pings is shown.

10. Feel free to look around at the different frames that were captured. You can expand any selected frame in the Frame Details pane. When you're done, close all open windows.

The filter removes all frames except for the frames using the ICMP protocol.

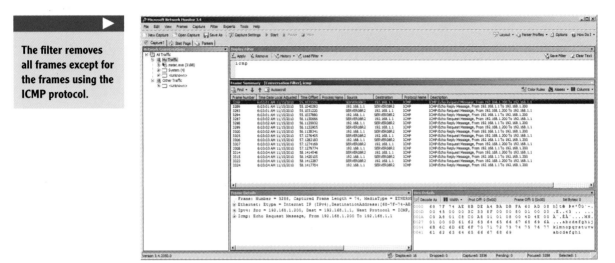

FIGURE 7.6 Displaying ICMP frames in Network Monitor

Preventing Fire Hazards

Another potential problem with cables is the potential hazardous fumes they can release when they catch on fire. The jacket or covering of some cables can be toxic to humans, so only certain types of cable are safe to use in different areas of a building.

Most buildings have spaces between the walls, below floors, and above ceilings used to circulate cooled or heated air. These spaces are called plenums. And, since it's such an open space, it's easy (and common) to run cables through this space. However, if these cables catch fire, the air circulates the fumes from the cables throughout the building.

Cable rated as *plenum safe* is designed specifically so that it will not release toxic fumes if it catches fire. Only plenum-safe cable should be used within plenums.

Plenum-safe cable is listed as UL 910 or ASTM E84 certified.

Understanding Cross Talk

Cross talk is data that crosses from one transmission line to another. This can result in a degraded signal, or worse, it can result in data jumping from one wire to another.

When data travels down a wire, it creates an induction field that is much larger in diameter than the wire. The induction field is a magnetic field that holds images of the actual signal. Figure 7.7 illustrates this induction field.

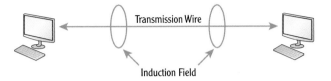

FIGURE 7.7 Induction field around a wire

Tools are available that can capture the signals from the induction field simply by placing the tool around the wire, similar to how you could close your forefinger and thumb around a wire. These tools capture the signals in the magnetic field without cutting into the cable.

Cross talk occurs when signals from one wire cross over to another through these induction fields. As an example, consider Figure 7.8. Cables connecting two classified computers are running side by side with cables connecting two unclassified computers. These signals cross from one wire to the other.

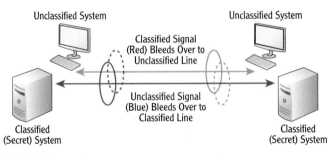

FIGURE 7.8 Cross talk between two wires

This cross talk results in two problems:

Corruption of Data   The cross talk can interfere with intended signals on the wire. This works similar to a collision and requires the retransmission of data.

Loss of Confidentiality   If confidential or secret data is transmitted on one wire but crosses to the other wire, the wrong people could pick it up. If unintended recipients learn the secrets, they aren't secret anymore.

Although shielded twisted pair (STP) provides some resistance against cross talk, it isn't a guarantee. Most systems that transmit classified data have specific requirements concerning the placement of wires transmitting classified and unclassified data. For example, an organization may specify that classified and unclassified wires can't be closer than 36 inches to each other.

Exploring Cable Types and Their Characteristics

You connect computers and devices to each other using different types of cables or media. The primary types of media you'll see in use today are as follows:

Twisted Pair   This is a single cable with four pairs of copper wires twisted around each other. *Twisted-pair* cables are limited to a distance of 100 meters, though you can use repeaters to extend the distance.

Fiber Optic   *Fiber-optic cable* is either glass or a type of plastic that carries light pulses. Fiber-optic cable has a lot of benefits over twisted pair, but it is more expensive. Fiber optic can carry signals distances up to 40 kilometers.

Wireless   Wireless networks connect computers together without wires. Instead, devices have transceivers to send and receive radio frequency transmissions. Wireless transmissions are limited to a smaller areas within a building, but multiple wireless access points can be connected together to make the network as large as desired.

> **The following sections provide specific details on distance, speed, and frequency for the different media. This section provides a short introduction of these characteristics.**

When deciding which media to use, you need to be aware of the different characteristics of each. As an example, fiber-optic cable is the most expensive but supports the longest cable runs. Fiber-optic cables can be as long as 40 km. You should be aware of the following primary cable characteristics:

Distance   This indicates how long a cable can be between connections, or how far wireless devices can be between each other. All twisted-pair cables are limited to no more than 100 meters. Fiber-optic cable can have much longer cable runs depending on the type of fiber-optic cable used. Wireless is limited to about 30 meters to 90 meters (100 feet to 300 feet) depending on the type of access used.

Speed   The speed indicates how much data can travel across the media measured in bits per second (bps). Higher data rate numbers indicate higher speeds and better network performance.

Frequency   The frequency refers to the transmission bandwidth. A higher signaling frequency equates to higher speeds on physical media. For wireless media, this indicates the primary frequencies used to transmit the data over the air.

Understanding Twisted Pair

Twisted-pair cable is the most commonly used cable type in networks today. It comes in multiple categories with different speed capabilities. A twisted-pair cable used in a network includes four pairs of copper wire. Each wire in the pair is twisted around each other, and the four pairs within a cable are then twisted around the other pairs. The four twisted pairs are then wrapped in a polyethylene or polyvinyl jacket.

The number of twists per meter in these cables is different for different categories of cables. Twists in the cable help minimize both cross talk and EMI. Additionally, the number of twists per meter determines the speed and frequency capabilities of the cable. Higher speeds and frequencies allow the cable to carry larger amounts of data.

However, all the twisted-pair categories have a maximum distance of 100 meters. In other words, the cable can't be longer than 100 meters between any two components. It is possible to extend this distance by using a repeater. The repeater amplifies the signal, allowing you to run the cable another 100 meters.

Table 7.1 shows the common twisted pair cable categories you'll come across in today's networks along with their basic characteristics.

◄ You don't need to know how many twists per meter a cable has, but you should know the characteristics of different cable categories.

◄ Category is commonly shortened to CAT. For example, Category 5E cable is Cat 5E.

TABLE 7.1 Twisted-pair categories

Type	Speed	Frequency	Comments
Cat 5	Rated at 100 Mbps	100 MHz	Largely replaced by CAT 5E today.
CAT 5E	Rated up to 1000 Mbps (1 Gbps Ethernet)	100 MHz	Cat 5E supersedes Cat 5 cables.
CAT 6	Rated up to 1000 Mbps (1 Gbps Ethernet) or up to 10 Gbps for shorter runs	250 MHz	Most new installations use this or Cat 6A today. Shorter Cat 6 runs up to 55 m provide speeds up to 10 Gbps.
CAT 6A	Rated up to 10,000 Mbps (10 Gbps Ethernet)	500 MHz	Improved resistance to cross talk and noise.
CAT 7	Rated up to 1000 Mbps	600 MHz	Shielded for manufacturing environments.

Twisted pair is also identified using the xxBaseT format. The xx indicates the speed. Base indicates that it uses baseband transmissions. Baseband uses a single frequency for transmission, while other methods such as broadband use multiple frequencies. The T indicates it is twisted pair. Some of the common designations are as follows:

10BaseT   10 Mbps twisted pair

100BaseT   100 Mbps twisted pair

1000BaseT   1000 Mbps twisted pair (1 Gbps)

10GBaseT   10 Gbps twisted pair

▶ The following are the primary problems that twisted pair is susceptible to:

Interference from EMI/RFI   Although the twists help prevent EMI and RFI problems, interference can still get in. Shielded twisted pair provides additional protection compared to unshielded twisted pair.

Cross talk   Twists also help prevent cross talk problems. Shielded twisted pair provides an additional layer of protection against cross talk. Also, many organizations have rules dictating what type of cables can be run next to each other.

Interception   It's relatively easy for someone to tap the cable and then add connectors to capture the signal. Wire-crimping tools are widely available, and experienced technicians can cut and splice a twisted-pair cable in just a couple of minutes.

Comparing Unshielded and Shielded Twisted Pair

Some UTP cables have foil wrapped around all the pairs and are called foiled twisted pair (FTP) or UTP with screening (S/UTP). This is not the same as STP.

Twisted pair comes in both shielded and unshielded versions. Unshielded twisted pair (UTP) includes the twisted wires encased in a polyethylene or polyvinyl sheath. Shielded twisted pair (STP) includes metal shielding over each pair of wires within the cable. This shielding helps prevent data from escaping beyond the cable from cross talk. It also helps prevent EMI and RFI from entering the cable.

Although the shielding does provide significant protection against EMI/RFI and cross talk, it does not eliminate it. The only way to be immune from these problems is to avoid using copper altogether. Fiber-optic cable is immune to these problems.

Comparing Straight-Through and Crossover Cables

Chapter 2 presented the concept of crossover cables. Straight-through and crossover cables are only used with twisted pair but can be found with both shielded and unshielded cables.

As a reminder, most cables are straight through. The wires going to the pins in a connector in one side of the cable are going to identical pins in the other side of the cable. In other words, pin 1 in one connector is wired to pin 1 in the other connector, pin 2 is wired to pin 2, and so on. Straight-through cables connect dissimilar devices on the network. For example, a computer connected to a hub, switch, or router would use a straight-through cable.

In contrast, crossover cables connect similar devices to each other. For example, you'd use a crossover cable to connect a router with a switch, a wireless access point to a modem, or a computer to another computer.

Crossover cables have specific pins in one connector crossed over to different pins in the other connector. Figure 7.9 shows these connections on opposite RJ-45 connectors in a single crossover cable. You can see in the figure the exact pins that specific wires connect to in a EIA/TIA 568B crossover cable.

◄

Gigabit devices use automatic crossover to sense when a crossover connection is needed. Because of this, Cat 6 or 6A crossover cables are rare.

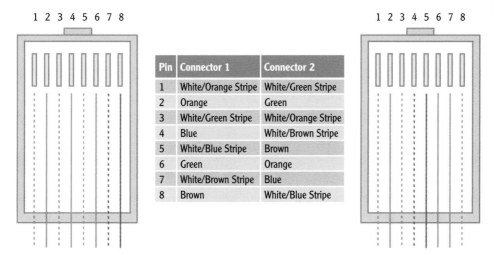

Pin	Connector 1	Connector 2
1	White/Orange Stripe	White/Green Stripe
2	Orange	Green
3	White/Green Stripe	White/Orange Stripe
4	Blue	White/Brown Stripe
5	White/Blue Stripe	Brown
6	Green	Orange
7	White/Brown Stripe	Blue
8	Brown	White/Blue Stripe

FIGURE 7.9 RJ-45 connector views of a crossover cable

Understanding Fiber Optic

Fiber-optic cable sends signals as light pulses rather than as electrical signals. As a results of it's not susceptible to many of the problems associated with twisted pair and can be used for much longer cable runs. There are two primary types of fiber-optic cable: *single-mode fiber* and *multimode fiber*.

Single Mode   Single-mode fiber (SMF) is smaller than multimode and is used for long-distance high-speed cable runs. A single SMF cable supports 10 Gbps for distances up to 40 km. Single mode uses a glass core.

Multimode   Multimode fiber (MMF) uses a plastic core and supports a wider variety of light sources. However, the speed and distance is less than the glass core SMF cable. A single MMF cable supports 100 Mbps for distances up to 2 km and up to 10 Gbps for distances up to 300 m.

Table 7.2 summarizes the characteristics of fiber-optic cable.

TABLE 7.2   Characteristics of fiber-optic cables

Type	Speed	Distance	Comments
Single-mode fiber	Up to 10 Gbps	Up to 40 km	Uses a glass core
Multimode fiber	Up to 100 Mbps	Up to 2 km	Uses a plastic core
Multimode fiber	Up to 1 Gbps	Up to 550 m	Uses a plastic core
Multimode fiber	Up to 10 Gbps	Up to 300 m	Uses a plastic core

> ▶
>
> MMF supports higher speeds at shorter distances but can get up to 100 Mbps only if the cable run is 2 km or less.

Compared to the 100 meter runs supported by twisted pair, fiber-optic cable provides significant improvement in the distance of the runs. Fiber also provides several other benefits:

Immune to Interference   Fiber is not susceptible to either EMI or RFI since the signals are sent using light pulses. In contrast, twisted pair is susceptible to electromagnetic interference (EMI) and radio frequency interference (RFI).

Immune to Crosstalk   Since fiber uses light pulses, it doesn't generate an induction field around the cable. This eliminates any problems related to cross talk.

Interception Is Difficult   Fiber-optic cable is difficult to cut and splice. It requires specialized equipment that isn't widely available and also requires special skills to ensure the splice works and is not detectable.

> Fiber-optic cable also has strict limitations on how much it can bend. This can also make a fiber-optic cable installation more expensive.
>
> ▶

Lightweight   Fiber cable carries much more data per pound. Individual cables carry more data than twisted pair, and the overall weight is much less. This makes fiber ideal in airplanes and ships where weight and space are both a concern.

The biggest drawback to fiber-optic cable is the cost. The actual cable costs more than twisted pair, and the technicians working on the cable require specialized training to work with the cable.

Understanding Wireless

Just as its name implies, wireless transmission doesn't use cables. Instead, the transmissions are broadcast over the air on specific frequencies. IEEE 802.11 standards define different wireless characteristics.

Table 7.3 shows there are four primary wireless standards.

TABLE 7.3   Characteristics of wireless standards

Standard	Speed	Frequency	Distance	Comments
802.11a	54 Mbps	5 GHz	About 30 meters (about 98 feet)	Less susceptible to interference
802.11b	11 Mbps	2.4 GHz	About 35 meters (about 114 feet)	Can configure specific channels
802.11g	54 Mbps	2.4 GHz	About 35 meters (about 114 feet)	Widely deployed
802.11n	300 Mbps	2.4 GHz or 5. GHz	About 70 meters (about 222 feet)	Newer and quickly overtaking 802.11g in popularity

Wireless devices provide a simple but valuable benefit. You don't have to run cables between devices in your network. Instead, you can add a wireless access point (WAP) to your network and use devices with wireless network interfaces. With just a little configuration, you have a running network.

A significant drawback with wireless is that the signals are broadcast over the air and susceptible to interference and interception. When placing the WAPs in a building, you need to ensure that the signal is reachable throughout the building. In a large business, you may place several WAPs to ensure full coverage.

The frequencies used by wireless networks are well known, and anyone with a wireless receiver can easily capture traffic. Even Microsoft's Network Monitor can be configured to capture wireless transmissions when it's run on a computer with a wireless NIC.

Because of this, wireless security is extremely important. Chapter 12 covers the different security protocols you can use to protect wireless transmissions. Older wireless security protocols, such as Wired Equivalent Privacy (WEP), were

Chapter 12 covers wireless networks in much greater depth. This section provides a short introduction and comparison with twisted-pair and fiber-optic cable.

Wireless transmissions can be degraded by many environmental factors. Actual distances for transmissions vary widely.

The coverage of the wireless network is referred to as its footprint. The footprint of a wireless network frequently extends outside the intended coverage area.

cracked long ago and provide very little security. Newer wireless security protocols, such as Wi-Fi Protected Access version 2 (WPA2), provide significant security when implemented correctly.

THE ESSENTIALS AND BEYOND

In this chapter, you learned about the potential problems of connecting computers on a network and the different types of media used to connect them. Interference comes in the form of EMI and RFI. Power spikes can destroy unprotected systems. Unprotected signals can be intercepted, captured, and analyzed using tools such as Microsoft's Network Monitor. Twisted pair is the most popular media, though it is susceptible to EMI/RFI, interception, and cross talk. Fiber optic is immune to interference and cross talk problems, and it is much more difficult to tap into to intercept the signals. Wireless is very easy to set up and configure, though it requires additional steps to protect the data transmission.

ADDITIONAL EXERCISES

▶ Identify the power source of the computer you're using. Determine whether it is a surge protector.

▶ Download Network Monitor from the Internet and install it if you haven't already. Capture some traffic on your network. Filter the traffic so that only TCP traffic is displayed.

▶ Locate the switch or router that your computer is connected to. Determine whether it is protected with physical security.

▶ Look at the cable used in your network. Determine whether it is plenum safe.

▶ To compare your answers to the author's, please visit **www.sybex.com/go/ networkingessentials**.

REVIEW QUESTIONS

1. What types of interference can cause problems for networks? (Choose all that apply.)

   A. EMI   C. STI

   B. RFI   D. PCI

2. A short-duration increase in AC power is a _____.

   A. power spike   C. power sag

   B. power surge   D. surge protector

(Continues)

THE ESSENTIALS AND BEYOND *(Continued)*

3. True or false. The purpose of a UPS system is to provide long-term power when power fails.

4. True or false. STP provides protection against interference and cross talk.

5. The maximum distance of a CAT 6 twisted-pair cable between two connections is _____ meters.

6. What is the speed of a CAT 6 cable?

   A. 10 Mbps   C. 1000 Mbps

   B. 100 Mbps   D. 10000 Mpbs

7. What does the *T* represent in a 100BaseT cable?

8. What tool can you use to capture traffic going across a network? (Choose all that apply.)

   A. Microsoft's Network Monitor   C. A network sniffer

   B. A protocol analyzer   D. A wire crimper

9. What frequency does 802.11g use?

   A. 2.4 GHz   C. 2.4 and 5 GHz

   B. 5 GHz   D. 9 GHz

## CHAPTER 8

Networking Computers with Switches

Switches are an important component in any wired network. At one point, switches were optional in most, but they have steadily replaced Ethernet hubs because of their extra capabilities. Additionally, advanced switches can perform functions of a router.

In this chapter, you'll learn the details of how a switch works and its benefits over a hub. You'll also learn about the differences between managed and unmanaged switches, between layer 2 and layer 3 switches, and how a switch can be used to create VLANs. Last, you'll learn some basics about switch speeds and switch security.

▶ **Connecting multiple computers**

▶ **Understanding physical ports**

▶ **Comparing hubs and switches**

▶ **Comparing managed and unmanaged switches**

▶ **Exploring switch speeds**

▶ **Understanding security options**

> The /24 represents CIDR notation. It indicates the subnet mask has the first 24 bits set to a 1. In other words, the subnet mask is 255.255.255.0.
>
> ▶

Connecting Multiple Computers

Chapter 2 introduced basic connectivity with hubs, switches, and routers. As a reminder, *switches* (or *hubs*) connect computers in a network. In larger organizations, routers connect multiple networks into a local area network (LAN).

Consider Figure 8.1. It shows three separate subnetworks of 192.168.1.0/24, 192.168.5.0/24, and 192.168.7.0/24. Each of the subnetworks has a central switch connecting the devices. A router connects the three.

Packets sent by computers on this network go through a switch first. The switch learns which computers are connected to which port. It uses this knowledge to determine the path for every packet it receives. In contrast, routers move packets between the subnetworks.

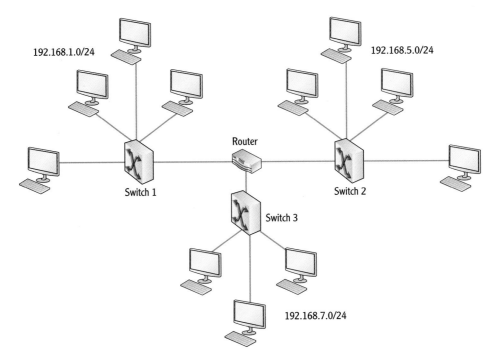

FIGURE 8.1 Using switches to connect computers

NETWORKS, SUBNETS, AND SUBNETWORKS

The terms *networks*, *subnetworks*, and *subnets* can easily be confusing. The terms are sometimes mixed together, and it's worth identifying the differences. In general, a network is two or more computers or other network devices connected together. When they are connected, they can share data and resources with each other.

Both a subnet and a subnetwork are a group of computers with the same network ID. Additionally, routers separate subnetworks and subnets from each other. However, there is a subtle difference between these two.

A subnet is a network that started as a classful network and was divided into multiple subnets. For example, you can divide a single Class C network of 192.168.1.0/24 into four subnetworks of 192.168.1.0/26, 192.168.1.64/26, 192.168.1.128/26, and 192.168.1.192/26. (The "Subnetting IPv4 Addresses" section of Chapter 5 explained subnetting.)

(Continues)

NETWORKS, SUBNETS, AND SUBNETWORKS *(Continued)*

Subnetworks use different classful IP ranges without subnetting them. For example, you can create one subnetwork with an address in 192.168.1.0/24, and a different subnetwork could have an address range in 192.168.5.0/24. This creates two subnetworks without subnetting a classful IP address. This is actually very common in private networks. There are more than enough classful IP address ranges for even very large organizations to use without subnettting.

Unfortunately, not everyone uses these terms in the same way. You'll often hear technicians call a subnetwork a *subnet* or simply a *network*. Some insist that they are all called *networks*. Some insist that a subnet is created only when a classful IP address range has been subnetted, and the rest are networks.

The debate will continue. However, the convention I'm using in this chapter is to separate subnetworks, subnets, and networks. If I called them all *networks*, then it would be easy for you to become confused between a local area network (composed of multiple subnetworks) and a network on one side of the router (which is only one subnetwork).

Although the terminology can be tricky, the primary message should still be clear. Switches connect and track computers within a subnetwork. Routers connect and track subnetworks.

> **Switches track the location of the computers on networks. Routers track networks or subnetworks, not computers.**

If the destination computer is on the same subnetwork, the switch forwards the packet to the destination computer. If the destination computer is on a different subnetwork, the switch forwards the packet to the router for routing to the correct subnetwork.

Notice that the switch is the central device for each subnetwork. It could be a hub, but for several reasons, switches have replaced hubs in many networks. Although most networks have switches connected as shown in Figure 8.1, many network line drawings omit the icon of the switch. For example, Figure 8.2 shows a network line drawing with the switches omitted.

Even though Figure 8.2 doesn't show the switches for each subnetwork, the computers have to be connected to a central device. They wouldn't all be connected directly to the router.

Understanding Physical Ports

►

Twisted-pair cable uses RJ-45 connectors. Each end of the twisted-pair cable has an RJ-45 connector, and the connector plugs into the port.

Switches have physical ports where physical cables plug in. For example, if the network is using twisted-pair cable, the switch will have RJ-45 ports that accept RJ-45 connectors. If the cable is fiber optic, the switch has physical ports that accept the fiber-optic connectors.

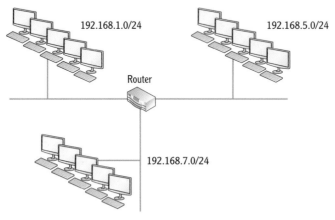

►

Uplinks connect two switches together or connect the switch to a router.

FIGURE 8.2 Using switches to connect computers

Most switches that connect end user computers have RJ-45 ports since twisted pair is the most commonly used media. Some switches include fiber-optic ports for uplinks.

►

Chapters 3 and 4 covered logical ports. These are numbers embedded in data packets.

Physical ports and logical ports are not the same. A physical port is something you can touch and accepts a cable. A logical port is simply a number that is embedded in a packet. For example, HTTP uses a logical default port of 80. When the packet reaches the destination computer, the logical port identifies the service or application that will process the data.

Identifying the Number and Type of Ports

The number of ports on a switch or hub varies according to the physical size of the device. Hubs are less expensive than switches and commonly have between 4 and 24 ports. This is usually enough for a small office/home office (SOHO) network. If selecting a device for a small business with 8 or 10 users, a 24-port device may be a reasonable investment, allowing for future growth.

Switches typically have between 8 to 64 ports. You can purchase switches in two separate designs:

Form Factor Switch   This has a set number of ports built into the switch, and the number of ports can't be changed. Form factor switches can have any number of ports, but 48 is the maximum for most form factor switches. These switches are great where simplicity is required.

Modular Switch   A modular switch starts with few to zero ports and can expand to hundreds of ports. You can then add plug-in modules to add ports. This is similar to a computer that can accept additional memory modules. For example, the computer may start with 1 GB RAM, but you can add RAM when your needs change. Similarly, you can buy a modular switch with a module that includes eight ports but then add modules to increase the number of available ports.

Selecting a switch design is based on several factors. For example, you will want to ensure you have enough ports for your immediate needs while also considering future growth requirements. Most modular switches require programming, which adds administrative overhead, while many form factor switches work right out of the box.

Identifying Ports in Drawings

When switches are included in network drawings or connection maps, the ports are usually labeled. This allows technicians to identify what port goes to what system. Switch ports are commonly labeled with E, F, or Gi followed by a number. For example, the following conventions are common:

E   The first 10 Mbps port is labeled as E0. This indicates Ethernet port 0. Some manufacturers represent the first Ethernet port on a modular switch as E0/0, which represents the first port on the first module.

F   The first 100 Mbps port is typically labeled as F0 or F0/0, a Fast Ethernet port. Compare this to the second port on the first module, which is labeled as F0/1. Fast Ethernet ports can also be labeled as Fa instead of just F.

Gi   The first 1000 Mbps port is labeled as Gi0/0, a gigabit port. Similarly, the first port on the second module is Gi1/0.

As an example, consider Figure 8.3. Based on how the ports are labeled, you can gain additional information about the switches. The ports on switch 1 are labeled

◄

You can add different types of modules to a modular switch. This includes modules for typical RJ-45 ports, wireless services, video services, and more.

Many computer technologies use zero-based numbering where the first item is a 0 instead of a 1. In a switch, the first port is 0 instead of 1.

◄

as E0 through E4, so it is a 10 Mbps switch. The ports on switch 2 are labeled as F0 through F4, so it is a 100 Mbps switch. The ports on switch 1 are labeled as G0 through G3, so it is a 1000 Mbps switch.

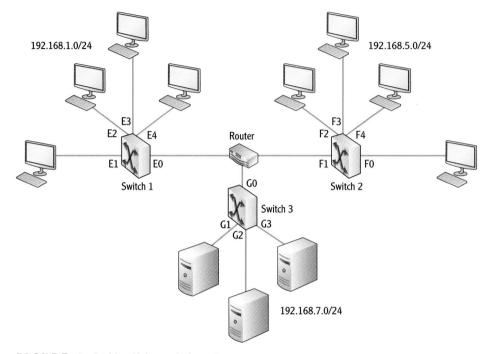

FIGURE 8.3 Identifying switch ports

Comparing Hubs and Switches

Chapter 2 introduced hubs, switches, and the concepts of broadcast and collision domains. Before going too far, it's worth repeating and expanding some of the key material.

A hub is a layer 1 device that connects multiple network devices. When using a hub, bandwidth decreases as you add more devices to the network since all devices share bandwidth equally. Any data sent into one port of a hub goes out all other ports. With a switch, each port is separated from each other. The ports do not share bandwidth with one another.

Hubs create a single collision domain and a single broadcast domain. Switches create multiple collision domains but share a common broadcast domain. Routers create separate collision and broadcast domains.

Understanding Collision Domains

A collision domain is a group of devices on the same segment that are subject to collisions. A hub creates a single collision domain. A switch creates multiple collision domains.

Ethernet Carrier Sense Multiple Access/Collision Detection (CSMA/CD) helps each device determine when they can send data across the network. The devices listen for traffic, and if they don't hear any traffic, they are free to send data. However, just as two people can start talking at the same time, two computers can start sending data at the same time.

Consider Figure 8.4. This shows several computers connected on the same segment. PC-1 and PC-4 are both sending traffic at the same time, and a collision occurs.

Collisions on the network degrade the network performance. Both computers must resend data each time a collision occurs.

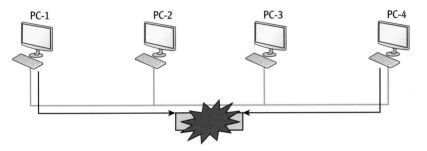

FIGURE 8.4 Collisions on a collision domain

CSMA/CD has a recovery mechanism for retransmission of lost data after a collision. First, a jamming signal is transmitted on the segment letting all devices know there has been a collision. Other devices postpone data transmission until the devices that had the collision resend their data. Once this process is complete, the network is reopened for business, and other devices may transmit their data.

If you think this creates a lot of network traffic, you are correct. Add collisions, and network performance will rapidly decrease.

You can reduce the number of collisions by increasing the number of collision domains. Since a hub has a single collision domain and a switch creates a separate collision domain for each port, you reduce collisions by replacing hubs with switches.

A hub has no intelligence. All traffic received on one port is flooded to all other ports.

Identifying a Collision Domain with a Hub

A hub connects multiple computers into a single collision domain. In other words, all devices connected with a hub contend for equal access to the same segment.

Figure 8.5 shows four computers connected with a hub. This is logically the same as Figure 8.4 shown earlier. Each computer uses CSMA/CD to listen before transmitting and can cause a collision if it sends data at the same time as another computer.

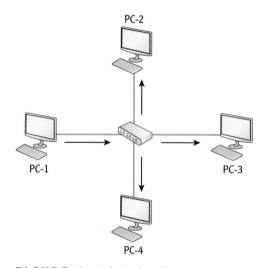

FIGURE 8.5 A single collision domain created by a hub

The hub acts as the central point in the network, and any traffic destined for another device will go to the hub first. In Figure 8.5, PC-1 sends data to PC-3. However, the hub forwards the packet to all computers connected to it. PC-3 will process the packet while PC-2 and PC-4 will discard it. However, this packet can cause a collision if any other computer sends data at the same time.

Identifying Collision Domains with a Switch

In contrast, Figure 8.6 shows how a switch creates multiple collision domains. Unicast traffic sent from the source computer is passed only to the destination computer. The switch creates an internal connection between PC-1 and PC-3. PC-2 and PC-4 don't receive the data.

If PC-2 sends data to PC-4 at the same time PC-1 is sending data to PC-3, it doesn't cause a collision. Instead, the switch makes an internal connection between PC-2 and PC-4.

A logical question is, "How does the switch track the computers connected to the ports?" That's a great question. The short answer is that a switch maps physical ports to computers' media access control (MAC) addresses.

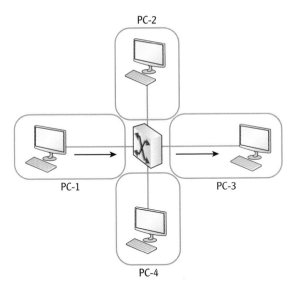

FIGURE 8.6 Multiple collision domains created by a switch

Mapping Ports to MAC Addresses

Chapter 3 introduced *MAC addresses*. As a reminder, a MAC address is a 48-bit address expressed in a hexadecimal format. For example, a MAC address looks like 00-23-5A-33-C4-CA.

Every network interface card (NIC) has a MAC address assigned to it. MAC addresses are typically burned into the card and unchangeable, though some NICs allow you to modify the MAC. Additionally, when a computer sends data to another computer, it always includes both its own IP address and its own MAC address as part of the source information.

A simple switch starts with very little knowledge when it's turned on. It knows what ports it has, but it does not know which computers are connected to which ports. However, as traffic is sent through the switch, it learns. It populates an internal *MAC address table* with the MAC addresses of each computer and maps them to the port to which they're connected.

Consider Figure 8.7. It shows a four-port switch with a computer connected to each port, and it shows their MAC addresses. Imagine this switch is just turned on. When PC-1 sends data to PC-3, the switch doesn't know what port PC-3 is on, so it sends the data to all ports. However, the packet from PC-1 includes the MAC address of PC-1. The switch silently says "gotcha" and starts populating the MAC table by logging port number F0 with the MAC address of PC-1.

Four bits are used to represent each hexadecimal character. Chapter 6 covered hexadecimal numbers in more depth.

Advanced switches (managed switches) are configurable. You can configure them with the MAC addresses of connected computers.

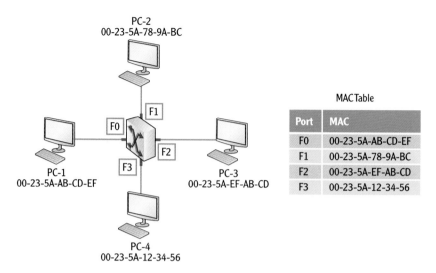

MAC Table

Port	MAC
F0	00-23-5A-AB-CD-EF
F1	00-23-5A-78-9A-BC
F2	00-23-5A-EF-AB-CD
F3	00-23-5A-12-34-56

FIGURE 8.7 Mapping ports to MAC addresses

When PC-3 answers, it includes the destination MAC address of PC-1 and the source address of PC-3. Again, the switch silently says "gotcha" and logs the MAC address of PC-3 with port F2 in the MAC address table. Since the switch knows that PC-1 is connected to port F0 (based on the MAC address), it internally switches the data from PC-3 to PC-1 on port F0. In a very short period, the switch will learn the MAC addresses of each computer along with their associated ports.

When the switch maps the MAC addresses to ports as traffic passes, the table is updated dynamically. However, an administrator can configure a managed switch with specific MAC addresses as static entries. Dynamic entries can be overwritten as time passes, but static entries remain.

Static entries are used for port security. Port security is explained later in this chapter.

Comparing Managed and Unmanaged Switches

Managed switches have configurable ports. You cannot configure ports on an unmanaged switch.

Switches can be configurable or nonconfigurable. If the switch must be customized in some way, then the administrator must be able to configure it. This requires additional knowledge on the part of the administrator and extra time. In other words, a configurable switch has administrative overhead.

A configurable switch is a *managed switch*. A nonconfigurable switch is an *unmanaged switch*. Determining what switch you need requires some basic knowledge of these two types of switches.

Understanding Unmanaged Switches

An unmanaged switch is just like a hub with respect to administrative overhead. There isn't any. You take the switch out of the box and plug it in, and it works.

The switch will monitor the traffic from each of the ports and build the MAC address table. As mentioned, the MAC address table maps the MAC addresses of the connected computers to their respective ports.

Even though an unmanaged switch doesn't require any administration, it does provide performance benefits over the simple hub. It still creates separate collision domains and increases performance on the network.

Unmanaged switches operate at layer 2 of the OSI Model.

> Chapter 3 presented the OSI Model. Layer 2 is the Data Link layer.
>
> ◄

Understanding Managed Switches

In contrast to an unmanaged switch, a managed switch can be configured. Managed switches are commonly managed using protocols such as Telnet or Secure Shell (SSH), and administrators can monitor and configure the switch remotely. As a reminder, SSH encrypts the traffic so that it can't be read if intercepted by a protocol analyzer or sniffer, while Telnet transmits in clear text.

Some of the management tasks that an administrator can perform are as follows:

> ◄
>
> Chapter 4 discussed PuTTY, a common application that uses SSH to administer managed switches from a remote location.

▶ Configure static entries in the MAC table

▶ Configure duplex settings (half-duplex or full-duplex) on ports

▶ Monitor performance of the switch using the Simple Network Management Protocol (SNMP)

▶ Configure the switch to send alerts called traps with SNMP when certain events occur

▶ Create a virtual LAN (VLAN)

▶ Configure port mirroring

> Port mirroring sends a copy of all traffic on the switch to a single port. Administrators can capture traffic on this port for monitoring with a packet sniffer.
>
> ◄

Although managed switches provide many more capabilities, they are also more expensive. Before spending the extra money for a managed switch, you should first ensure that your administrative staff can support them. If not, you may have a shiny new electronic toy with expensive extra features that no one knows how to use.

Managed switches can operate at layer 2 or layer 3 of the OSI Model.

> ◄
>
> Layer 2 is the Data Link layer. Layer 3 is the Network layer.

Comparing Layer 2 and Layer 3 Switches

A layer 2 switch has the primary purpose of segmenting collision domains at layer 2 of the OSI Model. Each port is segmented from the others. Layer 2 switches are hardware based, which makes them extremely fast. They use the integrated circuitry on the main board (the hardware) to move data between ports at lightning speed.

As you'd expect, a *layer 3* switch operates at layer 3 of the OSI Model. It includes standard switching functionality, but also contains routing capability to route layer 3 traffic just as if it were a router. Although the router is a great layer 3 device, it can be slow, because additional procesing of the packets must take place by the integrated software. A hardware-based switch is quicker.

Routers route traffic on layer 3. A layer 3 switch can route traffic on layer 3 like a router.

Only managed switches can be configured to route traffic on layer 3 like a router. Additionally, managed switches can be configured to create virtual local area networks. Unmanaged switches will work on layer 2 only.

As mentioned previously, a regular switch (a layer 2 switch) creates separate collision domains. It does pass broadcasts, so broadcast traffic goes to all ports on the layer 2 switch. In other words, a layer 2 switch does not create separate broadcast domains.

In contrast, a router does not pass broadcasts. The router creates separate broadcast domains. However, a layer 3 switch acts like a router and creates separate broadcast domains. You can use this to ensure traffic is routed to only certain ports on a switch without replacing the switch with a router.

Using a Managed Switch to Create a VLAN

A *virtual LAN (VLAN)* is like a LAN inside a LAN. However, just as the name implies, it is created virtually, not with extra physical hardware.

The benefits of creating a VLAN include the following:

- ▶ Improved LAN security, because broadcast traffic is limited to specific ports

- ▶ The ability to group workstations or servers based on needs, not physical location

- ▶ Improved network performance for each separate broadcast domain

Many other security measures could be taken, but this explanation is focused only on the creation of VLANs.

Imagine this scenario. You are the administrator for an organization that has several departments including the sales and finance departments. Recently financial data was leaked. The source of the leak is unknown, but security is being tightened everywhere financial data flows. Traffic from the computers in the financial department needs to be isolated with the least cost.

Figure 8.8 shows the configuration before creating the VLAN. Although the switch is actually hosting many more computers, the figure shows only four computers for simplicity's sake. There shouldn't be any surprises in this diagram to you except that it's drawn with the switch on one side and the computers on the other.

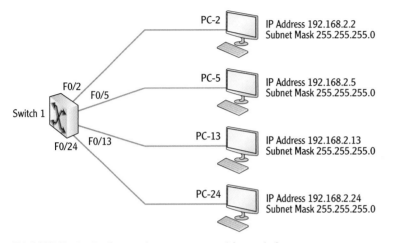

FIGURE 8.8 Connecting computers with a switch

The goal is to create two separate VLANs with this switch—one for sales and one for finance. VLANs need VLAN identifiers (VLAN IDs) and VLAN names, and Table 8.1 shows the VLAN configuration. The sales department will be on VLAN ID 2 using ports F0/0 through F0/11 and a network ID of 192.168.2.0/24. The finance department will be on VLAN ID 4 using ports F0/12 through F0/24 with a network ID of 192.168.4.0/24.

Network IDs are derived from the IP address and subnet mask. Chapter 5 explained how to calculate the network ID.

TABLE 8.1 VLAN configuration

VLAN ID	VLAN name	Port range	Subnet range	Subnet ID
2	Sales	F0/0-F0/11	192.168.2.0/24	192.168.2.0
4	Finance	F0/12-F0/24	192.168.4.0/24	192.168.4.0

Figure 8.9 shows this VLAN configuration. Even though the switch is shown twice, there is only one physical switch. However, it is using specific ports outlined in Table 8.1 to create the two VLANs.

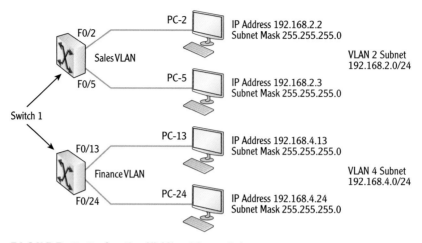

FIGURE 8.9 Creating VLANs with a switch

You would ensure that the financial computers are connected only to switch ports F0/12 through F0/24 and their IP addresses are changed so that they have a network ID of 192.168.4.0/24. Additionally, you need to ensure that all the sales computers are connected only to ports F0/0 through F0/12.

Although this example shows the basics of creating a VLAN, VLANs can be much more complex. For example, VLANs can be created to span multiple switches.

Consider Figure 8.10. This shows four departments connected with five switches. Each switch is dedicated to a specific department, but as the company grows, more salespeople are added than the office space can support. Some salespeople are sitting in the office space where the HR switch is connected. However, you can create VLANs so that these salespeople are virtually connected to the sales switch.

The following are some basic points to remember with VLANs:

▶ A VLAN must have at least two ports before traffic can flow, but it can have more.

 ▶ You can create 24 two-port VLANs on a 48-port switch.

 ▶ You can create two 24-port VLANs on a 48-port switch.

 ▶ You can create any mixture as long as each VLAN has at least two ports.

▶ All ports don't have to be used in a VLAN.

▶ VLANs can span multiple switches.

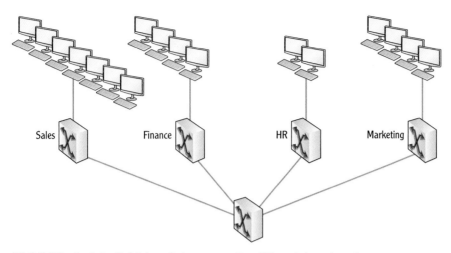

FIGURE 8.10 Multiple switches connecting different departments

Exploring Switch Speeds

A major consideration when managing and purchasing a switch is the transmission speed. This indicates the bandwidth of the switch, or how much data it can process at a time. Speeds are rated in megabits per second (Mbps) or gigabits per second (Gbps), per physical port.

You'll often hear the terms *bandwidth* and *speeds* used interchangeably. You can compare this to traffic on a highway. A single-lane road may be able to handle 100 cars an hour. However, if traffic increases and you need to handle 1,000 cars an hour, you can widen the road and add more lanes. The first 100 cars may or may not reach their destination any faster than before the road was widened, but as traffic increases, more cars will be able to get there faster because of the extra bandwidth of the road. Similarly, you can increase the amount of traffic a network can handle by increasing the bandwidth of the devices on the network.

The IEEE 802.3 standard identifies several basic speeds you're likely to see in networks today. Although more speeds are possible, Table 8.2 shows common speeds used with twisted-pair cables.

TABLE 8.2 Ethernet speeds

Protocol	Speed	Comments
IEEE 802.3	10 Mbps	10 million bits per second
IEEE 802.3u	100 Mbps	100 million bits per second

(Continues)

TABLE 8.2   *(Continued)*

Protocol	Speed	Comments
IEEE 802.3z	1000 Mbps	1000 million bits per second (1 gigabit)
IEEE 802.3an	10 Gbps	10 gigabits per second

There are three important speeds to pay attention to when looking at a switch:

▶ Transmission speed

▶ Uplink speed

▶ Backplane speed

These speeds are discussed in detail in the following sections.

Identifying Transmission Speeds

Switches are commonly represented with port speeds such as 10/100 Mbps or 100/1000 Mbps. The 10/100 means that a port may operate at either 10 Mbps or 100 Mbps, and the 100/1000 means that a port can operate at either 100 Mbps or 1000 Mbps.

The limiting factors are the capabilities of the end devices and the cable grade that is used. In other words, CAT 5 twisted-pair cable can't be used for 1000 Mbps, though CAT 5E can.

Similarly, if a computer has a 10 Mbps NIC, the switch can send data to the NIC only at 10 Mbps no matter how fast the switch is.

High-speed switches are available. Of course, they are more expensive. If you have a group of users who need to share large files, stream audio and video, or use Voice over IP (VoIP), it's worth getting the high-speed switches. If you do, you also need to ensure that the connecting cable and individual NICs meet the speed requirements.

If you are using a managed switch, you can manually configure individual ports for speed. Some ports could be set at 10 Mbps, some at 100 Mbps, and some at 1000 Mbps, as long as the switch supports all the speeds. Additionally, you can configure the ports individually for half-duplex or full-duplex.

Autosense for speed between the PC and the port is a common option with many switches. In other words, you don't have to set the speed, but the switch automatically determines the best settings for optimal speed.

Many switches use autosense to detect the speed of connected devices. For example, a switch rated at 100/1000 can operate at either 100 Mbps or 1000 Mbps on each port.

Chapter 7 presented different categories of twisted-pair cables.

Most network hardware available today uses full-duplex. However, you can downgrade a port to half-duplex for compatibility with legacy hardware.

Understanding the Uplink Port

An *uplink port* is a special port on a switch used to connect the switch to another switch or to another device. In contrast, other ports on the switch are called *access links*.

Uplink ports offer scalability by allowing you to add switches to the network in a daisy chain. You can also use the uplink port to connect the switch to a router for access to other subnets.

UPLINK PORTS AND CROSSOVER CABLES

An uplink port is wired so that a straight-through cable can be used to connect it to other switches or routers. However, if you're using a regular port, it's not wired to connect two switches, and you'll need to use a crossover cable.

Many new switches can automatically sense whether a crossover or straight-through connection is needed and configure the switch internally using Auto-MDIX. Other devices use the MDI/MDI-X button that you can toggle to change the port from straight-through to crossover.

The uplink port may be labeled as an uplink port. However, on some switches the port is not labeled but instead shares the capability with another port. For example, on some smaller switches, one of the ports may include a push button labeled as MDI/MDI-X (for medium dependent interface/medium dependent interface crossover). When MDI is selected, it works as a regular port. When MDI-X is selected, it works as an uplink port. If the MDI/MDI-X button is not available, you may need to use a crossover cable.

Many switches offer the ability to bundle access links together to act as a single link between switches. If your switch has a bundling option, you can configure multiple ports together as a single link. This uses the *link aggregation control protocol (LACP)*.

LACP defined in IEEE 802.3ax forms a single logical channel between devices with multiple physical links. For example, with LACP enabled, you could bundle five 100 Mbps ports as one logical link. This gives an effective throughput in this trunk of 500 Mbps. If full-duplex is used (and it normally is), your effective data throughput is 1 Gbps. Table 8.3 shows some possible speeds when bundling ports into a trunk.

◄ Chapter 7 identified the differences between crossover cables and straight-through cables.

Chapter 3 covered half-duplex and full-duplex. Most cables and network devices use full-duplex by default, but managed switches can be configured to match the existing hardware.

◄

TABLE 8.3   Trunking throughput speeds

No. of ports	Port speed	Duplex setting	Effective throughput at uplink
One	10	Half	10 Mbps
One	100	Full	200 Mbps
Five	100	Half	500 Mbps
Five	100	Full	1000 Mbps (Gigabit)

Identifying Backplane Speed

Another speed to consider with switches is the backplane speed. The backplane speed is the internal speed of the switch. The faster this speed is, the better the overall performance of the switch.

Backplane speed applies only to modular switches, not form factor switches. It measures how fast data is transferred between modules in the switch.

Depending on the manufacturer, backplane speed may be measured at a couple different points. The first would be the speed on the chassis where the modules plug in. This is sometimes referred to as the speed between application-specific integrated circuits (ASICs), or the ASICs speed. This is similar in concept to the bus speed on a computer.

The second backplane speed measurement is between ports on the different blades on the same chassis. This is slightly different from the ASICs speed and is sometimes referred to as the *port-to-port speed*.

Understanding Security Options

Security is never something that is done once and it's over. It's an ongoing process.

Security is required in any network. Any time data needs to be kept secret, security is required. In addition, a company without any proprietary data quickly becomes a company without revenue.

The basic security principle of security in-depth dictates that multiple layers of security are required. Additionally, security needs to be regularly reviewed and updated. Some of the common security steps you can take with switches are as follows:

▶ Keep network hardware protected with physical security (in a locked room, in a locked rack).

▶ Change default passwords on managed switches to a complex password.

▶ Never use blank passwords.

▶ Use a secure protocol (such as SSH) to remotely manage switches.

▶ Use SNMP version 3 (instead of just SNMP or SNMP version 2) for best security.

▶ Consider port security.

▶ Consider hardware redundancy for maximum availability of network resources.

These last two items (port security and hardware redundancy) are explained in more depth in the following two sections.

Understanding Port Security

Port security helps you restrict what devices can connect to ports on a switch. The danger is that if someone can walk into your organization and simply plug a computer into an RJ-45 jack in the wall, they can access your network. That's disconcerting to both administrators and organization executives.

One method of port security is to configure each port with the MAC address of a specific computer. Only that computer can connect. If a device with a different MAC attempts a connection, the switch refuses the connection. If you have five computers, this won't take much time. However, if you have 500 computers, it can be quite time-consuming and tedious.

An alternative is to configure the port to remember which MAC addresses it learned and to set a threshold for the maximum number of addresses allowed. For example, you may set the threshold at one or two addresses, and any MAC learned after that would trip an alarm. The alarm may notify an administrator using an SNMP trap (or error message) or may shut down communication with the port.

Another element of port security is ensuring that unused ports are not enabled. For example, you may have a 48-port switch that is cabled to 48 RJ-45 wall jacks in your organization. However, you are currently using only 40 of the RJ-45 jacks. The other jacks don't have computers attached. The switch ports where these jacks are connected should be disabled. This prevents someone from coming in, plugging in a computer to an empty jack, and accessing your network.

Planning Hardware Redundancy

The switch in a typical network configuration presents itself as a single point of failure. If the switch fails, *poof,* all the computers connected through the switch lose connectivity to network resources. However, you can build in fault tolerance by adding hardware redundancy.

◀

Only managed switches can use port security. Unmanaged switches can't be configured for specific MACs.

Fault tolerance means that a fault can occur and a system can tolerate it. Fault tolerance can be implemented at the disk level, the server level, the site level, and more.

◀

Hardware redundancy simply means that additional components are added to ensure that the failure of one component doesn't result in a complete failure. For example, many modular switches come with more than one power supply. If one power supply fails, the switch can continue to operate. In some switches, the power supplies are completely redundant, meaning that the switch will continue to operate with no loss of capability. In other switches, a failure of one power supply may affect only some of the ports on the switch but not all of them.

It's also possible to configure a fail-over state in a trunked environment with LACP. In other words, if one or more ports fail in the combined trunk, the capability can be switched to another port.

Obviously, adding redundant capabilities costs more money. The majority of the time, the redundant component is not actively utilized but is instead just there in case a failure occurs. When considering hardware redundancy for switches, you need to consider how critical connectivity is for the devices.

It may be that a failure of a particular switch results in immediate loss of critical resources and lost revenue. It's worthwhile adding additional redundancy for this switch. On the other hand, the loss of a switch may not be critical. You may be able to replace it within a day without any impact on the business's bottom line. In this case, the added cost of redundancy is not necessary.

THE ESSENTIALS AND BEYOND

In this chapter, you learned about many of the capabilities and inner workings of switches. You learned how the switch uses the MAC addresses to create a MAC address table. It then creates multiple collision domains by sending data only to the destination device based on the MAC address instead of to all devices connected to the switch. You also learned how some switches are managed and can be configured, while other switches simply work by plugging them in. Some switches operate as layer 2 and layer 3 switches, and you can create VLANs within a managed switch. Port security can control what devices can connect to a switch.

ADDITIONAL EXERCISES

▶ Draw a diagram of computers in your network up to the nearest router. Identify the different broadcast domains and the different collision domains.

▶ Locate a switch in your network. Count the number of normal ports it uses.

▶ Locate a switch in your network. Identify the uplink port. How is it labeled?

▶ Locate an active switch in your network. Identify the physical security used to protect it.

(Continues)

THE ESSENTIALS AND BEYOND (Continued)

To compare your answers to the author's, please visit **www.sybex.com/go/ networkingessentials**.

REVIEW QUESTIONS

1. A_____ switch is expandable. You can add ports by adding components.

2. You are looking at a drawing of a 100 Mbps switch and want to identify what device is connected to the first port. How will the port be labeled?

    A. E0   **C.** F1

    B. F0   **D.** Gi1

3. True or false. Layer 2 switches create separate broadcast domains.

4. Your network includes computers connected via hubs. You want to reduce the number of collisions to the least number possible. What should you do?

    A. You should replace the hubs   **C.** You should replace the hubs
         with bridges.   with switches.

    B. You should replace the hubs   **D.** You should replace the hubs
         with managed hubs.   with firewalls.

5. True or false. A managed switch requires less administrative overhead than an unmanaged switch.

6. A layer 3 switch functions just like a _____.

7. What does a switch maintain to track the location of computers?

    A. A MAC address table   **C.** A layer 3 table

    B. A routing table   **D.** A managed table

8. A switch has 48 ports. How many VLANs can you create with it?

    A. 2   **C.** 24

    B. 12   **D.** 48

9. A 100 Mbps switch is configured to combine five ports using LACP with full-duplex. What is the effective throughput at the uplink?

    A. 100 Mbps   **C.** 600 Mbps

    B. 500 Mbps   **D.** 1000 Mbps

10. You want to ensure that only known computers can connect to a switch. What should you implement?

## CHAPTER 9

Connecting Networks with Routers

Routers expand networks by allowing you to create multiple subnets or subnetworks. Routers are the traffic cops on a network that direct all the traffic from one subnetwork to another. At the very least, you need a router to access the Internet, and most networks in organizations include multiple routers.

Although the administration of routers is minimal in small networks, you should know some basics. For example, a router needs to know the path to all subnets in your network and the path to the Internet. Routers include a routing table that lists all of these paths, and the routing table can be updated manually or automatically. This chapter covers these topics and shows you how you can configure a Windows Server 2008 server as a software router.

▶ **Connecting multiple networks**

▶ **Routing traffic on a network**

▶ **Identifying transmission speeds**

▶ **Routing software in Windows Server 2008**

▶ **Understanding other routing protocols**

Connecting Multiple Networks

Chapter 8 covered switches and showed how switches connect multiple computers. In contrast, routers connect multiple networks so that computers on different networks can communicate with each other.

When talking about routers, you should understand some basic terms. These are explored throughout the chapter, but as introduction, they are defined here:

Hardware Router   This is a dedicated hardware device that routes packets. For example, Cisco makes several different models of routers used on internal networks and the Internet.

▶

Steps later in this chapter show how to configure Windows Server 2008 as a software router.

Software Router   This is a server that includes software used to route packets. For example, you can configure Windows Server 2008 as a software router.

Routing Interface   This is the interface where packets are received and transmitted. A router will have multiple interfaces but must have at least two.

Static Routing   *Static routing* means that routes to different subnets in the network are manually (statically) added to the router. If there are any changes to the network affecting the routes, an administrator must manually modify the routes.

Dynamic Routing   *Dynamic routing* means that routes to different subnets in the network are automatically (dynamically) updated on the router. Administrators need to configure routing protocols, but after that, the routers take care of keeping routes up to date themselves.

Routing Protocols   These protocols allow routers to communicate with each other and share routing information. Two primary *routing protocols* used on internal networks are *Routing Information Protocol version 2 (RIPv2)* and *Open Shortest Path First (OSPF)*.

Routing Table   This is a table maintained within a router that identifies all known subnetworks. The *routing table* also includes the path to these subnetworks.

Consider Figure 9.1. This shows a single router connecting four networks (labeled as A, B, C, and D). In this context, each of the networks is joined into a single local area network (LAN), and you can think of these joined networks as subnetworks in the overall LAN.

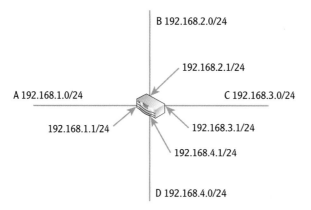

FIGURE 9.1 Using a router to connect networks

Each of the subnetworks has its own network ID that is different from the others. Additionally, the router has four separate interfaces with a single interface connected to each subnetwork.

Notice that the IP address assigned to the router interface in each of these subnetworks is the first IP address available. In other words, in the 192.168.1.0/24 subnetwork, the router interface is assigned the address of 192.168.1.1/24. It's common to assign the first address within a range to the router interface, but it is not required. No matter what address is assigned, though, it must have the same network ID as other devices in the subnetwork.

◄

Figure 9.1 doesn't show network devices. However, each of these subnetworks would host computers, servers, or other network devices.

Comparing Hardware Routers and Software Routers

Routers can be dedicated hardware routers, or they can be software routers. Although most routers in production networks are hardware routers, it is possible to configure Windows Server 2008 as a software router.

Windows Server 2008 includes all the software components to configure it as a software router. You don't need to purchase any additional software. The only item that is required is to have at least two network interface cards (NICs) installed. One NIC would connect to one network, and the other NIC would connect to another network. You then configure the server as a router, and it takes care of the rest.

Although it's much more common to use hardware routers, here are some examples of when you may want to use Windows Server 2008 as a software router:

◄

Sections later in this chapter show how to configure a Windows Server 2008 server as a software router.

Development Environment   You can create a temporary subnetwork without purchasing additional hardware. For example, if you want to isolate some computers in a separate subnet for testing or development purposes, a software router is an inexpensive alternative.

Replacement of Failed Router   If a hardware router fails, in smaller environments you may temporarily replace it with a software router until you purchase and receive a replacement.

Understanding Default Routes

A default route is the path that IP traffic takes when another path isn't identified. Most computers determine default routes based on their configured default gateway settings. Chapter 5 covered some basics of how TCP/IP determines whether traffic should go through a router. As a reminder, consider Figure 9.2 for the following scenarios.

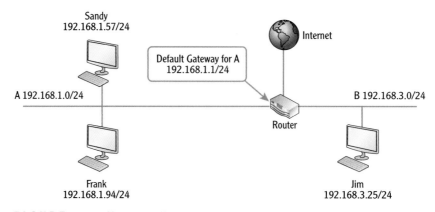

FIGURE 9.2 Moving traffic on a network

Imagine that Sandy wants to send data to Frank. TCP/IP will determine Sandy and Frank's network ID as shown in Table 9.1. Since the network IDs of both computers are the same (192.168.1.0), TCP/IP sends the traffic directly to Frank's computer.

TABLE 9.1 Determining the network ID of local computers

Computer	IP address	Subnet mask	Network ID
Sandy	192.168.1.57	255.255.255.0	192.168.1.0
Frank	192.168.1.94	255.255.255.0	192.168.1.0

Later, Sandy wants to send data to Jim. As you can see in Figure 9.2, Sandy and Jim's computers are on different subnetworks. TCP/IP determines this by calculating the network ID as shown in Table 9.2. Since the network IDs are different, TCP/IP realizes it must send the data to another network.

TABLE 9.2 Determining the network ID of remote computers

Computer	IP address	Subnet mask	Network ID
Sandy	192.168.1.57	255.255.255.0	192.168.1.0
Jim	192.168.3.25	255.255.255.0	192.168.3.0

More specifically, since the destination is on a different network, it must forward the data to the addresses of the default gateway. In Figure 9.2, the interface on router 2 with an IP address of 192.168.1.1 is the default gateway for subnetwork A. Notice that the default gateway has the same network ID as other computers on subnetwork A.

Some people call the router the default gateway. This is only partially correct. That's like calling an automobile a car door. Sure, an automobile does have a door, but the door is just one component. An automobile has much more to it. Similarly, the default gateway is one component of the router, and there is much more to the router.

◄

Similarly, any traffic destined for the Internet goes through the default gateway.

◄

The router in Figure 9.2 has three interfaces. The interface on subnetwork A is the default gateway for this network. The interface on subnetwork B is the default gateway for that network.

IDENTIFY THE DEFAULT GATEWAY AND ROUTERS

You can use the command-line tool `ipconfig` to determine your default gateway. You can launch the command prompt in most Windows systems by clicking Start ➢ Run, typing **cmd** in the Run box, and pressing Enter.

At the command prompt, enter **ipconfig**. The output will include information similar to the following:

```
Ethernet adapter Local Area Connection:

        Connection-specific DNS Suffix  . :
        IPv4 Address. . . . . . . . . . : 192.168.1.57
        Subnet Mask . . . . . . . . . . : 255.255.255.0
        Default Gateway . . . . . . . . : 192.168.1.1
```

The default gateway identifies the IP address of the near side of the router. Note this doesn't show the IP addresses of all the router's interfaces. It shows only the IP address of the interface on the same subnetwork.

Understanding Directly Connected Routes

Any subnetwork that is directly connected to a router is a *directly connected route*. For example, each of the subnetworks in Figures 9.1 and 9.2 is directly connected to a single router. Since the router is directly connected to these subnetworks, it inherently knows the path to them.

However, routers don't automatically know the paths to other subnetworks within a LAN. If a LAN includes multiple routers with multiple subnetworks connected to these different routers, you need to teach these routers about the other subnetworks. This is done either statically or dynamically. The next section discusses both static routing and dynamic routing.

Routing Traffic on a Network

Figure 9.3 shows a larger network with three routers and six subnetworks. This network includes both directly connected routes for each of the routers and indirectly connected routes. Can you name the directly connected routes for each of the routers?

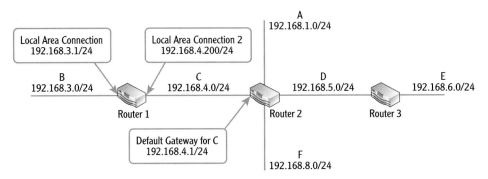

FIGURE 9.3 Multiple router network

▶ Router 1 knows about the directly connected subnetworks of B and C.

▶ Router 2 knows about the directly connected subnetworks of subnetworks A, C, D, and F.

▶ Router 3 knows about the directly connected subnetworks of subnetworks D and E.

For the network to be fully routed, each of the routers needs to know the paths to other networks. For example, if a computer in the F subnetwork needs to send data to a computer in the B subnetwork, router 2 needs to know how to get it there.

Creating Static Routes

When your network includes multiple routers, routers can be statically configured or dynamically configured. Administrators may manually add routes to a router to create statically configured routes. In a dynamically configured router, the administrator configures routing protocols, and these routing protocols automatically discover subnets on the network.

If you have only a few routes to add and you don't anticipate them changing, static routes can be the simplest method. It's also common to deploy some routers with some static routes, while others are configured dynamically.

Figure 9.4 shows the Routing and Remote Access (RRAS) console on a Windows Server 2008 server that has been configured as a router. In the figure, one static route to the 192.168.5.0 destination has been created. The dialog box in the foreground is adding a second static route to the 192.168.8.0 destination subnet. These routes support the network shown in Figure 9.3 earlier and are two of the routes that are needed on router 1.

Procedures at the end of this chapter show how to add RRAS to a Windows Server 2008 server and configure it as a software router.

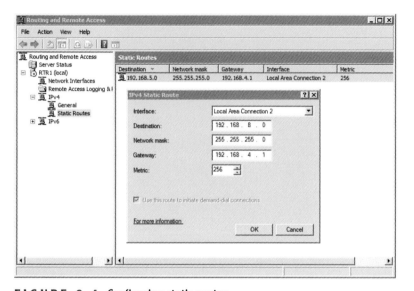

FIGURE 9.4 Configuring static routes

There are several key pieces of information in this figure worth pointing out:

Destination This identifies the destination subnetwork. The router doesn't name these by letters like you saw in Figure 9.3 but instead uses the network ID. If you look back at Figure 9.3, you can see these networks are identified by both a letter (such as A, D, E, and F) and a network ID.

Netmask This is the subnet mask of the network ID. Each of the subnetworks in Figure 9.3 has a CIDR notation of /24, indicating a subnet mask of 255.255.255.0.

Gateway This is the IP address of the destination router's network interface. Notice in Figure 9.3 that the path to other subnetworks from router 1 is through router 2 (except for the directly connected routes of B and C). The IP address of the router's NIC on subnetwork C is 192.168.4.1, so its IP address is entered here. It becomes the default gateway from router 1 and is also the default gateway for any computers on subnetwork C.

You can also enter routes to specific computers instead of to subnetworks. Routes to specific computers use a network mask of 255.255.255.255.

Interface   This identifies the NIC that should be utilized to connect to the specified destination by name. In this example, the NIC named Local Area Connection is on subnetwork B. The NIC named Local Area Connection 2 is on subnetwork C.

Metric   A metric represents a cost value to the route. If there are multiple paths to a network, the router calculates the least cost path to determine which path to take. In our example here, the metric doesn't matter since there is only one path to any of the networks.

> In large networks with multiple routers and multiple paths, the metric is important. It helps routers identify the best routes to different subnetworks.

While the figure shows the creation of two static routes, many more static routes must be created to support the network shown in Figure 9.3 earlier. Can you identify all the static routes that need to be created on each router?

▶ Router 1 needs four static routes (to A, D, E, and F) since it knows only about the two directly connected routes of B and C.

▶ Router 2 needs two static routes (to B and E) since it knows only about the directly connected routes of A, C, D, and F.

▶ Router 3 needs four static routes (to A, B, C, and F) since it knows only about the directly connected routes of D and E.

▶ This network has 10 static routes.

Instead of typing these static routes in manually, you can choose to configure dynamic routing instead.

Configuring Dynamic Routing

You can enable dynamic routing protocols on routers to enable them to learn the paths to other routers dynamically. After you configure the protocols, the routers talk to each other. Each router lets other routers know what it knows, and after a short time, each router knows the paths to all subnetworks on the network.

Table 9.3 briefly compares static and dynamic routing. In short, static routing has very few features. Dynamic routing provides more benefits.

TABLE 9.3   Comparison of static and dynamic routing

Features	Static routing	Dynamic routing
Discovery of remote networks (including new or changed networks)	Must be done manually	Done automatically

(Continues)

T A B L E   9 . 3   *(Continued)*

Features	Static routing	Dynamic routing
Information exchange with other routers	None	Information exchanged with routing protocol
Fault tolerance	None	Failure of routers can be detected and paths to networks modified (when multiple paths exist)

Since dynamic routing provides so many features over static routing, you may wonder why you'd ever use static routing. It depends in part on how many routers you have. If you have only two routers, it's much easier to configure the static routes once rather than adding and configuring a routing protocol.

A primary routing protocol used on Windows Server 2008 is Routing Information Protocol version 2 (RIPv2). RIPv2 is very easy to add and configure on a Windows Server 2008 server running RRAS. You simply add it, identify the NICs you want it to operate on, and you're done. The routers will automatically share their routing information with each other.

RIPv2 has replaced RIPv1 in most networks because of its many benefits. Table 9.4 compares RIPv1 and RIPv2.

◄

Many advanced routing protocols are available in larger networks and the Internet. This section focuses primarily on protocols used on smaller to medium-sized networks.

T A B L E   9 . 4   A comparison of RIPv1 and RIPv2

Features	RIPv1	RIPv2
Multicasting	Not supported	Supported
Classless routes	Supports only routes to classful networks	Supports routes to classful and classless networks
Authentication	None available	Allows routers to authenticate between each other prior to sharing routing data

Figure 9.5 shows the Windows Server 2008 RRAS console with RIPv2 added. Both the Local Area Connection and Local Area Connection 2 NICs have been added to the RIP node so that RIP operates on both. This router will now listen for RIP information from other routers and send RIP information to them through both of its interfaces.

◄

RRAS will send RIPv2 data and listen for RIPv1 and RIPv2 data by default. However, it can be configured for any combination of RIPv1 and RIPv2.

Although you can do more advanced configuration of RIPv2, the default configuration will work for most networks as long as the settings are configured in the same on other routers in the network. However, two settings are of primary importance:

► The Outgoing Packet Protocol is configured to use RIP version 2 broadcast by default. However, you can change this to RIP version 2 multicast (as shown in Figure 9.5) for better network performance.

► You can configure authentication by clicking the Activate Authentication check box and adding a password. All routers will need the same password. This ensures that only routers that can authenticate can access the routing information.

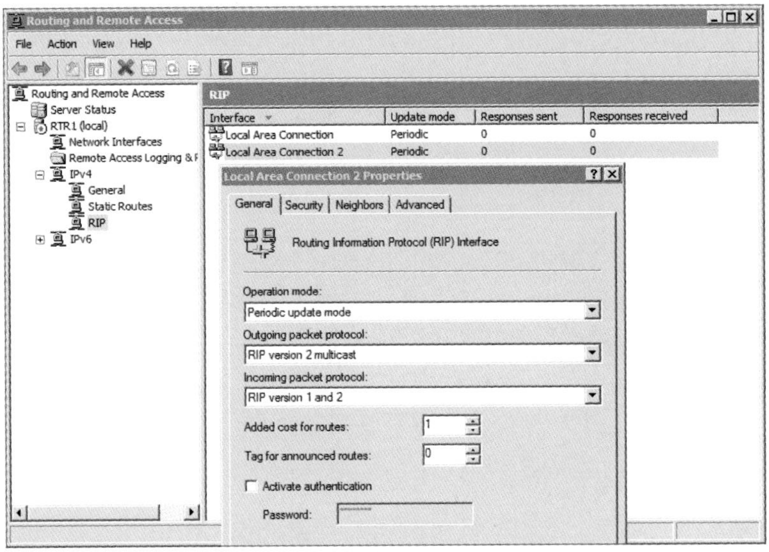

FIGURE 9.5 Configuring RIPv2 properties on a NIC

OPEN SHORTEST PATH FIRST

Open Shortest Path First (OSPF) is a common routing protocol used on internal networks with hardware routers. The method it uses to share routes between routers on the network is different from RIPv2. However, the result is the same. With OSPF, routers on the network will learn all routes and be dynamically updated when the network changes. RIPv2 and OSPF are not compatible with each other.

(Continues)

OPEN SHORTEST PATH FIRST *(Continued)*

Even though OSPF was available in Windows Server 2003, it was removed in Windows Server 2008. At the time I'm writing this, it remains out of Windows Server 2008 R2, though it's possible it may return in a future service pack.

If you have an existing network using OSPF and you want to add a Windows Server 2008 server as a router, you'll either need to configure the Windows server with static routing or need to convert the other routers to use RIPv2.

Understanding the Routing Table

Routers maintain routing tables that identify the path to other networks. Routing tables include the primary components shown in the "Creating Static Routes" section earlier in this chapter such as destination, interface, and gateway.

Figure 9.6 shows the routing table in a Windows Server 2008 RRAS console with a few key items highlighted. This computer has two NICs with IP addresses of 192.168.3.1 and 192.168.4.200.

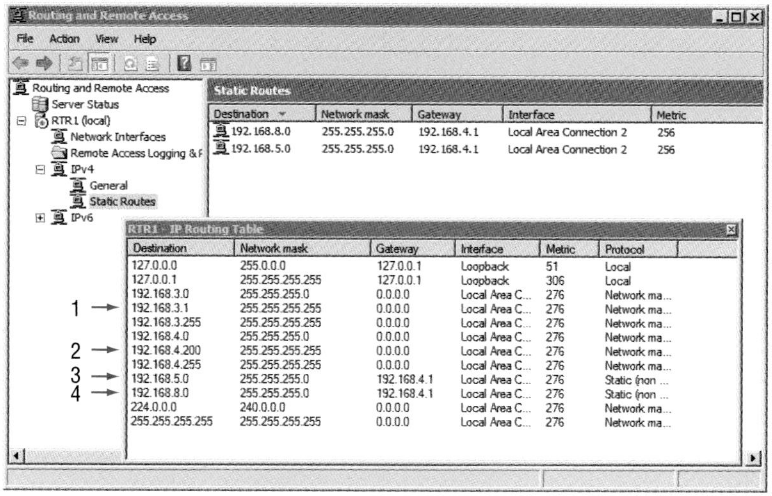

FIGURE 9.6 Viewing static routes in RRAS

The following list identifies the numbered items in Figure 9.6:

1. The NIC connected to the 192.168.3.0/24 subnetwork has an IP address of 192.168.3.1. Notice the network mask is 255.255.255.255, and the gateway is 0.0.0.0. This helps identify it as a directly connected route.

2. The NIC connected to the 192.168.4.0/24 subnetwork has an IP address of 192.168.4.200. Notice the network mask is 255.255.255.255, and the gateway is 0.0.0.0. This helps identify it as a directly connected route.

3. The path to the 192.168.5.0 subnetwork is via the 192.168.4.1 default gateway.

4. The path to the 192.168.8.0 subnetwork is via the 192.168.4.1 default gateway.

▶

You can execute the route print command at the command prompt of any Windows system to view the full routing table.

You can also view a routing table for any individual system. For example, Listing 9.1 shows a partial output of the route print command executed at the command prompt on a Windows Server with two NICs. The server is configured as a router connecting the 192.168.1.0/24 network and the 192.168.9.0/24 network.

Listing 9.1 Partial output of command C:\>route print

```
===========================================================================
Active Routes:
Network Destination        Netmask          Gateway       Interface  Metric
          127.0.0.0        255.0.0.0        On-link        127.0.0.1     306
          127.0.0.1  255.255.255.255        On-link        127.0.0.1     306
    127.255.255.255  255.255.255.255        On-link        127.0.0.1     306
        192.168.3.0    255.255.255.0        On-link      192.168.3.1     276
        192.168.3.1  255.255.255.255        On-link      192.168.3.1     276
      192.168.3.255  255.255.255.255        On-link      192.168.3.1     276
        192.168.4.0    255.255.255.0        On-link    192.168.4.200     276
      192.168.4.200  255.255.255.255        On-link    192.168.4.200     276
      192.168.4.255  255.255.255.255        On-link    192.168.4.200     276
        192.168.5.0    255.255.255.0    192.168.4.1    192.168.4.200     276
        192.168.8.0    255.255.255.0    192.168.4.1    192.168.4.200     276
          224.0.0.0        240.0.0.0        On-link        127.0.0.1     306
          224.0.0.0        240.0.0.0        On-link    192.168.4.200     276
          224.0.0.0        240.0.0.0        On-link      192.168.3.1     276
    255.255.255.255  255.255.255.255        On-link        127.0.0.1     306
    255.255.255.255  255.255.255.255        On-link    192.168.4.200     276
    255.255.255.255  255.255.255.255        On-link      192.168.3.1     276
===========================================================================
```

ROUTING TABLES AND MEMORY

The information for routing tables is stored in the router's memory. The routing tables shown in this chapter are trivial in size. They don't consume much memory. However, routing tables on Internet routers can contain tens of thousands of entries. These tables consume a significant amount of memory.

Identifying Transmission Speeds

Chapter 8 presented information on the speed of switches. As a reminder, the maximum speed of a switch determines the maximum speed that computers can send data through the switch. Switch speeds are measured in bits per second (bps, such as 100 Mbps).

Similarly, routers are also measured in bits per second, and the maximum speed of the router is the maximum speed that switches can send data through the network. One important consideration is the speed of routers that accept traffic from multiple switches.

Consider Figure 9.7. It shows a network with multiple routers and switches. Different routers will have to accommodate different amounts of data. For example, the router to the Internet may have high usage if all users regularly access the Internet. Even the router right below it (which is central to the network) will likely be substantially busier than other routers. The activity depends on where resources are placed in the network and the amount of usage for each of the subnetworks.

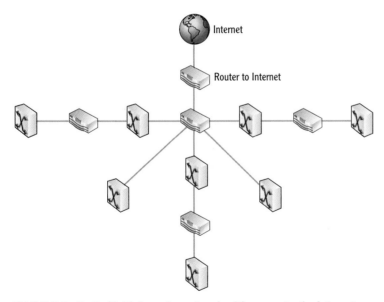

FIGURE 9.7 Multiple router network with access to the Internet

Common speeds for wired routers are 100 Mbps and 1000 Mbps. However, just as switches have increased in their speed capabilities, you can also buy higher-performance routers in the 10 Gbps range. Of course, higher speeds cost more money.

Routing Software in Windows Server 2008

You can add routing capabilities to a Windows Server 2008 server by enabling the Routing and Remote Access Services service. This is part of the Network Policy and Access Services role. Once the role is added, you can configure the service so that the server functions as a router.

ROUTING AND REMOTE ACCESS

The Network Policy and Access Services role has multiple uses. In addition to using it as a router as shown in this chapter, you can also use it to enable remote access for a network. Chapter 13 touches on using Network Policy and Access Services to create a dial-up or a virtual private network (VPN) server for remote access.

It's worthwhile repeating the obvious here. A router must have at least two separate interfaces. If you're creating a software router on a server, the server must have at least two network interface cards. Not all servers start with more than one NIC, but you can add NICs to most servers without too much problem.

Imagine that you manage a network with multiple computers and one or more servers. You decide that you want to move some of the computers from the primary network to a separate subnetwork for testing. This will create separate broadcast domains, and traffic on the testing network won't interfere with traffic on the primary network. Unfortunately, you don't have funding for a new hardware router. However, you do have a server and an extra NIC that you can use.

You can redesign the network so that it looks like Figure 9.8. You add the second NIC to the server, configure the server as a router, and rerun some of the cables.

Adding Routing Services to Windows Server 2008

The following steps show how to add the Routing and Remote Access Services service to Windows Server 2008:

These steps will also work on a Windows Server 2008 R2 server.

1. Click Start ➢ Administrative Tools ➢ Server Manager.

2. Click Roles, and select Add Roles.

3. Review the information on the Before You Begin page, and click Next.

4. Select Network Policy And Access Services. Click Next.

5. Review the information on the Network Policy And Access Services page, and click Next.

6. Click the Routing check box.
    A dialog box will appear as shown in Figure 9.9, prompting you to add the role services required for routing.

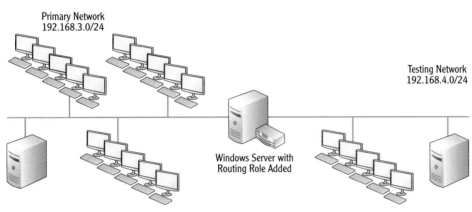

Primary Network
192.168.3.0/24

Testing Network
192.168.4.0/24

Windows Server with
Routing Role Added

Figure 9.8 doesn't show switches. However, switches are implied in both subnetworks. Even if you used a hardware router, you'd use two switches.

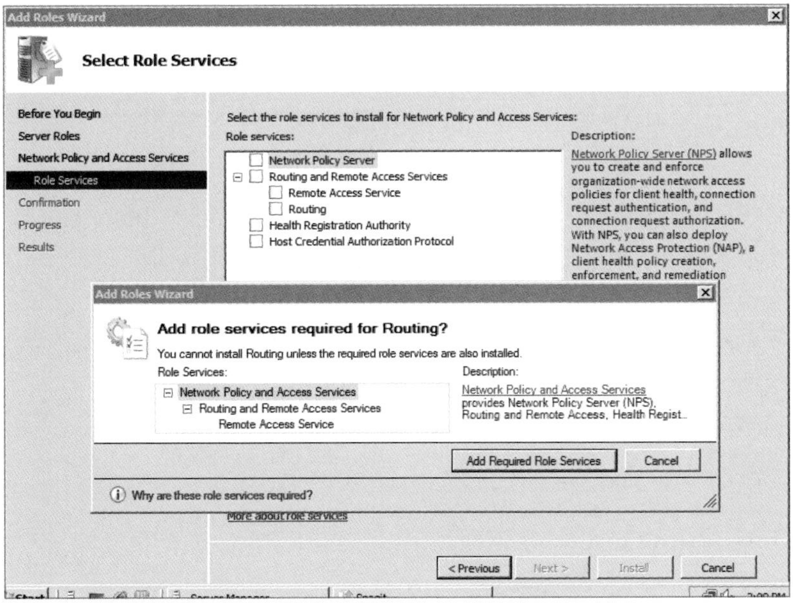

◀

FIGURE 9.8 Adding routing to Windows Server 2008

Even though you selected the Routing check box, it doesn't appear selected until you make a decision about adding the required role services.

◀

FIGURE 9.9 Adding routing to Windows Server 2008

USING VIRTUAL SYSTEMS FOR TESTING

You don't always have to use physical systems for testing. In fact, most IT professionals do a lot of testing, experimenting, and learning with virtual systems.

For example, if you're using Windows 7, you can use Windows Virtual PC. You can then install Server 2008 as a virtual machine running within Windows 7. You can even run multiple virtual systems at the same time (as long as you have enough memory), creating your own virtual network.

The Windows Server 2008 screenshots in this chapter were captured from a single Windows Server 2008 virtual server running within a Windows 7 operating system.

7. Click the Add Required Role Services button.
   Check boxes will appear next to Routing And Remote Access Services, Remote Access Service, and Routing.

8. Click Next.

9. Click Install on the Confirmation page.

10. After a moment, the install will complete. Click Close.

Configuring a Router on Windows Server 2008

Once you've added the RRAS service to a Windows Server 2008 server, you can then configure it. The following steps show the basic configuration:

1. Launch Routing and Remote Access by clicking Start ➢ Administrative Tools ➢ Routing And Remote Access.

2. Right-click the server, and select Configure And Enable Routing And Remote Access.

3. Review the information on the Welcome screen, and click Next.

4. On the Configuration page, select Custom Configuration, as shown in Figure 9.10. Click Next.

5. On the Custom Configuration page, select LAN Routing, as shown in Figure 9.11. Click Next, and then click Finish.

6. When prompted to start the Routing and Remote Access service, click Start Service.

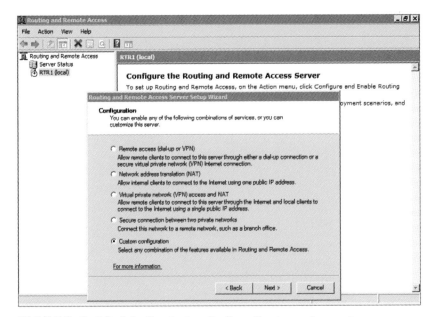

FIGURE 9.10 Selecting Custom Configuration to create a router

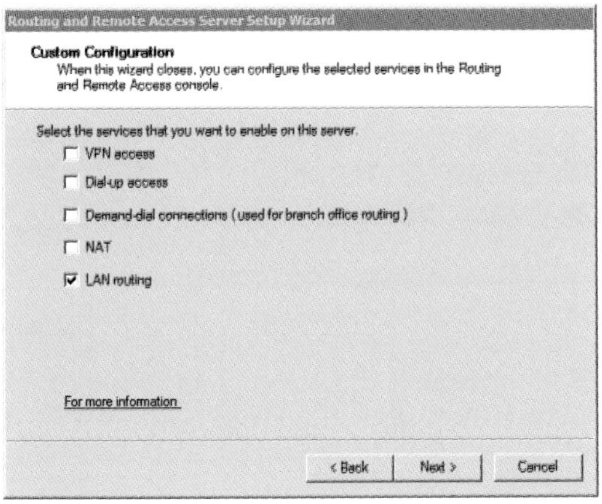

FIGURE 9.11 Selecting LAN routing when creating a router

At this point, the server is configured as a router. It will route traffic between the primary network and the testing network, and it will also create separate broadcast domains between the two networks.

Figure 9.12 shows the RRAS console with Network Interfaces selected. Notice the names of the interfaces are Loopback, Testing, PrimaryNetwork, and Internal. Loopback and Internal are part of the RRAS. However, Testing and PrimaryNetwork reflect the names of the networks directly connected to the router.

F I G U R E 9 . 1 2 Selecting LAN routing when creating a router

You may wonder how the directly connected networks were named, since none of the previous steps named them. These names are derived from the names of the network connections on the computer.

The default names of a network connection are Local Area Connection, Local Area Connection 2, and so on. However, you can rename them. These connections were renamed before creating the RRAS console. Local Area Connection was renamed to PrimaryNetwork, and Local Area Connection 2 was renamed to Testing.

You can rename NICs on a Windows Server 2008 server with the following steps:

1. Click Start, right-click Network, and select Properties.

2. Click Manage Network Connections.

3. Right-click a connection, and select Rename.

4. Type the name you want, and press Enter. The connection is displayed with a new name.

The name that will appear in the RRAS console is the same as the name of the NIC.

Even though the server is configured as a router, it can still be used for other services. Servers typically will be used for several roles simultaneously.

Understanding Other Routing Protocols

Primarily when you're talking about routing protocols in the context of internal routers, you're talking about RIPv2 or OSPF. However, other routing protocols that you can add to a Windows Server 2008 RRAS server are worth mentioning.

Figure 9.13 shows the dialog box within a Windows Server 2008 RRAS server you can access to add new routing protocols.

> If you rename the NIC, you may have to refresh the RRAS console before the new name appears.

> This is the same dialog box used to add the RIP protocol. After the RIP protocol was added to RRAS, it's no longer available to add as a new routing protocol.

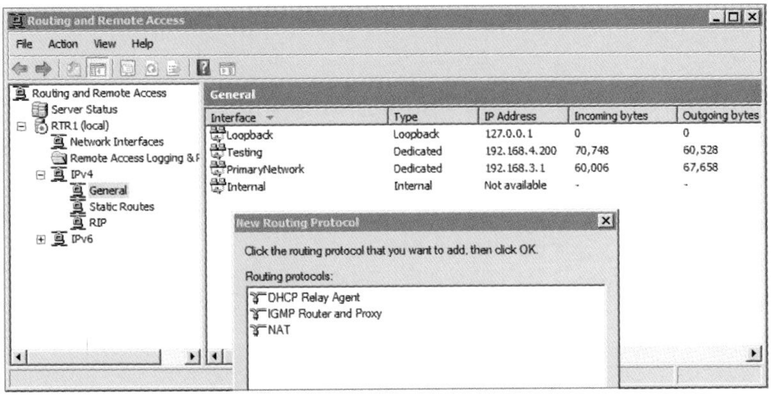

FIGURE 9.13 Adding a new routing protocol to Windows Server 2008

If you've installed RRAS on a server, you can access this dialog box with the following steps:

1. Launch RRAS by clicking Start ➤ Administrative Tools and selecting Routing And Remote Access.

2. Expand the server and IPv4.

3. Right-click General, and select New Routing Protocol.

Notice that there are several choices. The following section explains these additional protocols.

Using a DHCP Relay Agent

Chapter 1 introduced the Dynamic Host Configuration Protocol (DHCP), and Chapter 5 described DHCP in depth. As a reminder, a DHCP server provides DHCP clients with TCP/IP configuration such as an IP address, subnet mask, and more. DHCP automatically configures the DHCP client when the DHCP client first turns on and then again are various intervals.

DHCP uses special types of broadcasts known as BootP broadcasts. BootP broadcasts pass through routers using UDP ports 67 and 68. That is, of course, if the router is RFC 1542 compliant and can be programmed to allow these BootP broadcasts through.

Consider Figure 9.14. It shows a network with two subnets and one DHCP server. The router connecting the subnets is not RFC 1542 compliant. However, instead of installing a DHCP server on each subnet, you can install a DHCP relay agent on subnet B.

After adding the protocol, you also have to add the interface to the protocol node and configure it.

Routers that can pass DHCP broadcasts through UDP ports 67 and 68 are compliant with RFC 1542. Older routers are not RFC 1542 compliant and can't pass these broadcasts.

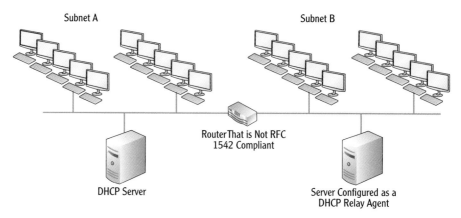

FIGURE 9.14 Using a DHCP relay agent

When a DHCP client in subnet B turns on, the following actions will occur:

1. The DHCP client sends a DHCP Discover message.

2. The DHCP relay agent hears the broadcast and forwards it to the DHCP server.

3. The DHCP server sends back a DHCP Offer to the relay agent.

4. The relay agent broadcasts the DHCP Offer on subnet B.

5. The DHCP client responds to the offer with a DHCP Request.

6. The relay agent hears the request and forwards it to the DHCP server.

7. The DHCP server sends back a DHCP Acknowledge to the relay agent.

8. The relay agent broadcasts the DHCP Acknowledge back to the DHCP client.

> **This is similar to the DORA process described in Chapter 5. The difference is that the proxy agent repeats the messages back and forth between the client and server.**

The default lease length for a Windows DHCP server is eight days, and clients renew the lease every four days. In other words, the DHCP relay agent won't have a lot of activity. If it's needed, you can easily install it on another server that is performing another role such as file or print server.

Using an IGMP Router and Proxy

You can add the IGMP Router and Proxy service to your router to have it act as a proxy for multicast traffic. For example, Microsoft's Windows Media Services generates multicast traffic on the network. With this service added, traffic from Windows Media Services (and other multicast traffic) can cross the routers to other subnetworks.

Using NAT

You probably remember that the Internet uses public IP addresses and that internal networks use private IP addresses. If you're using a router between the Internet and your internal network, you need to translate these addresses between private and public.

Network Address Translation (NAT) translates private IP addresses to public IP addresses and translates public ones back to private. You can add NAT within RRAS if the server will be used for Internet access.

If you look back at Figure 9.10 where the system was configured for LAN routing, you'll see you can also select the NAT check box to include NAT.

◄

Chapter 11 covers firewalls and proxy servers. It also includes an in-depth explanation on how NAT translates IP addresses.

THE ESSENTIALS AND BEYOND

Networks with Internet access include at least one router that provides a path to the Internet. Most networks include more than one router that provides paths to multiple other subnetworks. Each router includes a routing table that includes the paths to these other subnetworks. The routing table can be updated manually by an administrator (static routes), or routing protocols can update the routing table automatically (dynamic routing). Two common routing protocols used on internal networks are RIPv2 and OSPF. You can configure a Microsoft server as a software router by adding and configuring RRAS. RRAS supports RIPv2 but not OSPF.

ADDITIONAL EXERCISES

▶ View the routing table on a Windows computer.

▶ Determine the metric for the default path of your computer.

▶ Identify the IP address of the default gateway used in your subnetwork.

▶ Locate a router in your network. Identify as many directly connected routes as you can.

To compare your answers to the author's, please visit **www.sybex.com/go/ networkingessentials**.

REVIEW QUESTIONS

1. A router is configured in a network that includes multiple other routers. What routes does a router know by default?

    A. Directly connected routes   **C.** Dynamic routes

    B. Static routes   **D.** Routes added to the routing table

(Continues)

THE ESSENTIALS AND BEYOND *(Continued)*

2. You have added a second router to your network that includes three subnets. What's the easiest way to ensure that both routers know the routes to all subnets?

    A. Add OSPF to each router.   **C.** Add dynamic routes.

    B. Add RIPv2 to each router.   **D.** Add static routes.

3. True or false. A router determines the best path to another subnet based on the highest cost metric.

4. Where are routes known by a router?

5. Your network includes more than 50 hardware routers. What can you configure on these routers so that they will share routing information with each other? (Choose all that apply.)

    A. RIPv2   **C.** Routing protocols

    B. OSPF   **D.** ARP

6. True or False. Windows Server 2008 server supports RIPv2 and OSPF routing protocols.

7. A network includes a router that is not RFC 1542 compliant. Computers on one subnet use DHCP. What should you add to ensure computers on other subnets connected to the router can use DHCP?

    A. Another DHCP server   **C.** RIPv2

    B. DHCP relay agent   **D.** OSPF

8. True or false. You are adding a Windows Media Services server to your network that is using a Windows Server 2008 server as a router. You want to ensure that IP multicast traffic passes through the router. What would you add?

    A. OSPF   **C.** IGMP Router and Proxy service

    B. RIPv2   **D.** DHCP relay agent

## CHAPTER 10

Resolving Names to IP Addresses

You've learned a lot about TCP/IP in previous chapters. You know that TCP/IP uses IP addresses to route traffic from one computer to another. However, if you're like most people, you don't want to memorize IP addresses. Computers are much easier to identify when they have names.

Computers are named with host names and NetBIOS names. Each of these name types has special features. For example, computers on the Internet use host names, but internal networks can use either host names or NetBIOS names. Additionally, TCP/IP uses several different methods to resolve these names to IP addresses. The primary method used to resolve host names to IP addresses is with Domain Name System (DNS) servers. The primary method used to resolve NetBIOS names to IP addresses is with Windows Internet Naming System (WINS) servers. However, additional methods exist. This chapter covers the different types of names, the types of name resolution, and the steps TCP/IP uses to resolve names to IP addresses.

▶ **Exploring types of names used in networks**

▶ **Exploring types of name resolution**

▶ **Identifying the steps in name resolution**

Exploring Types of Names Used in Networks

Computers work with numbers. At the lowest level, the computers use ones and zeros assigned to individual bits. Every single piece of data that flows through a computer is reduced to simply ones and zeros.

However, you and I just don't think that way. Instead, we think in words. If someone asked you to memorize the MAC addresses or IP addresses of your favorite websites, you may find it a little challenging. However, if someone asked you to name your favorite websites, you could do so easily.

Thankfully, computers can also use names. However, there are many different elements built into networking to convert these names into the numbers used by the computers.

The following list shows the progression of how names are resolved to different types of addresses:

Name   Computers are assigned names, and you can usually reach a computer in a network using the name. These names can be either *host names* or *NetBIOS names*, or both, depending on where they are located. Only host names are utilized on the Internet, but both host names and NetBIOS names can be used on internal networks.

> Chapter 3 covered the seven layers of the Open Systems Interconnect (OSI) model.

IP Address   IP addresses are assigned to the network interface cards of computers. The IP address is used at the Network layer of the OSI Model to route traffic between subnetworks. Name resolution methods resolve the computer name to an IP address.

MAC Address   The media access control (MAC) address or physical address uniquely identifies the NIC. Each device on a network has an interface with a different MAC address. The MAC address is used at the lower levels of the OSI Model.

Bits   Bits are the lowest level of data. Data streams to and from computers using bits of ones and zeros.

The types of names given to computers and other network devices are either host names or NetBIOS names. As an introduction, Table 10.1 outlines some of the characteristics and differences of host names and NetBIOS names.

TABLE 10.1   Comparing host names and NetBIOS names

Characteristics	Host names	NetBIOS names
Length	Up to 255 characters	15 readable characters; 16th character identifies a service
Location	On Internet and internal networks	Only on internal networks
Primary name resolution method	Domain Name System (DNS)	Windows Internet Naming Service (WINS)
Namespace	Hierarchical (part of fully qualified domain name)	Flat namespace (single level names only)

Understanding Host Names

A host name is a user-friendly string of characters, or label, assigned to a computer or other network device. Host names are the primary name type used today. They are the only types of names used on the Internet and the primary name type used on many internal networks.

Host names can be as long as 255 characters. They can contain letters, numbers, periods, and hyphens.

When a host is part of a domain, the full computer name is the fully qualified domain name (FQDN). Figure 10.1 shows the host name and FQDN of a Windows Server 2008 server. The FQDN in a Windows system can be up to 255 characters as long as no more than 63 characters are used between each period.

Windows limits the length of host names in Windows systems to 63 characters. However, it's recommended to limit the length to 15 characters for compatibility with NetBIOS names.

System

View basic information about your computer

Windows edition

Windows Server® Enterprise

Copyright © 2007 Microsoft Corporation. All rights reserved.

Service Pack 1

System

Processor:	Intel(R) Core(TM)2 Duo CPU P8600 @ 2.40GHz 3 MHz
Memory (RAM):	1.50 GB
System type:	32-bit Operating System

Computer name, domain, and workgroup settings

Computer name:	Success1
Full computer name:	Success1.networking.mta
Computer description:	
Domain:	networking.mta

FIGURE 10.1 Viewing the computer name on Windows Server 2008

Notice that the computer name is Success1. This is the host name. The computer is a member of a domain named networking.mta. The full computer name (or FQDN) is success1.networking.mta.

Understanding NetBIOS Names

Network Basic Input/Output System (NetBIOS) names are 15 characters long. Even when the actual name is shorter (such as PC1), the NetBIOS name is padded with trailing spaces to make the name 15 characters long.

You can also view the host name of your computer from the command prompt by typing hostname and pressing Enter.

HOST NAMES, URLS, AND FQDNS

A uniform resource locator (URL) is the address used to access Internet resources such as websites. It includes the protocol and the fully qualified domain name (FQDN). For example, if you wanted to reach the website **www.bing.com**, you would use this URL: **http://www.bing.com**. The protocol is HTTP, and the FQDN is **www.bing.com**.

www is the host name, and it represents a web farm of computers that respond to that name. You probably know that you don't even have to use www, though. Instead, you can simply enter the address as **http://bing .com**, and it'll work. Of course, you can also skip the protocol in your web browser. For example, if you're using Internet Explorer (IE), you can simply enter **bing.com**. IE assumes you're using HTTP and fills that in for you.

DNS supports multiple computers with the same name and can resolve name requests to different servers in a round-robin fashion. DNS also supports alias names to allow computers to respond to different names. A single computer can be registered in DNS with multiple different names, and each name will resolve to the same IP address.

Chapter 6 presented the hexadecimal numbering system. As a reminder, it includes the numbers 0 to 9 and the letters *A* to *F*.

The NetBIOS name includes a hidden 16th byte. This 16th byte is a hexadecimal number that identifies services running on the system. Other systems and applications on the network use this information to determine how they can communicate with a system.

Table 10.2 shows common values for the 16th byte of a computer's NetBIOS name. These values identify services running on desktop and server operating system computers or provide other information about the computer.

In addition to tracking the name of the computer, NetBIOS tracks the name of the workgroup or domain that a computer has joined.

You can view NetBIOS names registered by a system using the nbtstat command. The following steps show how:

1. Launch a command prompt by clicking Start ➢ Run; then enter **cmd** in the Run box, and press Enter.

2. Enter **nbtstat -n**, and press Enter.

Listing 10.1 shows the output of the `nbtstat -n` command on a Windows Server 2008 server named success1. This computer is a domain controller within the networking.mta domain.

TABLE 10.2 Examples of the value and meaning of NetBIOS 16th byte for computer names

Hexadecimal value	Meaning	Comments
00	Workstation service	Used to create and maintain client network connections to other computers on the network
20	File server service	Indicates the computer can share files and printers over the network
23/24	Microsoft Exchange	Identifies a server hosting Microsoft Exchange

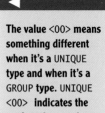

Microsoft Exchange is used in Windows environments for email.

Listing 10.1 Output of `nbtstat - n` command

```
C:\>nbtstat -n

Local Area Connection:
Node IpAddress: [192.168.3.1] Scope Id: []

          NetBIOS Local Name Table

     Name              Type         Status
    ---------------------------------------------
    SUCCESS1     <00>  UNIQUE     Registered
    NETWORKING   <00>  GROUP      Registered
    NETWORKING   <1C>  GROUP      Registered
    SUCCESS1     <20>  UNIQUE     Registered
    NETWORKING   <1B>  UNIQUE     Registered
```

The value <00> means something different when it's a UNIQUE type and when it's a GROUP type. UNIQUE <00> indicates the workstation service, and GROUP <00> indicates the domain name.

Notice the output for the computer name (SUCCESS1) has specific hex values listed. Similarly, the output for the domain name (NETWORKING from networking.mta) has hex values listed. Table 10.2 showed the meaning of these values for a computer name. Table 10.3 shows the meaning of some values for the domain.

TABLE 10.3 Examples of the value and meaning of NetBIOS 16th byte for domain names

Hexadecimal value	Meaning	Comments
00	Domain name	Indicates the name of the domain
1C	Domain controller	Indicates that the server is a domain controller in the domain
1B	Domain master browser	Indicates the computer is hosting the Domain Master Browser role, which is used by NetBIOS services in the network

Note that the value 00 means domain name when associated with GROUP, but it can also mean the workstation service when associated with UNIQUE.

Many more NetBIOS services can be assigned to any computer. The important point to grasp from this section is that each computer can have multiple NetBIOS names. Different NetBIOS names have different hex values to provide information about the computer.

Creating NetBIOS Names from Host Names

A Windows Server 2008 server's name is Success1. Is this a host name or a NetBIOS name? The answer is that it's both. When you name a computer, the name is used for both the host name and the NetBIOS name.

Duplicate NetBIOS names result in errors and communication problems with these computers. All computers on the same network need unique names.

If the name is 15 characters long or less, the computer will have the same host name and NetBIOS name. However, if the host name is more than 15 characters, Windows truncates the name to the first 15 characters for use as the NetBIOS name. This is important because it's possible to inadvertently give different computers duplicate NetBIOS names.

As an example, consider Table 10.4, which shows the host names and the resulting NetBIOS name derived from the host name. Some of the host names are more than 15 characters, resulting in duplicate NetBIOS names.

TABLE 10.4 NetBIOS names derived from host names

Host name	NetBIOS name	Comment
CPU1	CPU1	No problem
CPU2	CPU2	No problem
NetworkingComputer1	NETWORKINGCOMPU	Name truncated

(Continues)

TABLE 10.4 *(Continued)*

Host name	NetBIOS name	Comment
NetworkingComputer2	NETWORKINGCOMPU	Duplicate name
DC1	DC1	No problem
DC2	DC2	No problem
DomainController1	DOMAINCONTROLLE	Name truncated
DomainController2	DOMAINCONTROLLE	Duplicate name

> Although Windows host names can be 63 characters, you should limit them to no more than 15 characters for compatibility with NetBIOS.
>
> ◄

Notice that the shorter computer names are identical as both host names and NetBIOS names. However, since NetBIOS truncates the longer computer names to only the first 15 characters, some of the computers have duplicate NetBIOS names.

Viewing and Modifying a Computer Name

You can use the following steps to view a computer's host name, view its NetBIOS name, and modify the computer's name:

1. Log onto the computer. If you plan on changing the computer name, you will need to log on with an administrative account.

2. Click Start, type **cmd** in the Start Search box, and press Enter. This will launch a command prompt.

3. Enter **hostname** at the command prompt, and press Enter. This returns the host name of the computer.

> ◄
>
> These steps are written for a Windows Server 2008 server. However, they will also work on Windows 7 and some other Windows systems.

4. Click Start, right-click Computer, and select Properties. This will display a page similar to Figure 10.1 shown earlier in this chapter.

   Notice that you can view the computer name, the FQDN (as the full computer name), and the domain on this page. In Figure 10.2, the computer name is Success1, the FQDN is success1.networking.mta, and the domain is networking.mta.

5. On the System properties page, click Advanced System Settings. If prompted by UAC, click Yes or provide appropriate credentials.

6. Select the Computer Name tab. Click Change. Click More. Your display will look similar to Figure 10.2.

   Notice that you can view the DNS suffix of the computer and the NetBIOS computer name on this page. The suffix is automatically

> You can modify the primary DNS suffix. However, you cannot modify the NetBIOS name.
>
> ◄

added when a computer joins a domain, and the NetBIOS name is automatically created from the computer name.

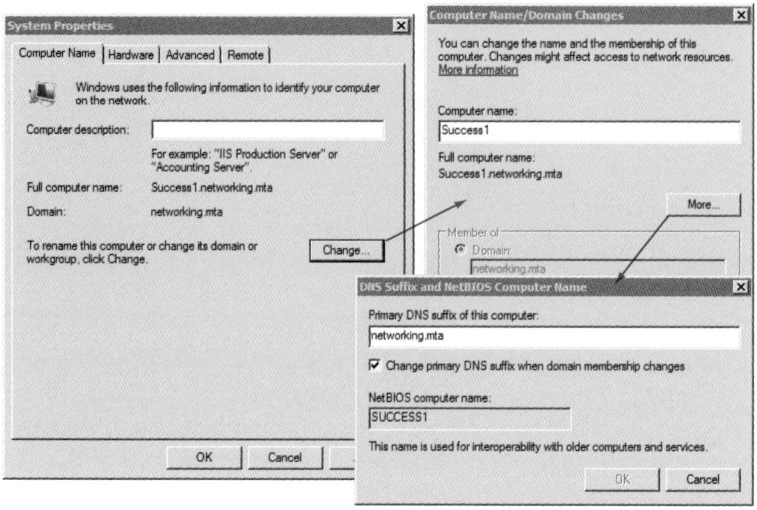

FIGURE 10.2 Viewing computer names

7. Click Cancel. If desired, you can modify the computer name by changing it on the Computer Name/Domain Changes page.

8. Close all windows.

Exploring Types of Name Resolution

Names have to be resolved to IP addresses on the Internet and within internal networks. Eight types of name resolution can be used. Table 10.5 introduces the different types, and the following sections describe them in more detail.

TABLE 10.5 Name resolution methods

Name resolution method	Resolves (host names, NetBIOS names, or both)	Comments
Domain Name System (DNS) server	Host names (Windows Server 2008 DNS can be configured to resolve NetBIOS names using GlobalNames zones)	DNS servers are on the Internet and internal networks; Microsoft domains require DNS.

(Continues)

TABLE 10.5 *(Continued)*

Name resolution method	Resolves (host names, NetBIOS names, or both)	Comments
Host cache	Host names	Host cache can be viewed with the `ipconfig /displaydns` command.
Hosts file	Host names	Located in `c:\windows\ system32\drivers\etc\` folder by default.
Windows Internet Name Service (WINS)	NetBIOS names	WINS servers are located only on internal networks.
NetBIOS cache	NetBIOS names	NetBIOS cache can be viewed with the `nbtstat -c` command.
Lmhosts file	NetBIOS names	Located in `c:\windows\ system32\drivers\etc\` folder when used.
Broadcasts	Both	The system simply sends a broadcast with the name asking the owner to reply with its IP address.
Link-local multicast name resolution (LLMNR)	Host names	This is a newer method similar to broadcast that works on internal networks.

Understanding Domain Naming Service

The *Domain Naming System (DNS)* is a service that resolves host names to IP addresses. These can be names of computers within an internal network or names of computers on the Internet. Clients send name resolution requests to a DNS server, and the DNS server responds with the IP address. The client computer then uses the returned IP address as the destination IP address for data traffic.

◄

DNS is essential on a Microsoft domain. Active Directory requires DNS to locate servers running specific services, such as domain controllers.

Figure 10.3 shows the DNS console on a Windows Server 2008 server. It shows several host (A) records with their names and IP addresses. When a system queries a DNS server with the name of a computer, the DNS server checks to see whether it has a matching host (A) record for the requested name in its database, and if so, it returns the IP address to the requesting client.

> Host records are sometimes listed as host (A) and other times as A (host). However, they are the same.

> Reverse lookup zones are optional. Some DNS servers don't host reverse lookup zones or support reverse lookups.

FIGURE 10.3 Viewing the DNS console

Notice that the server in Figure 10.3 also has a reverse lookup zone. Reverse lookup zones use pointer (PTR) records to do reverse lookups. In other words, you can pass the IP address to the DNS server and retrieve the name of the computer with that IP address.

DNS servers host multiple types of records beyond the A records. For example, an Active Directory domain must have service (SRV) records to locate domain controllers in the network. Table 10.6 outlines many of these records.

> SRV records are used for host names similar to how the 16th byte of NetBIOS names is used. Both identify specific services running on computers.

TABLE 10.6 Common DNS records

Record type	Usage
A (host)	Resolves host names to IPv4 IP addresses
AAAA (host)	Resolves host names to IPv6 addresses
PTR (pointer)	Resolves IP addresses to host names
CNAME (alias)	Resolves one host name to another host name, which allows multiple computer names to be resolved to the same IP address
MX	Used for mail exchange servers (email servers)

(Continues)

T A B L E   1 0 . 6   *(Continued)*

Record type	Usage
SRV	Required by Active Directory to locate servers running specific services (such as domain controllers)
NS	Identifies DNS name servers

A DNS server that holds records for a specific namespace (such as the networking.mta namespace) is authoritative for that namespace. In other words, it knows all the computers and the IP addresses in that namespace. If it doesn't have a record for one of these computers, no one else will either.

If a DNS server is not authoritative for a namespace, it can still resolve names by forwarding the name request to other DNS servers.

DNS is hierarchical. No single server knows the names and IP addresses for all the computers on the Internet. Instead, DNS servers are authoritative for different namespaces. Consider Figure 10.4, which shows the hierarchy of DNS servers on the Internet. They are explained as follows:

DNS Root Servers   At the top of the hierarchy are DNS root servers. There are only 13 DNS root servers in the world. These servers know only the addresses of DNS servers that are authoritative for top-level domains such as .com, .net, .org, and so on. If you ask it for the address of training.microsoft.com, it won't know. However, it will know the address of the DNS servers that are authoritative for the .com namespace.

Top-Level Domain DNS Servers   Next are the top-level domain DNS servers. Top-level domain DNS servers know the addresses of second-level domain DNS servers in their namespace. For example, a .com DNS server knows the addresses of servers that are authoritative for the Microsoft.com namespace. However, a .com DNS server doesn't know anything at all about .net, .org, or any other top-level domain namespace.

Second-Level Domain DNS Servers   Below the top-level domain DNS servers are the second-level domain DNS name servers. These servers are authoritative in the second-level DNS namespace. For example, Microsoft has several servers that are authoritative in the Microsoft.com domain. The DNS servers in the Microsoft.com namespace know only about Microsoft.com. They wouldn't know anything about other namespaces such as sybex.com.

Third- and Lower-Level Domain DNS Servers   Third-level and lower-level domain DNS servers are possible. However, these are needed only when the FQDN includes these lower levels. For example, Microsoft may have a DNS server dedicated to the

◄

Multiple DNS servers are available for each of the top-level domains. If one DNS server in the .com namespace fails, others in the .com namespace can still answer queries.

training.microsoft.com namespace. This DNS server can resolve all the host names in the training.microsoft.com namespace. Other companies may not have third-level DNS servers. Instead, the second-level server resolves the names for all the company's resources on the Internet.

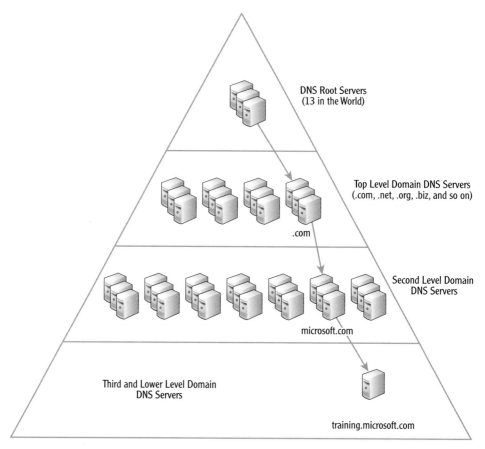

DNS Root Servers
(13 in the World)

Top Level Domain DNS Servers
(.com, .net, .org, .biz, and so on)

.com

Second Level Domain
DNS Servers

microsoft.com

Third and Lower Level Domain
DNS Servers

training.microsoft.com

FIGURE 10.4 DNS hierarchy

DNS queries to the Internet start with a query to one of the DNS root servers. For example, imagine if a client is trying to reach a web server named **www.sybex .com** from an internal network named `networking.mta`. The record for the **www .sybex.com** web server won't be on the internal DNS server. However, the internal DNS server can make queries to the Internet to retrieve the name.

Figure 10.5 and the following steps show how this works in practice.

1. The client passes the request to the DNS server to resolve www.sybex. com. Assume that the DNS server has just turned on and doesn't have any information except for the address of the DNS root servers.

2. Since the top-level domain is .com and the DNS server doesn't have the IP address of a DNS server in the .com domain, it queries a DNS root server. The DNS root server responds with the IP address of a DNS server that is authoritative for the .com namespace.

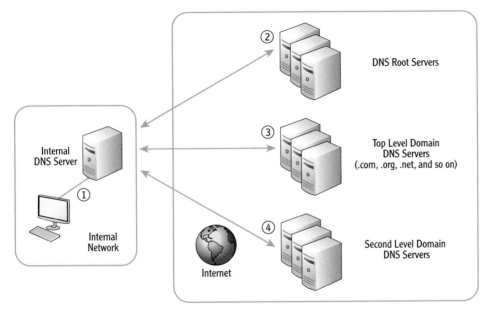

If the DNS server has been on for a while, it will have cached information, and it may be able to skip some of the steps.

FIGURE 10.5 Resolving a DNS query on the Internet

3. Next, the internal DNS server queries the .com DNS server for the address of a DNS server that is authoritative in the sybex.com domain. The top-level domain DNS server responds with an IP address.

4. Finally, the internal DNS server queries the sybex.com DNS server for the IP address of the web server named www.

DNS servers cache responses in their internal memory. In other words, after a DNS server queries a root DNS server for an address of a .com DNS server, it keeps this information. The next time it needs to query the .com server for an address, it just looks in cache for this information.

RESOLVING NETBIOS NAMES WITH DNS

Windows Server 2008 supports a new type of zone called a GlobalNames zone. In networks where there are very few NetBIOS applications, you can use GlobalNames zones for single label names, just as if they were NetBIOS names.

When a GlobalNames zone is used, DNS can resolve both host names and NetBIOS names. GlobalNames zones are used only on internal Microsoft networks. On the Internet, DNS can only resolve host names.

Viewing the Host Cache

Every time a computer receives a name resolution response from a DNS server, it places the result in the local host cache. The host cache is an area of memory on any computer that is dynamically updated with host name and thier corresponding IP addresses.

The host cache is also called the *DNS resolver cache*, since many of the entries are created when DNS is queried to resolve a host name. However, the host cache also includes data from the hosts file (described in the next section).

> The host cache on an end user's computer is different from the DNS cache on a DNS server. However, they work the same. Cached data doesn't need to be queried again.

You can view the host cache on any computer from the command prompt by using the following steps:

1. Launch a command prompt by clicking Start ➤ Run; enter **cmd** in the Run box, and press Enter.

2. Enter **ipconfig /displaydns**, and press Enter.

> The actual output includes many more entries. However, only a few entries are shown here to conserve space.

Listing 10.2 shows the partial output of the ipconfig /displaydns command on a Windows Server 2008 server.

Listing 10.2 Output of ipconfig /displaydns **command**

```
C:\>ipconfig /displaydns

Windows IP Configuration

    1.0.0.127.in-addr.arpa
    ----------------------------------------
    Record Name . . . . . : 1.0.0.127.in-addr.arpa.
    Record Type . . . . . : 12
    Time To Live  . . . . : 86400
    Data Length . . . . . : 4
    Section . . . . . . . : Answer
```

```
PTR Record  . . . . . : localhost

localhost
----------------------------------------
Record Name . . . . . : localhost
Record Type . . . . . : 1
Time To Live  . . . . : 86400
Data Length . . . . . : 4
Section . . . . . . . : Answer
A (Host) Record . . . : 127.0.0.1

bing.com
----------------------------------------
Record Name . . . . . : bing.com
Record Type . . . . . : 1
Time To Live  . . . . : 580
Data Length . . . . . : 4
Section . . . . . . . : Answer
A (Host) Record . . . : 65.55.175.254
```

Notice the first record is a PTR record (reverse lookup record) for the local computer using the loopback address of 127.0.0.1. The second record is an A (host) record for localhost record that is mapped to the loopback address of 127.0.0.1. You will usually see these two entries for any Windows 2008 computer.

The third record for bing.com is a record returned from a DNS server and placed in cache. Notice that it has a Time To Live section. Every record returned from a DNS server includes this, and it indicates how long the data will remain in cache. The value of 580 indicates that it will remain in cache for another 580 seconds. Any queries to bing.com will use this IP address as long as it remains in cache. After the timeout period, it is removed from the cache and requires another query to DNS to resolve it.

Viewing the Hosts File

The hosts file is a simple text file located in the `c:\windows\system32\drivers\etc` folder by default. The hosts file maps the names of computers to IP addresses. The benefit is that mapped records in this file are automatically placed in the host cache.

Listing 10.3 shows the contents of a host file on a Windows Server 2008 server.

Listing 10.3 Hosts file

```
# Copyright (c) 1993-2006 Microsoft Corp.
#
# This is a sample HOSTS file used by Microsoft TCP/IP for Windows.
```

The 127.0.0.1 and localhost records come from the hosts file on Windows computers.

◄

You can remove cached items from the host cache with the `ipconfig / flushdns` command. However, this does not remove items in cache from the hosts file.

◄

◄

You can place entries in a hosts file to bypass DNS queries for specific hosts. If the entry is in the hosts file or in cache, DNS is not queried.

```
#
# This file contains the mappings of IP addresses to host names. Each
# entry should be kept on an individual line. The IP address should
# be placed in the first column followed by the corresponding host name.
# The IP address and the host name should be separated by at least one
# space.
#
# Additionally, comments (such as these) may be inserted on individual
# lines or following the machine name denoted by a '#' symbol.
#
# For example:
#
#      102.54.94.97     rhino.acme.com          # source server
#       38.25.63.10     x.acme.com              # x client host

127.0.0.1        localhost
::1              localhost
```

Notice that the beginning of the file consists of comments preceded by hash marks (#). The only two entries are the 127.0.0.1 and ::1 lines. These lines map the localhost name to the IPv4 loopback address of 127.0.01 and to the IPv6 loopback address of ::1.

All entries in the hosts file are immediately placed in cache, and they stay there constantly. Hosts file entries do not time out and fall out of cache.

Understanding WINS

Windows Internet Name Service (WINS) is a service you can add to a server to resolve NetBIOS names to IPv4 addresses. A WINS server can resolve only NetBIOS names, not host names.

You'll find WINS servers on internal Microsoft networks. Non-Microsoft networks may include NetBIOS servers to resolve NetBIOS names, but they can be other types of NetBIOS servers. WINS is Microsoft's implementation of a NetBIOS server.

You may remember that DNS is hierarchical. It uses multilevel names such as root level, top level, and so on. Because of this, DNS is highly scalable. DNS on the Internet efficiently resolves the IP addresses of billions of computers. It works as efficiently with these billions of computers as it will on an internal network with just a few dozen computers.

In contrast, WINS is not hierarchical. Instead, it's a flat database that supports only single-level names. WINS does not scale well and couldn't possibly work with billions of computers. As more computers are added to a WINS server, it can get bogged down.

> If you enter ping localhost at the command prompt, the localhost name is resolved to either 127.0.0.1 or ::1, depending on whether ping is using IPv4 or IPv6.

> Don't be fooled by the word *Internet* in WINS. WINS is not used on the Internet at all. It is used only on internal Microsoft networks.

Since DNS performs so much better than WINS and because WINS does not support IPv6, WINS is being phased out. However, it is still being used in many networks today since many applications still use NetBIOS names.

Figure 10.6 shows the TCP/IP properties for a network interface card (NIC) on a Windows system. Notice that you can configure the name of a DNS server on the same page as you configure the IP address of the NIC. However, you have to click the Advanced button and select the WINS tab to add the IP address of a WINS server.

If your network includes multiple WINS servers, you can add the IP addresses of each one.

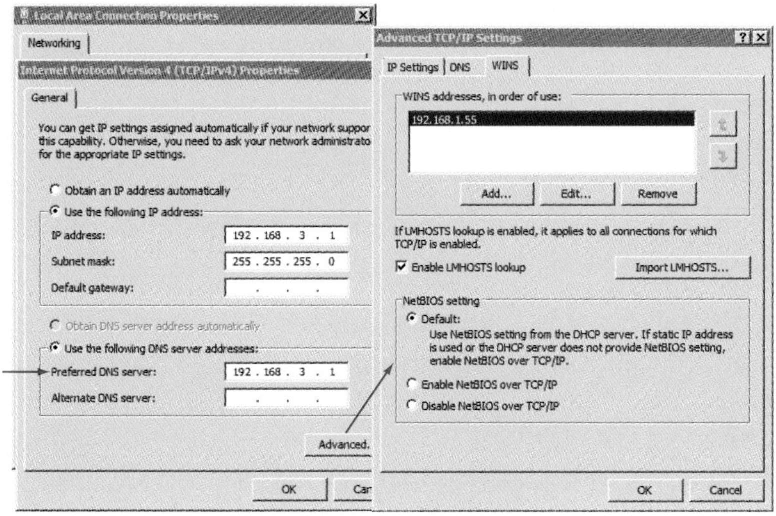

◄

Although you can configure the IP address of DNS and WINS servers manually, most networks use DHCP to configure these addresses automatically.

FIGURE 10.6 Configuring a computer to use WINS

Viewing the NetBIOS Cache

Just as any host name that is resolved by DNS is placed in cache, NetBIOS names resolved by WINS are also placed in cache. DNS names are placed in the host cache, and WINS names are placed in the NetBIOS cache.

You can view the NetBIOS cache using the nbtstat -c command, as follows:

1. Launch a command prompt by clicking Start ➢ Run; then enter **cmd** in the Run box, and press Enter.

2. Enter **nbtstat -c**, and press Enter.

Listing 10.4 shows the cache of a Windows 2008 server that recently resolved the name of a file server (named FS1) to the address of 192.168.1.117.

Listing 10.4 **Output of** nbtstat -c

```
C:\>nbtstat -c

Local Area Connection:
Node IpAddress: [192.168.3.1] Scope Id: []

            NetBIOS Remote Cache Name Table

    Name              Type      Host Address    Life [sec]
    -------------------------------------------------------------
    FS1            <20>  UNIQUE    192.168.1.117      562
```

The R in the
nbtstat -R
command must be
uppercase. This is
one of the few times
when a command
prompt command is
case sensitive.

▶

Notice that the table in Listing 10.4 includes a Life (sec) column. This lists how long (in seconds) the entry will remain in cache. It is similar to the Time To Live entry for the hosts cache. After the time expires, the entry will fall out of cache, and another NetBIOS query will be needed to resolve the IP address. You can flush the NetBIOS cache with the nbtstat -R command.

Understanding the Lmhosts File

▶

The last popular use
of the lmosts file was
in Windows NT 4.

The lmhosts file is similar to the hosts file except that you map NetBIOS names to IP addresses. The hosts file maps host names to IP addresses. Although the lmhosts file was used quite often in the early days of Microsoft networking, it is rarely used today. Windows 7 and Server 2008 products don't even include a working lmhosts file in operating systems.

You can view the lmhosts.sam file (a sample lmhosts file) in the same location as the hosts file: c:\windows\system32\drivers\etc. If you want to use an lmhosts file, you need to create one. The name of the file must be lmhosts without any extension.

Understanding Broadcast Name Resolution

Another method of name resolution is *broadcast*. In other words, a system can simply send a request on the segment with a name. Any host that has that name replies with its IP address.

Remember, though, that broadcasts don't pass routers, so the use of broadcasts for name resolution works only when the computers are on the same segment.

LLMNR has been
available in Windows
since Windows Vista
and Windows
Server 2008.

▶

Understanding Link-Local Multicast Name Resolution

Link-local multicast name resolution (LLMNR) is similar to broadcast, but it can resolve both IPv4 and IPv6 addresses. It works for hosts on the same local link.

Chapter 5 described Automatic Private IP Addresses (APIPA) in the 169.254.0.0 range. APIPA addresses are assigned to DHCP clients when a DHCP server can't be reached. APIPA addresses don't include DNS addresses, and the primary method of name resolution for APIPA clients is via broadcasts. Chapter 6 described link-local addresses that are similar to APIPA addresses but for IPv6. Link-local addresses have a prefix of fe80 hexadecimal.

If a system is using a link-local IPv6 address, LLMNR can be used in place of DNS for name resolution. It will work for other hosts that have the same link-local address prefix of fe80.

Identifying the Steps in Name Resolution

Applications and services on networks resolve computer names to IP addresses. Some of the applications and services are host based, and some are NetBIOS based. In other words, some expect that the computers have host names, and some expect that the computers have NetBIOS names. This is important because it affects the steps in name resolution.

The application or service determines the steps used in name resolution, based on whether it expects a host name or a NetBIOS name.

The following two sections show the steps in name resolution for host names and NetBIOS names.

Identifying Steps in Host Name Resolution

When an application or service assumes that a name is a host name, it will take the following steps to resolve it:

1. Windows first checks to see whether the queried name is the same as its host name. If so, it uses its own IP address.

2. Next, Windows checks the host cache. If the name is in cache, it doesn't check any further.

3. If the name isn't in cache, Windows queries DNS. If a system is configured with both a preferred and an alternate DNS server, it queries the preferred DNS server. An alternate DNS server is queried only if the preferred DNS server doesn't respond.

4. Next, Windows checks the NetBIOS name cache.

5. If the name isn't in the NetBIOS name cache, Windows will query a WINS server. If multiple WINS servers are configured, Windows will query each WINS server until it either resolves the name or runs out of WINS servers to query.

These first three steps are the primary steps for host name resolution. If necessary, NetBIOS methods can be used to resolve the name.

6. If WINS doesn't resolve the name, Windows will attempt to resolve the name using broadcast. This succeeds only if the computer is on the local subnet.

7. Last, Windows will check the lmhosts file, if it exists.

The preceding steps are used if the application assumes that the name is a host name. However, if the application assumes that the name is a NetBIOS name, then it performs the steps in a different order, as shown in the next section.

Identifying Steps in NetBIOS Name Resolution

If the application or server assumes that the name is a NetBIOS name, it will use the following steps by default:

1. First, Windows checks the NetBIOS name cache.

2. If the name isn't in the NetBIOS name cache, Windows will query DNS for a name in a GlobalNames zone (GNZ).

3. If a GNZ isn't being used or can't resolve the name, then Windows will query a WINS server. If multiple WINS servers are configured, Windows will query each WINS server until it either resolves the name or runs out of WINS servers to query.

4. If WINS doesn't resolve the name, Windows will attempt to resolve the name using broadcast. This succeeds only if the computer is on the local subnet.

5. If the broadcast can't resolve the name, Windows then checks to see whether the queried name is the same as the computer's NetBIOS name.

6. Next, Windows checks the host cache.

7. Last, Windows queries DNS.

Although the preceding steps are the default, different steps and orders are possible. Windows systems use NetBIOS over TCP/IP (NetBT). The NetBT node type can be modified to use different combinations. Table 10.7 shows the different node types available in Windows.

You can view which NetBT node type your system is configured to use with the ipconfig /all command. Listing 10.5 shows a partial output of the ipconfig /all command. Notice the node type is listed as Hybrid. This shows that it will use WINS by default and then use broadcast.

TABLE 10.7   NetBIOS over TCP/IP (NetBT) node types

Type	Comments
B-node (broadcast)	Sends only a broadcast
P-node (peer-to-peer)	Queries only a WINS server
M-node (mixed)	Combines B-node and P-node
	Uses broadcast by default
H-node (hybrid)	Combines B-node and P-node
	Uses WINS by default
Microsoft enhanced B-node	Uses broadcast and then the lmhosts file

◀

Windows 7 and Windows Server 2008 use the H-node (hybrid) by default.

Listing 10.5   Partial output of `ipconfig /all`

```
C:\>ipconfig /all

Windows IP Configuration

        Host Name . . . . . . . . . . . . : Success1
        Primary Dns Suffix  . . . . . . . : networking.mta
        Node Type . . . . . . . . . . . . : Hybrid
        IP Routing Enabled. . . . . . . . : Yes
        WINS Proxy Enabled. . . . . . . . : No
        DNS Suffix Search List. . . . . . : networking.mta
```

THE ESSENTIALS AND BEYOND

The two types of computer names are host names and NetBIOS names. Computers on the Internet use host names. Internal networks use either host names or NetBIOS names. The primary name resolution method for host names is DNS. The primary name resolution method for NetBIOS names in Microsoft networks is WINS. Other name resolution methods include the host cache, hosts file, NetBIOS cache, lmhosts cache, broadcast, and LLMNR.

ADDITIONAL EXERCISES

▶ Identify the host name and FQDN (if applicable) of your computer.

▶ Identify the NetBIOS name of your computer.

(Continues)

THE ESSENTIALS AND BEYOND *(Continued)*

▶ View the host cache on your computer.

▶ View the NetBIOS cache on your computer.

To compare your answers to the author's, please visit **www.sybex.com/go/ networkingessentials**.

REVIEW QUESTIONS

1. What is the type of name used for computers on the Internet?

    A. DNS name   **C.** WINS name

    B. NetBIOS name   **D.** Host name

2. What type of computer names are assigned to Microsoft systems on a Microsoft network? (Choose all that apply.)

    A. DNS names   **C.** WINS names

    B. NetBIOS names   **D.** Host names

3. True or false. The primary name resolution method for NetBIOS names is DNS.

4. True or false. Any entries in the Windows hosts file automatically appears in the host cache.

5. How can you view the host cache (or DNS resolver cache)?

    A. Enter **nbtstat -n** at the command prompt.

    B. Enter **nbtstat -c** at the command prompt.

    C. Enter **ipconfig /displaydns** at the command prompt

    D. Enter **ipconfig /flushdns** at the command prompt.

6. True or false. The Windows Internet Naming Service (WINS) operates on the Internet.

7. What command can you enter at the command prompt to remove DNS resolved entries from the host cache?

    A. Enter **ipconfig /flushdns** at the command prompt.

    B. Enter **ipconfig /displaydns** at the command prompt.

    C. Enter **nbtstat -n** at the command prompt.

    D. Enter **nbtstat -c** at the command prompt.

8. A system has an IPv6 address with a prefix of fe80. It does not have an IPv4 address. How is the computer name resolved to an IP address for this computer?

## CHAPTER 11

Understanding Network Security Zones

Security is an important consideration with any network. Some areas of a network are more vulnerable to attacks than other areas. This increased risk requires increased security. Different areas of a network are categorized in zones with varying levels of security required in different zones.

The Internet is the riskiest zone. Internal networks, or intranets, are the safest. Between these two, you can create perimeter networks as a buffer zone. One of the primary methods of separating the zones is with firewalls. This chapter covers these different zones and provides some information on firewalls in general and Microsoft firewalls in particular.

- ▶ **Understanding risks on the Internet**

- ▶ **Exploring an intranet**

- ▶ **Understanding firewalls**

- ▶ **Identifying a perimeter network**

- ▶ **Understanding extranets**

Understanding Risks on the Internet

I'm betting you've used the Internet once or twice, but it's still worth mentioning here. It's the largest network in the world and continues to grow by leaps and bounds with no end in sight.

Several things have been mentioned about the Internet throughout this book, and it's worth consolidating them here in the context of network security zones:

The Internet Is the Riskiest Security Zone Attackers from anywhere in the world can attack computers on the Internet, and they do. In 2009 and 2010, malware authors created 20 million new strains of malicious software (an average of 63,000 a day). Infected systems join massive botnets and participate in attacks on other computers.

All Internet Addresses Are Public   Internet Protocol (IP) addresses used on the Internet are public IP addresses. In other words, they are accessible from any other computer with access to the Internet. In comparison, IP addresses on internal networks are private.

The Internet Is TCP/IP Based   The TCP/IP protocol suite is the standard used on the Internet. Most internal networks use the same TCP/IP protocol suite for easy interaction on the Internet.

The World Wide Web (WWW) Travels Over the Internet   The primary protocol used to transfer web pages is the Hypertext Transfer Protocol (HTTP). Note that the WWW isn't the Internet. Rather, you can think of the WWW like a semitruck delivering goods and the Internet as the highway that the truck travels on. Other protocols traveling over the Internet include the File Transfer Protocol (FTP) and Simple Mail Transfer Protocol (SMTP).

BOTNETS AND MALWARE

Malicious software (malware) includes viruses, worms, Trojan horses, and other software designed with malicious intent. In the early days of computers, malware would often cause harm to a user's computer such as destroying data or destroying a user's hard drive. Some were less benign and simply popped up a message like "Legalize Marijuana" on a certain day.

However, malware has changed. Today, the primary purpose of most malware is to have a computer join a *botnet*.

Botnet is short for *robot network*, implying an automated network. Infected computers become a member of a botnet as a clone or zombie. The terms *clone* and *zombie* are interchangeable. Botnets are networks of these clones or zombies that can be secretly controlled at will by the attackers. Attackers manage computers on the Internet with command and control software that can issue orders to them. These zombies check in periodically and do the bidding of the attacker. It's not unusual for the attackers to have almost as much control of the user's computer as the user does.

Zombies may send spam on behalf of the attackers, steal identities, or steal financial data. Zombies also participate in massive *distributed denial of*

(Continues)

BOTNETS AND MALWARE *(Continued)*

service (DDoS) attacks on the Internet. A DDoS is a simultaneous attack on a single system or server by multiple attackers.

Any computer with access to the Internet (even computers within private networks) can become a zombie. Users are often unaware their computers are infected as zombies. Indeed, this is one of the strengths of botnets. They don't harm the user's computer but instead enlist it in their army. Today, it's not unusual for a botnet to have tens of thousands or even millions of zombies at their beck and call.

The best defense is antivirus software that is always on and regularly updated.

Exploring an Intranet

An *intranet* is nothing more than a LAN by a different name. A stricter definition is that an intranet is a private network that uses TCP/IP protocols to share resources within the network.

From a network security perspective, the intranet is the safest network security zone. It includes clients on the internal network and has substantially fewer risks than computers placed directly on the Internet. Administrators control these computers and can implement many layers of security on them.

However, don't think that computers within an intranet are risk free. They aren't. The only way to keep a computer free of risks is to leave it powered off. Of course, it isn't very useful without power.

Intranets have private IP addresses. Chapter 5 listed these usable private IP address ranges, but as a reminder, here they are:

> 10.0.0.1 through 10.255.255.254
>
> 172.16.0.1 through 172.31.255.254
>
> 192.168.1.1 through 192.168.255.254

You may remember that private IP addresses can only be used on internal networks, and they are never used on the Internet. However, most users within intranets need to access the Internet. Since private IP addresses are used in intranets and public IP addresses are used on the Internet, networks need some method of connecting the two. Enter NAT.

◄

You can also think of an intranet as an internal network that uses the same protocols found on the Internet.

Understanding Network Address Translation

Network Address Translation (NAT) is a service that translates private IP addresses to public IP addresses and translates public back to private.

Consider Figure 11.1. It shows a private intranet with connectivity to the Internet via a router that is running NAT. The router does basic routing, and the NAT service translates the private and public IP addresses.

> **The router in the figure also has a firewall. Firewalls are explained in more depth later in this chapter, but it's common to implement firewalls between the Internet and intranet.**

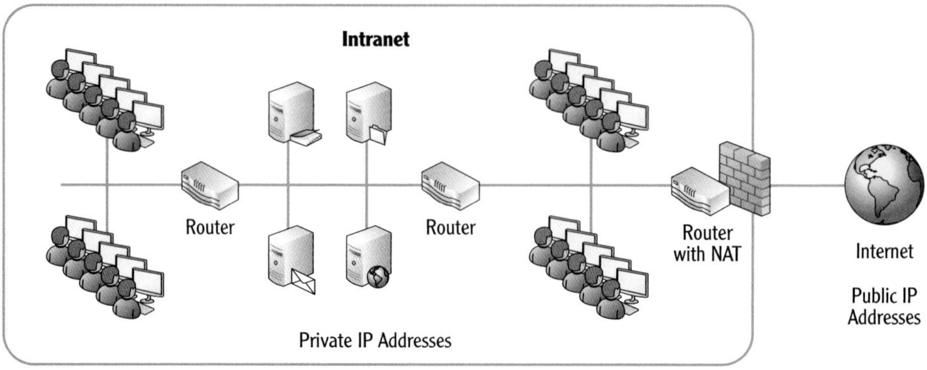

FIGURE 11.1 An intranet connected to the Internet

All the computers on the intranet have private IP addresses, and of course, the Internet has public IP addresses. The router with NAT has a private IP address assigned to the interface connected to the intranet and a public IP address assigned to the interface connected to the Internet.

Port Address Translation (PAT) is a popular way that NAT is implemented. PAT is sometimes called Network Address Port Translation, but more often than not, it's simply called NAT. The following explanation shows how the PAT version of NAT works.

Imagine that a user named Dawn on the intranet is trying to access Bing.com via the router. NAT will take the following actions:

1. It receives the request and logs the source IP address and port (Dawn's computer) and logs the destination IP address and port (Bing.com) in an internal table.

2. NAT then creates a new packet to forward the request to Bing.com. It keeps the destination IP and port but changes the source IP address to its own public IP address. It also changes the source port to an unused

port. At this point, the NAT table, with only one entry, looks something like this:

Source IP	Source port	Destination IP	Destination port	NAT source port
192.168.1.5	49155	Bing.com	80	49212

3. NAT sends the request to Bing.com. Bing.com returns the web page to the NAT server with the NAT source port (49212) included.

4. NAT looks at the source port and compares it to its internal NAT table. It sees that it's mapped to Dawn's computer with an IP address of 192.168.1.5 and then sends the page back to her computer.

You may be wondering why NAT created its own source port. That's a great point. It needs a way to identify the original requestor, and it does so with different source ports. Suppose that Jack was accessing Bing.com searching about feng shui at the same time Dawn was accessing Bing.com searching about firewalls. The NAT server would receive two answers from Bing.com. Without changing the source port for each request, there wouldn't be any way for NAT to determine who should receive which response from Bing.com.

The following table shows the NAT table with two entries. In this example, Dawn has an IP address of 192.168.1.5, and Jack's computer has an IP address of 192.168.1.22. NAT creates different source ports for each request in the internal NAT table. When Bing.com returns the data on firewalls requested by Dawn, it includes the source port created by NAT. NAT then uses this information to ensure that the request is forwarded back to Dawn's computer.

> The NAT table is stored in the system's memory. If it's a router running NAT, it's stored in the router's memory. If it's a proxy server, it's stored in the server memory.
> ◀

Source IP	Source port	Destination IP	Destination port	NAT source port
192.168.1.5	49155	Bing.com	80	49212
192.168.1.22	49158	Bing.com	80	49213

> Chapter 4 covered the different ports. It included the well-known ports between 0 to 1023, the registered ports from 1024 to 49151, and the dynamic ports to 65,535.
> ◀

You may be wondering how the source ports are generated. Most systems generate source ports from the dynamic port range of 49,152 to 65,535. Only ports that aren't currently being used are selected.

NAT provides several benefits:

Hides Internal Computers   Since the computers don't have public IP addresses, they can't be directly accessed by Internet sources.

Reduces Costs   If NAT wasn't used, you'd have to purchase public IP addresses for all internal computers. This is simply an unnecessary cost since it's so easy to install NAT.

Extended the Lifetime of IPv4   Since companies can use a single public IP address for hundreds or thousands of internal computers, the public IPv4 address range wasn't depleted earlier.

Although NAT can use a single public IP address, it's also possible to use multiple public IP addresses. Consider a large network with thousands of users. A single connection to the Internet may not be enough to adequately serve all of these clients. Instead, additional connections can be added with additional public IP addresses.

Static NAT uses a single public IP address, and all connections are mapped to this single IP address. Dynamic NAT uses a two or more public IP addresses. Any user's request from a private IP address can be dynamically mapped to any one of the public IP addresses. One benefit of dynamic NAT is that it is able to balance the load among the different public IP addresses.

Understanding Proxy Servers

> Microsoft sells a proxy server product called Microsoft Forefront Threat Management Gateway (Forefront TMG). It was previously called Internet Security and Acceleration Server (ISA).

Instead of just using NAT, many organizations use *proxy servers*. A proxy server acts on behalf of the client computers in the internal network to retrieve web content from the Internet. A proxy server often includes NAT, but it does more.

Proxy servers provide three important benefits:

> A proxy server isn't a replacement for antivirus software within a company. However, it is useful as part of a defense-in-depth security strategy.

Caching   If one user requests a page from a site, the proxy server will retrieve the page and return it to the user. It also keeps a copy of the page in its local memory, or cache. If another user then requests the same page, the proxy server retrieves the page from memory and serves it to the second user. This saves Internet bandwidth since the same content doesn't have to be retrieved repeatedly.

Filtering   The proxy server can use filtering lists to restrict access to certain websites. For example, if an organization wants to ensure that employees don't access gambling sites, a filter list can list these sites, and the proxy server will then block all access to these sites.

Content Checking   Some proxy servers can verify that the content is valid. For example, the proxy server can check web pages for malicious content, such as embedded malware or malicious scripts. If the web server includes a certificate for secure HTTPS pages, the proxy server can check the certificate's validity.

Consider Figure 11.2. Notice in the figure that a proxy server is between the Internet and the other computers in the intranet. This is a common configuration for many midsize and large organizations.

The proxy server will retrieve any requests that are allowed. It will block requests for pages identified in its block list.

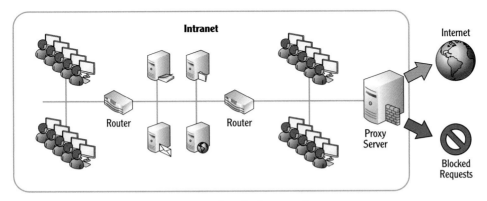

FIGURE 11.2 An intranet connected to the Internet via a proxy server

PROXY SERVER FILTERS

Some companies sell subscriptions to filter lists. These companies have web bots that constantly crawl the Web to identify content. The content is categorized, and the web pages are then added to specific lists. For example, one list might be for gambling and include all known gambling sites. Another list might be for pornography and include all known pornography sites.

Organizations can then subscribe to the different lists. These lists are added to the proxy server, and any requests to access a site on a list are blocked.

Some organizations are more proactive and create lists of only acceptable websites. If a user tries to access any website that isn't on this list, access is blocked.

For example, if a client wanted to access a web page on the Internet, the internal process would take the following steps:

1. The client computer forwards the request to the proxy server.

2. The proxy server checks the internal filter.

   a. If the page is on a block list, the request is not filled. Instead, the user will usually see a web page indicating that accessing this page is against the company policy.

   b. If the page is allowed, the web server will attempt to retrieve it from the Internet. It often uses the same NAT process shown previously in this chapter.

3. When the web page is received, the proxy server checks the content to ensure it's valid. Suspect content can be blocked with a warning to the user that the page is suspect.

4. The proxy server places valid web pages in cache. Pages in cache are served to other users from cache without retrieving them from the Internet again.

5. The web page is sent to the client that originally requested it.

Client computers need to be configured to use the proxy server. For example, most Windows computers use Internet Explorer. Figure 11.3 shows the proxy server settings on Internet Explorer. In this example, the IP address of the proxy server is 192.168.1.251, and it is listening on port 8080.

► **Administrators can set these settings manually or automate the settings.**

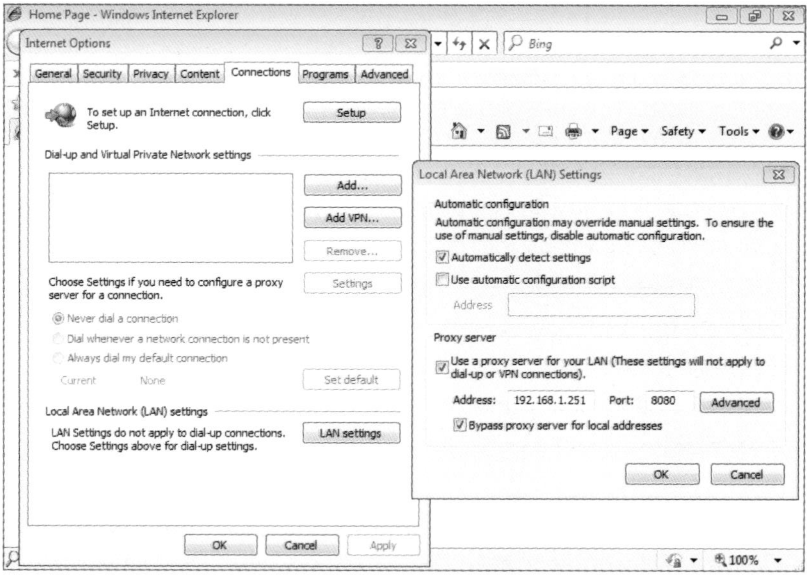

FIGURE 11.3 Configuring proxy server settings in Internet Explorer

An additional setting shown in the figure is Bypass Proxy Server For Local Addresses. This ensures that requests to web servers on the internal network (the intranet) don't have to go through the proxy server.

You can access the settings in Figure 11.3 by following these steps:

1. Launch Internet Explorer.

2. Select Tools and then Internet Options.

3. Click the Connections tab.

4. Click the LAN Settings button.

Understanding Firewalls

Chapter 2 introduced firewalls. As a reminder, a *firewall* provides protection to both networks and individual systems by controlling the traffic that can flow in or out. A host-based firewall controls the traffic for an individual host or computer. A network-based firewall controls the traffic for a network.

Microsoft's Forefront Threat Management Gateway (Forefront TMG) is a network firewall. It's an additional server product you can purchase and install on a server. Forefront TMG was previously known as Internet Security and Acceleration (ISA) Server.

Firewalls have been widely improved over the years. The most basic firewall is simply a router with rules that define what traffic is allowed and what traffic is blocked. This is also known as a packet-filtering firewall.

Packet-Filtering Firewall   A packet-filtering firewall filters packets based on IP addresses, ports, and some protocols. For example, if you want to allow only HTTP traffic (which uses port 80), you can create a rule to allow incoming traffic on port 80. If you only wanted to allow traffic through a firewall from specific computers, you could create rules based on their IP addresses.

Stateful Filtering   Traffic is filtered based on the state of the network connections. In other words, the firewall is able to examine packets in different conversations and make decisions based on connection states. Both TCP and UDP traffic is analyzed. If traffic isn't part of a known connection, it is blocked.

Content Filtering   Some firewalls can block traffic based on the content. For example, malware is often delivered via spam embedded as a zip file and other types of attachments. Content filtering is often performed on email servers also in order to filter spam and its attachments.

Application Layer Filtering   Traffic is filtered based on an application or service. The firewall has a separate component for each application protocol (such as

◀

Forefront TMG has multiple security purposes. As mentioned earlier, it can be used as a proxy server.

◀

Chapter 4 covered ports, including many of the commonly used well-known ports.

Microsoft's Forefront TMG firewall performs packet filtering, stateful filtering, content filtering, and application layer filtering.

◀

HTTP or FTP) that it will filter. These firewall components examine the traffic using that protocol to allow and block certain types of traffic. For example, HTTP Get commands (which allow retrieval of documents or files) could be allowed, while Put commands (which would post documents or files) can be blocked. In practice, application layer filters are CPU intensive and used sparingly.

Most firewalls use an implicit deny policy. In other words, all traffic that has not been explicitly allowed is blocked. As an example, consider Figure 11.4. This shows a partial listing of programs and their Windows Firewall settings on a Windows Server 2008 system.

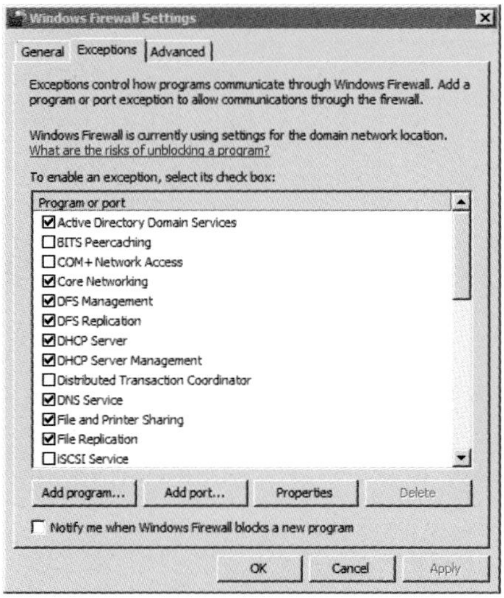

FIGURE 11.4 **Allowing programs through the Windows Firewall**

Each item that is checked is explicitly allowed. If an item is not selected, it is blocked.

You can access the screen shown in Figure 11.4 on a Windows Server 2008 system by following these steps:

1. Click Start ➢ Control Panel.

2. Click Security.

3. Select Allow A Program Through Windows Firewall.

Exploring the Windows Server 2008 Firewall

Today's Windows operating systems have the Windows Firewall built in as a host-based firewall. Following Microsoft's principle of secure by default, the Windows Firewall is enabled by default.

Early versions of the Windows Firewall allowed you only to create rules to control inbound packets. However, since Windows Vista and Windows Server 2008, you have been able to control both inbound and outbound traffic.

Another feature of Windows Firewall in current Windows operating systems is the use of different rules based on where your computer is operating. For example, you could have a Windows 7 computer running in a home network, in a corporate domain network, or in a public wireless networks such as a coffee shop or airport. Each of these network locations has different levels of risk. Windows sometimes automatically detects this network location. Other times, you identify it when you first connect. Either way, Windows implements firewall rules to increase or decrease security based on the network location settings.

The Windows Firewall has been included since the release of Windows XP. It has been enabled by default since Windows XP Service Pack 2 (SP2).

NETWORK DISCOVERY IN WINDOWS

Windows systems allow computers to discover each other. When network discovery is enabled, your computer can discover other computers on the network, and other computers can discover your computer. When it's off, it prevents other computers from seeing your computer.

Network discovery doesn't prevent connections. For example, a computer with network discovery disabled on a public wireless network will still be able to access the Internet by going through a known wireless router. However, network discovery does enable specific firewall rules, which makes it more difficult for other computers to discover a Windows computer running in a public network.

The different network locations are as follows:

Public This is a public location such as in a coffee shop or airport. Users often connect via wireless connections, and other users are completely unknown. The other users could be friendly or malicious. Attackers can try to hack into systems in a public network to steal data. Since a public network is the riskiest network location, the Windows Firewall provides the highest level of protection and helps prevent computers from being discovered on the network. Network discovery is disabled.

Home   This indicates a small, protected network where you know and trust other devices on your network. Network discovery is enabled. Users in a home network can join a homegroup, which is a special type of workgroup in newer Windows operating systems.

Work   This is similar to the home network location. Network discovery is enabled, and computers can discover each other. Computers can be a member of a workgroup but not a homegroup.

Domain   Computers that are joined to a domain are automatically configured for a domain network location. Administrators control these settings using domain tools.

There are two basic graphical user interfaces (GUIs) you can use to manipulate the firewall in Windows Server 2008. The basic GUI is in the Control Panel, and the second tool is the Windows Firewall with Advanced Security GUI which is located in the Administrative Tools section.

Figure 11.5 shows the Control Panel view of the firewall in a Windows Server 2008 R2 system. Notice that the connection for the domain networks is Connected. This indicates the computer is joined to a domain and that the firewall is using the settings for a domain. You can also see that the firewall is On, and it's configured to block all incoming connections that haven't been explicitly allowed.

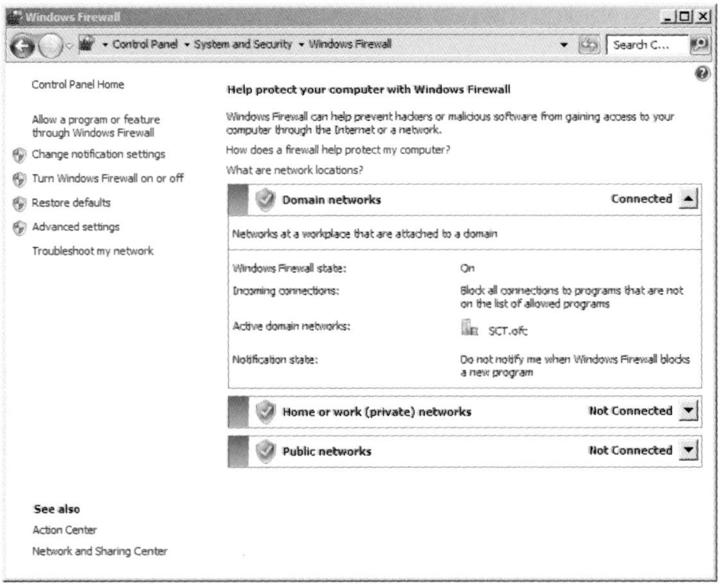

> In Windows Vista and Server 2008, home and work network locations are the same and expressed as home/work. In Windows 7 and Server 2008 R2, they are separated.

FIGURE 11.5   Basic Windows Firewall GUI in Windows Server 2008 R2

You can access the screen shown in Figure 11.5 by following these steps:

1. Click Start, and select Control Panel.

2. Click Check Firewall Status.

Figure 11.6 shows the Windows Firewall with Advanced Security GUI in Windows Server 2008 R2 with the New Inbound Rule Wizard started. The inbound rules are selected, and all the rules with a green circle are enabled to allow the traffic. The ones that are grayed out are not enabled. Notice in the left pane that there are also outbound rules and connection security rules that you can manipulate.

> **Connection Security Rules use Internet Protocol Security (IPSec). IPSec can encrypt data traveling on the wire.**

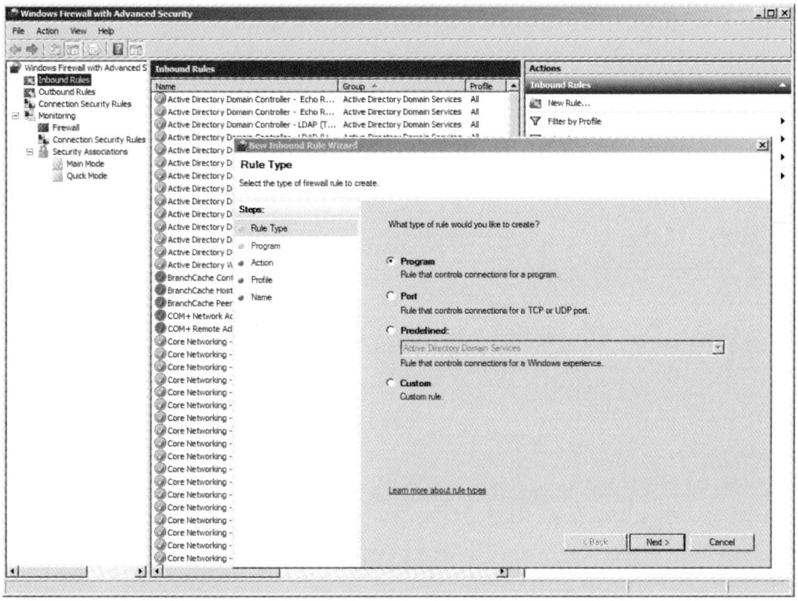

FIGURE 11.6 Windows Firewall with Advanced Security GUI in Windows Server 2008 R2

Although Windows Server firewalls include many built-in rules, you can also add your own rules. In the figure, the New Inbound Rule Wizard was started by clicking New Rule in the Actions pane (on the right).

You can access the screen shown in Figure 11.6 by following these steps:

1. Click Start ➢ Administrative Tools ➢ Windows Firewall With Advanced Security.

2. Select Inbound Rules.

3. Click New Rule in the Actions pane (on the right).

Identifying a Perimeter Network

▶

Internet-facing servers are any servers accessible from the Internet. They include web servers, mail servers, FTP servers, and more.

▶

A perimeter network is often called a *demilitarized zone* (DMZ) or a buffer zone. This is especially true when it's created with two firewalls.

A *perimeter network* is an area between the Internet and an intranet that hosts servers accessible from the Internet. It provides a layer of security protection for these Internet-facing servers and isolates these servers from the internal network.

Consider Figure 11.7. It shows a perimeter network hosting a web server and a mail server. Notice that the perimeter network is between two firewalls. This is a common configuration, but there are others.

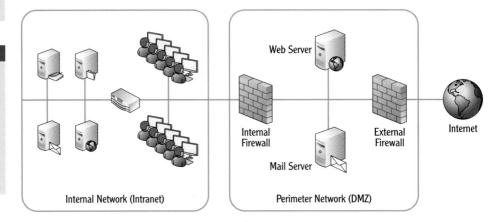

FIGURE 11.7 Using a perimeter network

An important point to realize about the perimeter network is that servers placed here are accessible from anywhere on the Internet to anyone who has access to the Internet. However, the perimeter network does provide protection.

As an example, consider the web server. A typical web server serves web pages using HTTP on port 80 and HTTPS on port 443. The external firewall will filter traffic to this web server and can block all traffic to this server that isn't using either port 80 or port 443. This can prevent many potential attacks from ever reaching the server.

From a risk perspective, the perimeter network is a little safer than the Internet. However, since servers in the perimeter network are still accessible from anywhere on the Internet, there is still a significant amount of risk, especially when compared with the intranet. Additionally, if a server in the perimeter network is compromised, the internal firewall will protect resources on the intranet.

You can also create a perimeter network with just a single firewall. Figure 11.8 shows an example of perimeter network created with just a single firewall. Notice that the mail server and web server are still isolated from both the Internet and the intranet. The firewall controls what packets can reach the perimeter network and what data can reach the intranet.

Although this configuration is less expensive since only a single firewall is used, it's also much more complicated to configure. An administrator must configure rules to route traffic to specific NICs. Since these rules are more complex than the rules for two firewalls, there's a greater chance of error.

A significant benefit of a two-firewall perimeter network is that you can use two separate vendors. For example, one firewall can be Microsoft's Forefront TMG firewall, and another firewall can be from another vendor. Although vulnerabilities may occur in any system, it's unlikely that both firewalls will be vulnerable at the same time. Also, although an attacker may be an expert on either of the firewalls, it's less likely that an attacker will be an expert on both at the same time.

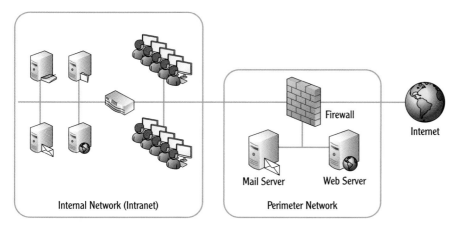

FIGURE 11.8 A single firewall perimeter network

Understanding a Reverse Proxy Server

Some organizations implement *reverse proxy servers* to increase security and performance of web servers. A reverse proxy server is an additional server in the perimeter network. It isolates these web servers from direct access on the Internet, providing a layer of protection from Internet attackers.

Consider Figure 11.9. This shows a reverse proxy server used with a web server. The reverse proxy server receives the requests from the clients and forwards them to the web server. The web server sends the web pages back to the proxy server, and the proxy server sends them to the clients.

Just as a regular proxy server can cache requests, the reverse proxy server can also cache requests. This reduces some of the load on the web server. However, since all the pages are still served over the Internet link, it doesn't reduce Internet usage.

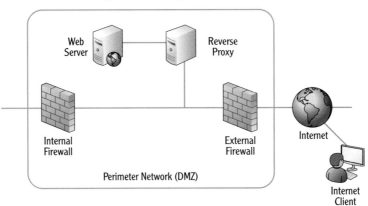

Using A Reverse Proxy Server

FIGURE 11.9 A single firewall perimeter network

Clients don't need to be configured to use a reverse proxy. Indeed, clients will rarely ever know a reverse proxy is in use. It is simply transparent to the end users.

Understanding Guest Networks

Guest networks are another type of perimeter network used by larger organizations. A guest network is an isolated portion of the internal network that can be used by guests or visitors.

Depending on how the guest network is configured, visitors may not need to provide any credentials to access the guest network. However, their access on the network is usually very limited. The primary access that is usually granted from a guest network is Internet access.

Guest networks are also becoming popular in home wireless networks. For example, Cisco's Valet Wireless Router allows you to create a separate password you can give to visitors without giving the primary password that is used for other connections. When the visitor leaves, you can change the visitor password or disable visitor access.

Figure 11.10 shows the Cisco Valet Wireless router's Guest Access Settings page. Notice you can also modify how many guests can connect.

FIGURE 11.10 Guest network configuration

Understanding Extranets

An *extranet* is an area between the Internet and an intranet that hosts resources for trusted entities. These resources are available via the Internet. An extranet is often physically the same as a perimeter network. The difference is in the intent and the scope of access and resources that are made available. Specifically, an extranet is configured so that only trusted partners or customers have access to a company's resources in the extranet. These trusted partners typically need access to areas of a company's network such as private websites or databases that would not be accessible publically. This allows the company to extend access to their internal resources to trusted entities outside the intranet.

Figure 11.11 shows a drawing of an extranet. You may notice that this looks very similar to Figure 11.7. However, keep in mind that the difference between an extranet and a perimeter network is based on the intent. The perimeter network hosts servers that are accessible to any Internet clients from anywhere on the Internet. Extranets are available only to specific clients.

For example, a boating parts company sells and ships parts to boat builders. The parts company may want some customers to be able to access their accounts, check availability of parts, place orders, and track status. It can add a web server to an extranet and restrict access to specific customers.

◄

Extranets are often created to share data between two companies that have business relationships or partnerships.

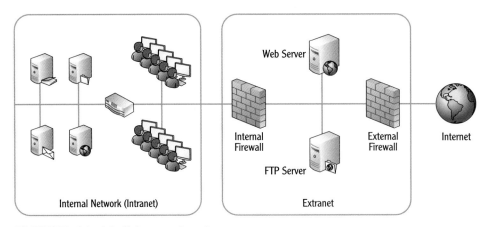

FIGURE 11.11 Using an extranet

By only allowing access to their web server via an extranet, they can control who is granted access to the extranet's website. This prevents unwanted users (such as competitors) from viewing information the company doesn't want to make public.

THE ESSENTIALS AND BEYOND

This chapter covered basic security zones in networks. The Internet is the riskiest security zone. Any resources placed directly on the Internet are accessible from anywhere in the world and are subject to attack from anywhere in the world, as long as the attacker has access to the Internet. The intranet is an internal network and is considered the safest zone when compared to other zones. Firewalls typically separate the intranet from the Internet. Microsoft desktop and server operating systems include host-based firewalls built into the operating system. Additionally, Microsoft sells a network-based firewall server product called Forefront TMG. A perimeter network (also known as a DMZ) usually includes two network-based firewalls, and Internet-facing servers are placed between the two firewalls. The firewalls control traffic to and from resources in the perimeter network. Extranets are perimeter networks created to provide access to internal resources to specific trusted entities. Guest networks are perimeter networks created to provide temporary network access to visitors.

▶ Determine whether your computer is using a proxy server.

▶ Determine whether a software firewall is enabled on your computer.

▶ The network location determines what firewall rules are enabled on Microsoft operating systems. Determine what network location your computer is using.

▶ Draw a perimeter network, and draw an extranet. Describe the differences.

(Continues)

To compare your answers to the author's, please visit **www.sybex.com/go/ networkingessentials**.

REVIEW QUESTIONS

1. Which network security zone represents the highest risk?

    A. Internet   C. Perimeter network

    B. Intranet   D. Extranet

2. What service translates private IP addresses to public IP addresses and translates public IP address back to private?

3. An organization wants to restrict which web pages employees can access on the Internet using company computers. What should be implemented?

    A. NAT   C. Proxy server

    B. Firewall   D. Reverse proxy server

4. True or false. A DMZ provides a layer of security for Internet-facing servers.

5. How many firewalls are used to create a perimeter network? (Choose all that apply.)

    A. One   C. Three

    B. Two   D. Four

6. What allows computers to locate each other in a Microsoft network?

    A. Firewall   C. Network discovery

    B. Public network location D. Proxy server

7. You want to provide access to some internal resources to a business partner via the Internet. No one else should have access. What should you create?

## CHAPTER 12

Understanding Wireless Networking

Wireless networks allow you to create a network without running cables. You can also expand an existing wired network by adding a wireless access point as a bridge for wireless clients to your wired network. Two important pieces of knowledge you'll need are an understanding of current wireless networking standards and an understanding of wireless security methods.

IEEE 802.11 includes several different wireless standards, including 802.11a, b, g, and n. To get the most out of your wireless network, you need to use compatible protocols. Some work together, but others don't. IEEE 802.11n provides the greatest flexibility and speeds.

Wireless security had a rocky start, and early wireless security methods weren't secure at all. However, wireless security has increased significantly over the years, and it is possible to create a more secure wireless network today. You just need to know how.

When you have networks in buildings separated by long distances, you can use point-to-point wireless bridges to connect them, even if the buildings are miles away.

▶ **Exploring basic wireless components**

▶ **Comparing networking standards and characteristics**

▶ **Comparing network security methods**

▶ **Using wireless networks**

▶ **Understanding point-to-point wireless**

Exploring Basic Wireless Components

Wireless networking is virtually everywhere today: homes, airports, restaurants, and hotels. Even some cities offer citywide wireless Internet access. With newer technologies, we are seeing wireless speeds near that of gigabit.

Before digging in to the details of wireless standards and security methods, it's important to understand some of the basics of wireless networks. This section covers these topics:

▶ Using wireless access points and adapters

▶ Naming the wireless network

▶ Comparing CMSA/CD and CSMA/CA

Using Wireless Access Points

A *wireless access point (WAP)* is a device that is located between a wired LAN and wireless clients. It bridges the two networks, giving the wireless clients access to the wired network. When a WAP is used, the wireless network is working in infrastructure mode.

Consider Figure 12.1, which shows a basic wireless network with a WAP bridging the wireless clients to a wired network.

> When a WAP is not used, clients connect using ad hoc or peer-to-peer mode. Ad hoc wireless has additional security risks beyond WAP-based networks.

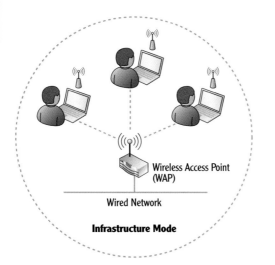

FIGURE 12.1 Wireless network using infrastructure mode

Once the wireless clients connect, they are able to access resources on the wired network through the WAP. The number of clients you can connect to the WAP depends on bandwidth. As you add more wireless clients, performance slows down for all the wireless clients. Just as with wired networks, high-bandwidth speeds are desirable in wireless networks. Different standards support different speeds, with 802.11n providing the best performance today.

Wireless clients have wireless adapters that must be configured to connect to the WAP. Many laptops include a built-in adapter, but there are also USB wireless adapters that you can plug into a USB port and adapter cards that you can plug into a slot inside the computer. The adapter must be configured with settings that are compatible with the WAP.

Naming the Wireless Network

Every wireless network includes a *service set identifier (SSID)*. The SSID is simply the network name. You can name a wireless network just about anything you want as long as you don't exceed the maximum length of 32 characters.

Any wireless device that connects to the WAP uses the SSID, and the SSID is one of the primary items you need to know when configuring wireless devices. Most WAPs include a setup screen that allows you to name the SSID. For example, Figure 12.2 shows a setup screen for the Cisco Valet wireless router.

Cisco Connect

Change Valet name and password

Valet name:

HomeSweetHome

1 - 32 characters

Password:

X78cx#24

8 - 63 characters

Change   Cancel

> Even though the setup screen uses a more user-friendly name of "Valet name," this is the SSID. Notice it can be up to 32 characters.

FIGURE 12.2 Wireless router setup screen

Most WAPs also give you the option of turning SSID broadcast off or leaving it on. When SSID broadcast is on, the WAP broadcasts the name of the wireless network. One benefit is that other wireless devices can easily see it and connect, as long as other security settings are configured properly.

> Many people consider this point debatable. However, if you're taking a Microsoft exam, don't disable the SSID broadcast for security reasons.

There was a time when IT professionals consistently recommended disabling SSID broadcast. However, Microsoft recommends against this. Let me repeat that. Microsoft recommends that SSID broadcast is not disabled but instead that the WAP should be configured to broadcast its SSID.

WHAT'S THE DIFFERENCE BETWEEN A WAP AND A WIRELESS ROUTER?

A WAP provides connectivity to a wired network for wireless clients. You can think of this as a bridge between the wireless clients and the wired clients.

In contrast, a wireless router is a WAP with additional components. It includes routing components to route traffic between different networks (such as from the Internet through an ISP to a private network). The wireless router often includes a switch component so that you can plug in wired connections to the wireless router and provide connectivity for them.

When you need wireless connectivity in an enterprise, a simple WAP (instead of a wireless router) will often be enough. The WAP connects the wireless devices to the wired network. Other devices on the wired network provide services such as routing and Internet access.

In summary, a wireless router always includes the basic capability of a WAP in addition to routing capabilities. It usually includes even broader capabilities such as that of a switch and DHCP. However, a wireless access point does not include additional capabilities.

There are few reasons Microsoft makes this recommendations:

Disabling SSID Broadcast Doesn't Enhance Security   Wireless security is primarily provided by authentication and encryption. Disabling the SSID broadcast doesn't help or hinder either authentication or encryption.

Disabling SSID Broadcast Does Not Truly Hide the SSID   Since the frequency ranges used by different wireless protocols are well known, any receiver can capture frames sent by the wireless devices. The SSID is included in probe requests sent by clients, and attackers can use wireless sniffers to discover the SSID.

Disabling SSID Broadcast Requires Clients to Broadcast the SSID   When you disable SSID broadcast on the WAP, clients must initiate the connection. Since clients don't know whether they are close to a wireless network, they must constantly send out probes looking for WAPs until they connect. When a client is away from the network (such as in a coffee shop, hotel, or airport), it is sending out probes as often as every 30 seconds with the SSID name. You can disable automatic connection, but this requires additional work on the part of the user.

The different security methods are explained later in this chapter. Older methods are WEP and WPA. The current method is WPA2.

You'll also need to configure the wireless device with the security used by the WAP. This usually includes setting the passphrase and configuring it to use WPA2.

Comparing CSMA/CD and CSMA/CA

Ethernet uses Carrier *Sense Multiple Access Collision Detection* (CSMA/CD). If a collision occurs, it detects it, and the two parties then retransmit the data.

Wireless networks cannot detect collisions, so they use *Carrier Sense Multiple Access/Collision Avoidance* (CSMA/CA) instead. CSMA/CA prevents a wireless node from transmitting when another node is doing so.

In other words, if one computer wants to send data to another, it will first listen to see whether anyone else is transmitting. If no other device is transmitting, it will send data. However, if it hears data transmissions, it will wait for a random period and recheck the airwaves. This method of transmission reduces the chance of a collision in a wireless environment.

An optional method of improving this process is with Request to Send/Clear to Send (RTS/CTS) packets. Figure 12.3 shows how this works.

Chapter 3 introduced CSMA/CD, and Chapter 8 explained it in much more depth.

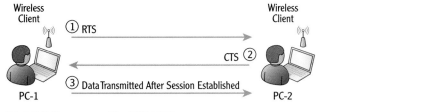

FIGURE 12.3 The RTS/CTS process

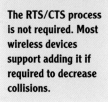

The RTS/CTS process is not required. Most wireless devices support adding it if required to decrease collisions.

In the figure, PC-1 first sends an RTS frame to the other computer asking whether it's clear. PC-2 then sends back a CTS frame indicating it's clear to send. All nodes within hearing distance (including the intended recipient) allow the sender adequate time to send the packet.

Comparing Networking Standards and Characteristics

Although wireless technologies have grown significantly in the past few years, there really aren't that many standards that are commonly used. Chapter 7 introduced the common wireless standards, and Table 12.1 shows them here with some of their characteristics. The following sections in this chapter explore these standards in more depth.

TABLE 12.1 Current wireless standards

Standard	Speed	Frequency	Comments
802.11a	54 Mbps	5 GHz	Less susceptible to interference
802.11b	11 Mbps	2.4 GHz	Can configure specific channels
802.11g	54 Mbps	2.4 GHz	Widely deployed
802.11n	300 Mbps	2.4 GHz or 5 GHz	Newer and quickly overtaking 802.11g in popularity

Comparing FHSS, DSSS, and OFDM

Any devices that use radio frequency (RF) signals are susceptible to interference. For example, some cordless phones use this same frequency band as many wireless devices. When more than one device transmits on the same frequency at the same time, it causes interference. For a wireless LAN, this interference can negatively affect performance.

To combat the interference problems, wireless technologies adapted different methods of transmitting data on these bands. They are as follows:

> ▶ Frequency-hopping spread spectrum (FHSS)

> ▶ Direct-sequence spread spectrum (DSSS)

> ▶ Orthogonal frequency division multiplexing (OFDM).

Since these are often referenced for the different technologies, it's worthwhile explaining them.

FHSS hops between frequencies in a pseudorandom pattern. It starts with a center frequency known to the transmitter and receiver and then quickly changes, or *hops*, between different frequencies. The transmitter and receiver synchronize these hops so they know what frequency is next.

These random frequencies are in 1 MHz increments and do not use more than 1 MHz at any given time. FHSS was introduced with the original 802.11 specification but isn't used with any of the current IEEE 802.11 specifications. It is used with Bluetooth wireless networking.

IEEE 802.11b uses DSSS. It uses the full bandwidth (or spectrum) of the transmitted frequency and can use one of 11 possible channels in the United States, as shown in Figure 12.4.

FHSS made it difficult for unintended recipients to receive the data, but it wasn't that effective at limiting interference problems.

Bluetooth is a wireless technology used for short distances creating personal area networks (PANs). A PAN transmits data to devices that a person is carrying or wearing.

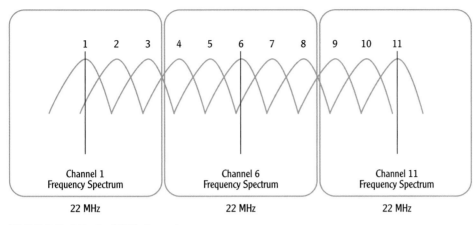

FIGURE 12.4 DSSS channels

Each DSSS channel has a spectrum of 22 MHz. Channel 1, channel 6, and channel 11 can each be used without interfering with each other. This is useful if you have multiple wireless access points located close to each other for different networks. DSSS uses the center frequency of the channel and then modulates the signal out from the center frequency consuming the entire 22 MHz spectrum. DSSS is resistant to interference, and it allows multiple users to share a single channel.

OFDM splits the radio frequency signal into smaller subsignals and transmits data simultaneously across these different frequencies. Each subsignal includes a separate data stream. You can compare this to multiplexing used with cable TV. A single cable includes multiple TV channels, and a TV can tune to any single channel. 802.11a and 802.11g use OFDM. 802.11n uses an enhanced OFDM by combining it with multiple antennas.

> WAPs used as wireless repeaters use the same center channel. WAPs physically close to other WAPs for different wireless networks use different channels.

IEEE 802.11

IEEE created 802.11 as the first Wi-Fi standard in 1997. It maxed out at a speed of 2 Mbps, with an actual throughput of less than .7 Mbps, which was simply too slow for most applications. It used FHSS.

It was also highly susceptible to radio interference from other devices using the 2.4 GHz frequency. This includes devices such as baby monitors, cordless telephones, video cameras, microwave ovens, and Bluetooth devices.

Combined with the slow speed and high susceptibility to interference, the original specification was never widely adopted.

WIRELESS GOVERNING BODIES

Four governing bodies overlook wireless technology. They are the Federal Communications Commission (FCC), Institute of Electrical and Electronics Engineers (IEEE), International Organization for Standards (ISO), and the Wi-Fi Alliance.

IEEE   The IEEE sets the ISO standards for the wireless IEEE 802.11 family to ensure consistency. You can visit the IEEE and ISO websites at www.ieee .org/index.html and www.iso.org/iso/home.html.

Wi-Fi Alliance   The Wi-Fi Alliance is the trade association that promotes wireless technology. It approves products that meet their interoperability guidelines, and these products can use the Wi-Fi logo. For more information on the Wi-Fi Alliance, you can visit its website at www.wi-fi.org.

FCC   The Federal Communications Commission (FCC) regulates wireless frequencies and modulation types. The FCC also regulates the use of unlicensed Instrument, Scientific, and Medical (ISM) frequency bands that are used in Wi-Fi communications. You can view the FCC website at www.fcc.gov.

IEEE 802.11a

IEEE designed 802.11a with a different frequency band to avoid the interference in the crowded 2.4 GHz frequency band. Instead, IEEE uses 5 GHz. It can achieve a raw speed of 54 Mbps, which was significantly higher than the max of 2 Mbps for 802.11. However, the higher frequency of 5 GHz had a trade-off of a shorter range.

The advertised range of 802.11a is approximately 30 meters (100 feet). However, you were only able to achieve the full 54 Mbps speed at close ranges of between 50 feet and 100 feet.

Unfortunately, this different frequency also caused logistics problems. The 5 GHz components were difficult to manufacture, and first-generation components often didn't live up to the advertised specifications. Because of this, the release of 802.11a was slow. IEEE 802.11a and IEEE 802.11b actually made it to market at about the same time.

> **The maximum range of wireless is achievable only in ideal conditions. Obstructions such as walls and trees absorb the signal, reducing the distance.**

WIRELESS SPEEDS AND DISTANCES

The advertised speeds of different wireless devices represent the maximum speeds in ideal conditions. In the real world, these speeds are rarely achievable.

For example, IEEE 802.11g advertises a speed of 54 Mbps. If the wireless access point is 5 feet away from the wireless device, you can probably achieve a speed of 54 Mbps. However, if you move the wireless device farther and farther away, at some point errors creep into the transmission.

Devices automatically correct for errors by slowing down the transmission speed. If there are errors at 54 Mbps, the devices try slower and slower speeds until they are able to achieve an error-free transmission. In other words, depending on the distance, interference from other transmissions, and obstructions, an advertised speed of 54 Mbps could be reduced to 6 Mbps.

IEEE 802.11b

IEEE 802.11b was another improvement over the original IEEE 802.11 specification. Like 802.11, it operates at 2.4 GHz but increased the speed from 2 Mbps to a speed of 11 Mbps. The increase in data throughput speed from 802.11's 2 Mbps was a major performance increase. The migration to 802.11b was rampant.

As mentioned previously, 802.11b uses DSSS, which improved the reliability of the signals. Also, DSSS has configurable channels. For example, if your neighbor is using channel 6 at full power, you can change your network to channel 1, and neither network will interfere with other. Changing to a lesser used channel increases performance without any additional cost.

IEEE 802.11g

IEEE 802.11g uses OFDM, which brought a significant increase in speed up to 54 Mbps. It uses the same 2.4 GHz frequency as 802.11b, making both b and g wireless devices compatible with each other.

Users loved the increased speed, and 802.11g quickly became a favorite, both in homes and businesses. IEEE 802.11g is widely available, but the advances of 802.11n will likely overtake 802.11g devices in market share within a couple of years.

Because of the manufacturing problems with 802.11a's 5 GHz components, more users adopted 802.11b than 802.11a.

◄

802.11b devices can work with 802.11g devices, but connections between them will operate at the slower 11 Mbps speed.

◄

◄

Some devices are advertised as a/b/g compatible. They can operate at 5 GHz for 802.11a devices and operate at 2.4 GHz for 802.11b and 802.11g devices.

As mentioned, 802.11g increased the speed to 54 Mbps. One of the reasons for this speed increase is the change in the modulation type. IEEE 802.11g uses OFDM. The average distance for maximum performance is still rated between 80 feet and 100 feet, but some vendors advertise distances as great as 150 feet. The maximum distance will always vary depending obstructions, RF interference, and even atmospheric conditions.

IEEE 802.11n

The need for speed brought 802.11n to our wireless networks. It advertises speeds of up to 300 Mbps and includes the possibility of reaching 450 Mbps. The improvements in speed are primarily because of equipment changes.

IEEE 802.11n uses *maximum-input maximum-output* (MIMO) antenna technology. MIMO includes multiple antennas at both the receiver and the transmitter to minimize errors and increase the data throughput. An intriguing improvement is the concept of smart antennas. These intelligent ears grab multiple streams of data and combine them to ensure lightning fast speed.

These multiple antennas also increase the distance of 802.11n devices. Even as far as 300 feet away, tests indicate that 802.11n networks still operate as high as 70 Mbps.

Even though 802.11n wasn't formally approved by IEEE until late in 2009, devices based on proposed draft versions of the standard started hitting the market in 2007. The Wi-Fi alliance began certifying products in 2007 based on the 802.11n proposal.

Another benefit is that IEEE 802.11n is backward compatible with 802.11a, 802.11b, and 802.11g devices. It is important to realize that being backward compatible does not mean that the older devices will operate at the newer speeds. If you want to achieve the 300 Mbps speed, both the WAP and the wireless device need to be 802.11n.

> ▶
>
> **Actual data throughput is usually closer to 180 Mbps, but this is still much better than a perfectly operating 802.11g wireless network at 54 Mbps.**

> ▶
>
> **Many companies wanted to be first to market 802.11n products to grab market share. By late 2009, there were already many 802.11n devices available.**

Comparing Network Security Methods

One of the biggest concerns with wireless is security. Since the signals are broadcast over the air, they are easily intercepted. However, multiple security technologies are available today. Some are better than others are, and some aren't secure at all. It's important to know which security methods to implement in different wireless networks.

When wireless networks were first created, they had a primary goal of being easy to use. Designers wanted to make it easy for devices to connect to each other and easy to transmit data between each other. The designers did a good job with this goal.

Later, they decided to add some security features. Unfortunately, their first attempt at security was not very successful. Because of this, many people still think of wireless networks as not being secure. However, it is possible to provide strong security for wireless networks today.

If you plan on using a wireless network, you need to know what security methods are available. More, you should know what methods are actually secure. Table 12.2 introduces the wireless security methods, and the following sections explore them in more depth.

TABLE 12.2 Wireless security methods

Security method	Security level	Comments
Wired Equivalent Privacy (WEP)	Low, cracked in 2001	Not recommended for use unless nothing else is available.
Wi-Fi Protected Access (WPA)	Medium, cracked in 2008	Interim fix for WEP until release of WPA2.
Wi-Fi Protected Access 2	Strong	WPA2 support is required for all Wi-Fi certified devices.
802.1x	Strongest when used with WPA2	802.1x (also known as Enterprise mode) authenticates clients before granting wireless access.

Figure 12.5 shows the wireless security page of Cisco wireless router. This model supports several different security modes. Notice that WPA and WPA2 both support Personal and Enterprise modes.

The figure also shows a RADIUS mode. RADIUS is short for Remote Authentication Dial-in User Service. IEEE 802.1x can use RADIUS and has a back-end server to provide authentication.

Wired Equivalent Privacy

Wired Equivalent Privacy (WEP) was the first security model used on IEEE 802.11 wireless networks. Its intent was to offer privacy equivalent to a wired Ethernet network. The key here is the word *intent*. It failed.

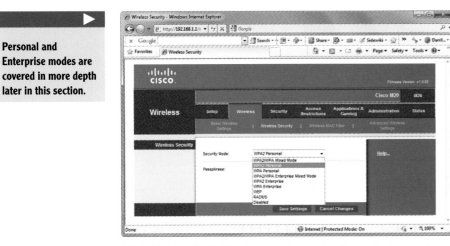

Personal and Enterprise modes are covered in more depth later in this section.

FIGURE 12.5 Viewing security modes for a wireless router

WIRELESS NETWORK THEFTS

Hardly a day goes by when network security (or the lack of it) isn't mentioned in the news. Wireless security has been especially problematic in the past. Early attempts to lock down wireless networks were woefully lacking, and many businesses simply didn't understand the risks. They transmitted some data using insecure methods, and other transmissions didn't use any security at all.

For example, in 2003 and 2004, hackers stole information from more than 45 million credit cards from TJ Maxx and Marshalls stores. Wireless networks transmitted all of this information. Customers who returned merchandise without receipts had to provide driver's license numbers, and it's estimated that 455,000 of these customers had their data stolen. This represents one of the biggest wireless thefts (if not the biggest), but there have certainly been many more.

Hackers were able to capture these wireless transmissions and harvest the data. Some data was sent without any security. Other data was sent using the insecure WEP. The stolen data was used to steal identities and make fraudulent charges on the credit cards.

Instead, attackers learned ways to listen to the data, capture it, and decrypt it. WEP had multiple faults including the following:

Its Use Was Optional   Instead of a secure by default strategy, WEP had to be enabled. Many wireless users didn't understand its use and didn't enable it.

Weak Encryption   WEP used RC4, which is a stream cipher. Attackers are able to crack RC4 using freely available software downloaded from the Internet.

Poor Key Management   Encryption keys are secret strings of data used to encrypt and decrypt data. They must be secret between the parties, changed often, and not repeated. However, keys used by WEP are not secure. An eavesdropping attack can determine the encryption key within a minute.

Cracking Software Widely Available   Once attackers understood the cracks, they wrote and distributed tools to attack wireless networks.

◄

The Payment Card Industry Security Standard Council sets standards for credit card processing. They prohibit the use of WEP on any wireless networks processing credit cards today.

WAR DRIVING

War driving is the act of driving a car through an area and scanning for wireless networks. Attackers war drive to locate wireless networks and determine the security used to protect them. When attackers locate wireless networks with weak security, they sit in their car with a wireless receiver and capture the wireless transmissions.

Attackers use modified antennas to improve the reception. For example, you can create a rudimentary directional antenna with a can. You remove the top of the can, empty it, and then run a wire from the can to the wireless receiver. You can then point the can in different directions to capture wireless signals. This directional antenna significantly increases the reception distance. Now, instead of an attacker sitting in the parking lot or outside your home, they can be further away.

Wi-Fi Protected Access

Wi-Fi Protected Access (WPA) was the initial security improvement over WEP. WPA works on WEP-designed hardware without any additional cost to the consumer. This usually required a flash upgrade to upgrade the firmware on existing WEP hardware.

◄

Flashing the wireless device is similar to flashing the BIOS on a computer. It installs new software in the programmable read-only memory (PROM).

The intent behind WPA was to improve upon WEP's weaknesses and reduce the complexity of configuration. You learned earlier that one of WEP's weaknesses was manual key management. It was optional but cumbersome and oftentimes avoided. With WEP, you can use the same key for as long as you choose, but when you do change the key, it has to be changed on all devices within your wireless network. It increased the administrative workload, and many users simply overlooked this step.

TKIP changes keys without requiring the user to change the passphrase. In WEP, similar keys were reused for encryption until the passphrase was changed.

With WPA, rekeying the encryption keys are mandatory, and with each data frame, a new key is created automatically. Temporal Key Integrity Protocol (TKIP) managed the keys and provided several other technical improvements.

You can configure WPA in two different modes:

- ▶ Personal mode, or preshared key (PSK) mode
- ▶ Enterprise mode

Personal mode requires manual configuration similar to WEP but not with the upkeep of changing the key. The initial shared key is a string of characters such as a password or passphrase. Once you enter the initial shared key, TKIP is responsible for encryption and automatic rekeying, which eliminates the need for manual rekeying.

You can configure a Windows Server 2008 server as an 802.1x server. 802.1x authentication servers are covered in more depth later in this section.

Enterprise mode requires authentication with a back-end server known as an 802.1x server. After authentication, the access point negotiates a separate and unique key with each client.

The significant difference between WPA Enterprise and Personal mode is in authentication. With WPA Personal mode, every wireless client uses the same passphrase, which doesn't individually identify any of the clients. Any client with the passphrase is granted access. With WPA Enterprise mode, authentication takes place at an authentication server, and each client requires a specific account and credentials (such as a username and password).

WPA is still better than WEP. However, the preferred security solution for wireless networks today is WPA2.

It may not be obvious, but the primary purpose of WPA was to provide a temporary secure solution while designers created a more secure solution. Designers fully expected that researchers or attackers would crack WPA. They were right. Researchers cracked WPA in 2008.

WPA2

WPA2 is the updated version of WPA and is standardized as IEEE 802.11i. WPA2 supports encryption with the Advanced Encryption Standard (AES) algorithm. The U.S. government adopted AES as their encryption standard, and it is considered the strongest symmetric encryption available.

AES is an extremely strong and widely respected encryption algorithm. Many different applications encrypt data with AES, including nonwireless applications.

One drawback to WPA2 is that it requires hardware that is different from the hardware used with WEP and WPA. At this point, all new hardware is WPA2 compatible, but you may run across older hardware that isn't compatible. If so, you can use the older TKIP with WPA2.

WPA2 supports both Personal and Enterprise mode just like WPA. Personal mode uses a preshared key, and Enterprise mode requires an 802.1x server.

WPA2 Personal Mode   WPA2 Personal (or WPA2-PSK for preshared key) is for home users and small businesses that are not using an authentication server. Anyone that has the passphrase and name of the network can connect. It combines the passphrase and the network name to create unique encryption keys for clients.

WPA2 Enterprise Mode   WPA2 Enterprise Mode uses 802.1x for authentication. This requires a back-end server such as a Windows Server 2008 server running Network Policy Access Services to authenticate clients. Wireless clients are not granted access to the wireless network unless then can authenticate.

Using an IEEE 802.1x Authentication Server

IEEE 802.1x provides port-based security. In short, it provides an authentication mechanism for either 802.3 (wired Ethernet) or 802.11 networks. 802.1x includes three elements in the authentication process:

- ▶ Supplicant: Client

- ▶ Authenticator: Access point

- ▶ Authentication server: Running RADIUS and EAP

Consider Figure 12.6. It shows the wireless client as the supplicant, the WAP as the authenticator, and a back-end server as the authentication server.

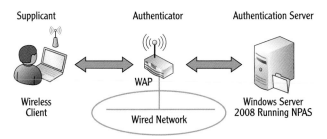

F I G U R E   1 2 . 6 **WPA2 enterprise authentication**

The authenticator acts like a security guard and ensures the supplicant has adequate credentials before providing access to other networks. When the supplicant first connects, the access point sends the credentials to the authentication server,

The Wi-Fi Alliance requires all new wireless devices to support WPA2 in order to be certified with the Wi-Fi logo.

Authentication means the clients must provide credentials such as a username and password. More advanced authentication can require smart cards or fingerprints.

In a Microsoft environment, the authentication server will often check the credentials against an Active Directory database. Active Directory hosts accounts and their credentials.

and the authentication server checks the credentials against its database. If the credentials are valid, the authentication server confirms them to the authenticator, and the authenticator grants access to the client.

You can add the Network Policy and Access Services (NPAS) role to a Windows Server 2008 server and configure it as an 802.1x server. Any clients that are not authenticated will not be allowed access to the network. You can also configure NPAS to grant nonauthenticated clients across to isolated networks.

Figure 12.7 shows a Windows Server 2008 server with the NPAS role added.

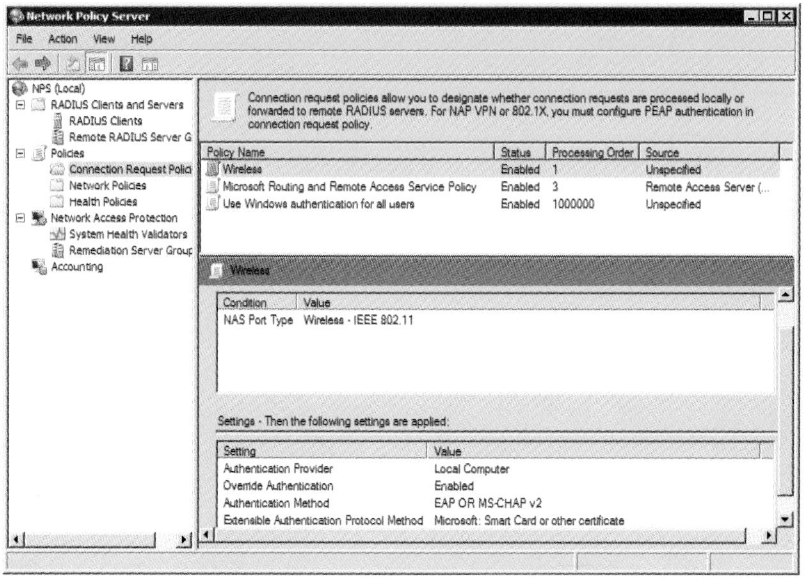

> **The configuration of NPAS is beyond the scope of this book. However, Network Access Protection is covered in the Microsoft Windows Security Essentials book in this series.**

FIGURE 12.7 Network Policy Server role in a Windows Server 2008 server

You can see a Wireless policy in Figure 12.7 (named *Wireless*). It is configured with a value of Wireless – IEEE 802.11 to authenticate 802.11 wireless clients. Additionally, it is configured to authenticate the clients using EAP or MS-CHAPv2. EAP supports the usage of smart cards, and MS-CHAPv2 is a secure method of authenticating username and passwords.

Using Wireless Networks

Wireless networking offers many advantages over wired network configuration such as ease of installation and elimination of wires. Once the wireless network is configured, users can share resources such as files, folders, printers, and more, just as they can in a wired network.

MAC FILTERING DOES NOT PROVIDE REALISTIC SECURITY

On many wireless routers, you can configure media access control (MAC) address filtering. The goal is to ensure that only computers with the specified MAC address can access the wireless router. On the surface, this sounds very secure since MAC addresses are theoretically unique.

However, it's very easy for an attacker to spoof a MAC address. In other words, the attacker can modify packets so that it looks like the attacker's packets are coming from an approved MAC address. Although using MAC filtering doesn't cause any harm, it won't stop an experienced attacker from entering your network.

More and more wireless networks are popping up in both homes and businesses today. The following sections expand on the use of wireless in these different environments.

Home Wireless Networks

The primary piece of equipment used to create a wireless network in a home (or small business) is a wireless router. It's important to realize that a wireless router has many different components:

Wireless Access Point   The wireless access point provides connectivity for the wireless devices. It includes a bridge to bridge the wired and wireless devices together.

Switch   The switch provides connectivity between wired and wireless devices. All of the devices connected to the switch ports have the same network ID and share the same broadcast domain.

Router   In a home network, the router is usually connected directly to the cable modem or to another Internet connection. It routes traffic from the internal switch to the Internet (and back).

DHCP   DHCP provides IP addresses and other TCP/IP configuration information to all the devices on the switches network.

Figure 12.8 shows the rear view of a wireless router with the extra components. The first four ports are typical wired ports that connect with the wireless router's switch component. The device also connects wireless connections through the switch. DHCP provides TCP/IP information to all the ports connected to these switch ports and has assigned addresses to a wired computer, a wireless printer, and a wireless laptop.

You can connect wired and wireless devices using the wireless router's WAP and switch components without connecting it to a WAN. This creates a private network.

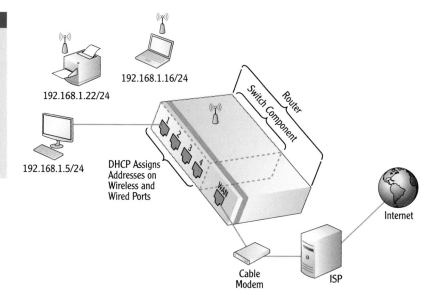

FIGURE 12.8 Wireless router rear view

The routing component routes any traffic destined for the Internet through the WAN port. This usually connects to a DSL modem, cable modem or other broadband device to the Internet service provider (ISP).

Many wireless routers use the range of 192.168.1.0/24. The wireless router uses 192.168.1.1 and is the default gateway for computers connected via the wireless router. The router routes traffic from the switch to the WAN port, and the WAN port provides connectivity to the Internet via an ISP.

You can configure most routers through a web interface. Figure 12.9 shows one of the pages in the web interface for a Cisco M20 wireless router. This is the Basic setup page with some items highlighted.

1. This is the URL using the IP address of the router (192.168.1.1).

2. The router is using DHCP to receive a public IP address from the ISP.

3. The router's internal private IP address is 192.168.1.1.

4. The device name is the first 15 characters of the SSID (the network name). If the SSID is 15 characters or less, the device name will be the same.

5. DHCP settings indicate how many IP addresses the wireless router can issue and the range of addresses. In the figure, the range starts at 192.168.1.100 and issues 50 addresses.

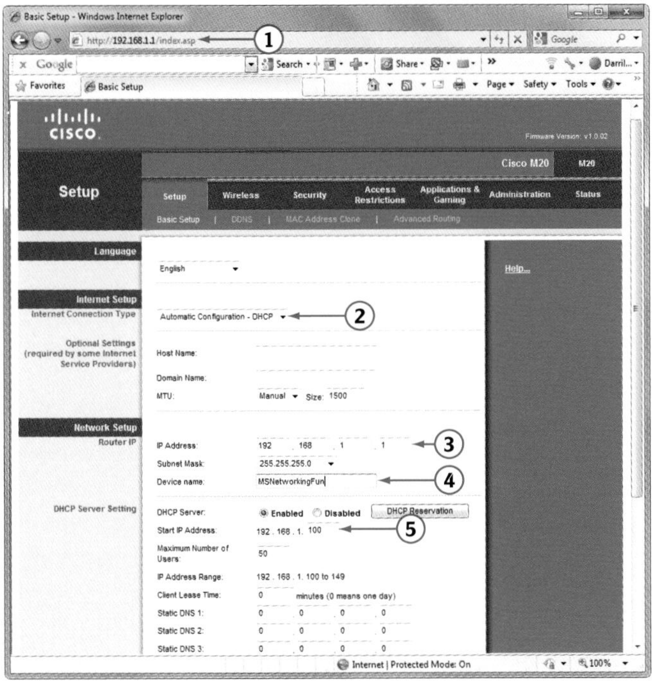

FIGURE 12.9 Cisco M20 web interface

All wireless routers have default IP addresses, administrator names, and default passwords. Table 12.3 shows some of the defaults for common brands.

TABLE 12.3 Common wireless router defaults

Brand	Default IP address	Administrator name	Default password
Cisco	192.168.1.1/24	admin	admin
Linksys	192.168.1.1/24	Admin or blank on older systems	admin
Netgear	192.168.0.1/24	admin	password
3COm	192.168.1.1/24	admin	admin

Most wireless routers today are extremely simple to set up. About all you really need to do is enter or change the network name (SSID), change the administrator password from the default, and choose the security method (usually WPA2 Personal). Many have installation wizards that lead you through the process.

It's important to change the default password of the administrator account. If not, an attacker can access the network and make changes, even out locking the owner.

Many wireless routers have additional capabilities. For example, some include a VPN that allows you access a home network from a remote location.

Wireless Networks in a Business

Wireless networking in the business environment has grown exponentially in recent years with no end in sight. The advantages to wireless networking in a business are as follows:

▶ Reduced costs compared to wired networks

▶ Better flexibility over wired networks

▶ Greater mobility between offices

▶ Improved scalability

The primary difference between using wireless networks in a home or small office and using wireless in a business is that businesses will usually use wireless access points only, and not wireless routers.

Configuring a wireless network in a business is very similar to configuring a wireless network at home. You need to name the network with an SSID and configure the security. As a reminder, the most secure security you can use in a business wireless network is WPA Enterprise, which uses 802.1x for authentication.

One difference in businesses is the use of repeaters. Since a business can be considerably larger than a home, a single WAP may not cover the entire business. Instead, you add additional WAPs as repeaters.

There are two terms worth defining in the context of wireless repeaters:

Basic Service Set (BSS)   A BSS is a wireless network composed of one WAP and one or more wireless devices. For many wireless networks, a single WAP is enough.

Extended Service Set (ESS)   An ESS is a wireless network with more than one WAP, with each WAP supporting one or more wireless devices. Additional WAPs act as repeaters and extend the range of the wireless network. All devices in the ESS use the same SSID, and the same broadcast channel.

Figure 12.10 shows an ESS network. WAP2 is extending the range of the wireless network.

The key to success when adding repeaters is device placement. If a repeater is placed too far from the root WAP, a device may get dropped while roaming. If repeater is placed too close, the two WAPs may interfere with each other. In Figure 9.6, a repeater has been added at approximately 100 feet (about 30 meters) from the root access point, which is a reasonable distance, but testing may dictate that you need to adjust the distance.

> Computers connected in ad hoc mode (a wireless network without a WAP) form an Independent Basic Service Set (IBSS).

> The placement of WAPs in business networks also becomes a network security issue, because the signals can easily bleed outdoors and across parking lots and streets.

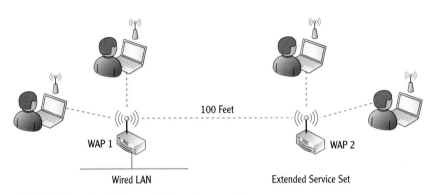

FIGURE 12.10 Extended service set with a repeater

The repeater ensures that users who are out of range of the root WAP will still have adequate signal strength to stay connected. As users roam between repeaters, wireless devices will connect with the strongest signal automatically, allowing for optimal performance.

Understanding Point-to-Point Wireless

Point-to-Point (P2P) wireless is useful when you need to connect two networks using wireless technologies instead of traditional wired connections. It's sometimes cost prohibitive to run cable between two points. The distance between points may be a few hundred feet, or a few miles, with 25 miles typically being the maximum.

For example, Figure 12.11 shows a main office with a newly leased building 10 miles down the road. Each building includes an internal network, but they need connectivity between each other.

Many technologies support the P2P wireless bridge. These include microwave, infrared, and laser-optics radio transmission. Most of these are limited to line of sight, but there are other considerations.

The first step in configuring a wireless bridge is performing a site survey. This is to ensure that the area is free from radio frequency interference and line-of-sight obstructions. Wireless radio waves in the 2.4 and 5.0 GHz range do not penetrate building structures or trees very well. You also need to know the height of the transceivers on both buildings because this affects the distance. Higher buildings allow longer distances.

If the area is clear of radio interference and physical obstructions, you still don't have a green light. The area underneath and above the line of direct sight has to be considered. This area is the Fresnel zone, as shown in Figure 12.12.

Cell phones roam in this way. They automatically switch between wireless towers to the tower providing the strongest signal.

P2P wireless connections are also called wireless bridges or P2P wireless bridges. They bridge two or more wired networks with a network connection.

Line of sight indicates that there is a clear path between the two bridges. The curvature of the earth limits the line of sight.

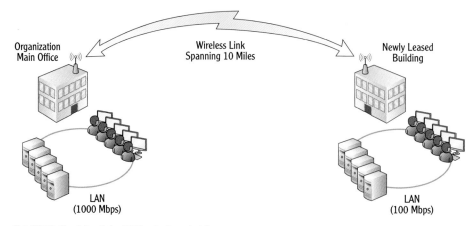

FIGURE 12.11   P2P wireless bridge

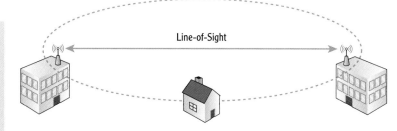

FIGURE 12.12   Evaluating the Fresnel zone

The *Fresnel zone* is the area underneath and above the direct line of sight between the two points. In the figure, a house is penetrating the lower boundary of the Fresnel zone. Structures within the Fresnel zone have a tendency to absorb radio waves, and blockage greater than 40 percent will render your wireless connection unreliable.

Another consideration with the bridge is alignment of the directional antennas between the two points. It will require special equipment and expertise to have these two antennas focused toward each other.

Bridge antennas are typically the dish type (parabolic) directional antennas or Yagi directional antennas. A directional antenna has the best performance in a specific direction and can be pointed or directed at specific locations. In contrast, omni-directional antennas receive signals from all directions.

THE ESSENTIALS AND BEYOND

In this chapter, you learned about many of the wireless components, standards, and security methods. A WAP bridges wireless devices to a wired network. A wireless network has an SSID, which is simply the name of a wireless network. Several different wireless standards are used, including 802.11a, b, g, and n. 802.11a uses a frequency of 5 GHz. 802.11b and g use 2.4 GHz, and 802.11n uses either 2.4 GHz or 5 GHz. Security standards include WEP (old and insecure), WPA (cracked in 2008), and WPA2 (strong). You can increase security by using WPA2 with 802.1x, which adds authentication. In businesses, you can extend a wireless network by adding repeaters. You can also connect two buildings that are miles apart by using Point-to-Point (P2P) wireless bridges.

ADDITIONAL EXERCISES

▶ Draw a network for a home network that includes wired connections and wireless connections and provides connectivity to the Internet.

▶ Imagine that you came across a WRT54G router but you don't have the username and password. Look on the Internet to learn how to reset this router.

▶ List the different types of wireless standards including their speeds and frequencies.

▶ List the different types of security methods used with wireless.

REVIEW QUESTIONS

1. Which of the following statements about the service set identifier (SSID) are true? (Choose all that apply.)

    A. The SSID is an alphanumeric value that identifies the vendor's device type.

    B. The SSID is an alphanumeric information field with a maximum value of 32 bits.

    C. The SSID is a logical network name for a wireless network.

    D. The SSID identifies the security encryption method.

2. True or false. 802.11 networks use CSMA/CD.

3. What frequency does an 802.11a network use?

    A. 11 Mbps

    B. 54 Mbps

    C. 2.4 MHz

    D. 5 GHz

4. Which of the following frequency ranges does 802.11b use?

    A. 2.4 GHz

    B. 4.1 GHz

    C. 2.4 MHz

    D. 5 GHz

(Continues)

THE ESSENTIALS AND BEYOND *(Continued)*

5. What frequency does an 802.11n network use? (Choose all that apply.)

   A. 54 Mbps   C. 2.4 MHz

   B. 300 Mbps   D. 5 GHz

6. What is the maximum speed of an IEEE 802.11b network?

   A. 2 Mbps   C. 54 Mbps

   B. 11 Mbps   D. 300 Mbps

7. True or false. IEEE 802.11n networks can operate at speeds as high as 300 Mbps.

8. Of the following security methods, which one is the most secure?

   A. WEP Personal Mode   C. WPA2 Personal Mode

   B. WEP Enterprise Mode   D. WPA2 Enterprise Mode

9. True or false. A WAP and a wireless router are the same thing.

10. Your company is planning to lease a second building, which is about 2 miles away. You're asked how the networks between the two buildings can be connected. What would you suggest?

    A. Add roaming WAPs.   C. Extend the network by adding additional WAPs.

    B. Connect the buildings with a P2P bridge.   D. Run a twisted pair between the buildings.

## CHAPTER 13

Understanding Internet Access Methods and Wide Area Networks

Homeowners, home offices, and small offices may connect to the Internet by utilizing one of multiple methods. These range from the most basic dial-up connections to the popular broadband cable, but there are other types of connections available to select from. This chapter introduces Internet access methods and identifies their characteristics, such as speed and availability.

Enterprises use these and other connectivity methods to access the Internet and to connect offices via wide area network (WAN) links. WANs connect remote offices together, even when they are a significant distance apart from each other. Some common methods used to create WANs are Integrated Services Digital Network (ISDN) connections, T1 and T3 lines in the United States, and E1 and E3 lines in Europe.

▶ **Comparing connectivity methods used in homes and SOHOs**

▶ **Comparing connectivity methods in enterprises**

▶ **Exploring remote access services**

▶ **Using RADIUS**

Comparing Connectivity Methods Used in Homes and SOHOs

Users in homes and small offices and home offices (SOHOs) connect to the Internet using a wide variety of methods depending on what is available in their area. Table 13.1 introduces these different connectivity methods, and the following sections describe them in more depth.

TABLE 13.1   Home and SOHO connectivity to Internet

Method	Speed	Availability
Dial-up	@50 Kbps	Anywhere phone lines exist
Broadband cable	Up to 30 Mbps	Urban areas that have cable TV
DSL	Up to 24 Mbps	Must be close to a telephone company central office (generally within 2 miles)
Satellite	Typically up to 10 Mbps	Widely available but requires unobstructed view to satellite

Worldwide Interoperability for Microwave Access (WiMAX) is a technology available in some cities. It provides a wireless alternative for broadband cable and DSL and get speeds up to 40 Mbps.

It's possible to provide Internet sharing for each of these methods. In other words, a single router or computer connects to the Internet using one of the methods listed in Table 13.1, and this connection is shared among all the computers in the network. This is a little more challenging with dial-up since it's so slow to start with, but it's very common with the other methods.

Using a Dial-up Connection

In rural areas, dial-up is often the only reliable method available to access the Internet.

Dial-up connectivity methods use the *plain old telephone service* (POTS). A user connects a modem to their telephone line and then connects to the remote network by dialing out through the phone line. You can use dial-up methods to connect to the Internet via an *Internet service provider* (ISP) or directly to a remote access server for connectivity to a company's internal network.

Compared to other technologies used today, dial-up is very slow. It has a theoretical maximum speed of 56 Kbps, but typical speeds are less than 50 Kbps. However, dial-up is much cheaper than other methods, and it's available anywhere phones are available. ISDN technology (described later in this chapter) is an alternate form of dial-up Internet access occasionally used for home networking. However, it is more expensive and not widely available because of special installation requirements.

Connecting with DSL

Digital subscriber line (DSL) connections are popular in some urban areas. They use telephone lines but send the data digitally instead of using an analog signal. One benefit is that you can use the telephone for voice at the same time you're using the telephone line for DSL access.

Figure 13.1 shows typical DSL connectivity. You connect a router (or a single computer) to the DSL modem. A DSL splitter splits the lines so that the phone line can be used at the same time as the DSL modem. The signal travels over the telephone lines to a telephone company's central office, which then connects to the Internet.

One limitation of DSL is that the end user must be relatively close to the central office. Improvements in recent years have extended this distance, but in general, the DSL modem must be located within two miles of the central office. The digital signal can't travel as far on the telephone lines as an analog voice signal. Users that are close to the central office are able to get higher speeds on the connection.

The DSL splitter may include DSL filters, or you may need to include one. The DSL filter removes digital noise from the telephone line that can be quite aggravating.

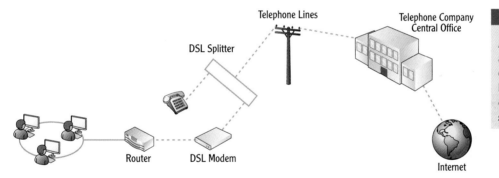

A *central office* is a nearby telephone exchange switch building that processes the digital signals.

FIGURE 13.1 DSL connectivity

DSL lines can be as fast as 24 Mbps for downstream data and 3 Mbps for upstream data. However, these are premium speeds often available only at a premium price. You can usually get a slower speed of about 1 Mbps for downstream data at the basic price.

There are many variations of DSL commonly referred to as xDSL. These variations use different technologies to improve the performance. They include asymmetric DSL (ADSL), symmetric DSL (SDSL), and very-high-bit-rate DSL (VDSL). Many businesses use one of these types in what is commonly called *business-class DSL*.

Compared to dial-up speeds, the DSL speed provides significant improvements.

MODEMS CONVERT DIGITAL AND ANALOG SIGNALS

A modem modulates and demodulates a signal. Traditional phone lines can transmit analog signals, but they can't transmit digital signals. Computers can understand digital data (ones and zeros), but they can't understand analog signals.

The following graphic shows the digital and analog signals in relation to the computer and modem.

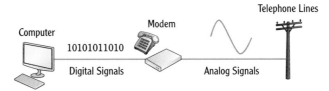

The modem modulates the analog signal with the digital signal. In other words, it uses a specific frequency sine wave and adds variations on the analog signal to represent the digital signal. When the modem receives signals, it demodulates the signal by removing the digital data from the analog signal. It then sends the digital data to the computer.

Other modems use this same process. For example, broadband modems perform a similar modulation and demodulation process.

Employing Broadband Cable

Communications companies often include Internet access through the same cable that provides cable TV. It's called *broadband cable* because the same cable transmits multiple signals across a broad frequency spectrum.

Part of this is obvious. You don't need a separate cable for every TV channel. Instead, the cable delivers all of the channels, and you only need to tune your TV to view the desired channel. The TV tuner strips out all the other TV channels. Similarly, you can add a cable modem to strip out all the TV channels and leave only the Internet access signal.

Figure 13.2 shows the basic connectivity for broadband cable. A router (or a single computer) connects to the cable modem. A cable splitter splits the signal between the cable modem and the TV, with TV signals going to the TV and the Internet signal going to the cable modem. The cable company hosts ISP servers for Internet access.

Speeds of broadband cable vary greatly. Although they're often advertised as high as 30 Mbps, users rarely get those speeds. For one thing, users share the same bandwidth with their neighbors. If several neighbors are uploading or downloading data at the same time, all the connections will be slower than if only one user was using the connection.

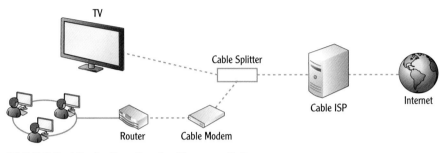

FIGURE 13.2 Broadband cable connectivity

Some ISPs offer tiered services. For example, if you pay the minimum price, you can get speeds up to 3 Mbps. Pay a little more, and you can get up to 15 Mbps. Or you can pay top dollar to get the top speed.

Another addition in broadband is fiber. This is similar to broadband cable, but the fiber-optic lines can carry significantly more data than traditional cable (up to 100 Mbps in some cases), and it is quicker. This increases the capability for all users sharing the same line.

Connecting via Satellite

The use of satellite Internet access is expanding, especially in rural areas where only dial-up access is available. A satellite transceiver is able to upload and download data from a satellite, and the satellite provides Internet access via an ISP, as shown in Figure 13.3. The satellite modem connects the transceiver to a router for a group of computers, or it can also connect to a single computer for a home user.

Speeds vary wildly, in both advertised speeds and the actual speeds that users report. Upload or uplink speeds (from the transceiver to the satellite) typically have a maximum advertised speed of 10 Mbps, though the actual uplink speeds are usually closer to 256 Kbps.

Download or downlink speeds (from the satellite to the transceiver) sometimes have maximum advertised speeds as high as 1000 Mbps (1 Gbps). However, these quick speeds are usually available only for users willing to pay a steep premium.

ISPs often cap speeds with bandwidth-throttling techniques. This prevents a single user from consuming bandwidth at the expense of other users.

Originally, satellite access required a phone line (called *terrestrial transmit*) used to upload data. Today, most transceivers include direct upload capability.

Compared to dial-up speeds, even the slowest satellite links provide great improvement for users in rural areas.

Many satellites are in geostationary orbits. A geostationary orbit always appears to be in the same stationary location from any point on the earth, even though the earth and the satellite are zipping through space at phenomenal speeds. As long as you have a clear unobstructed view to the location of the satellite, you can use satellite Internet access.

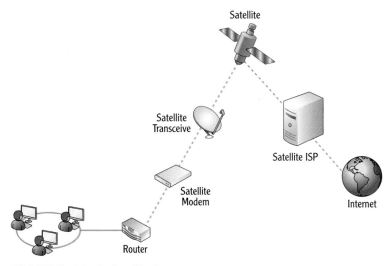

FIGURE 13.3 Satellite Internet access

One drawback to satellites is that they are susceptible to interruptions because of precipitation. Rain and snow can interfere with the signal. This can reduce speeds or completely block the signal. Another drawback is latency because of the amount of time it takes for signals to travel back and forth to the satellite. For example, when a user clicks the mouse, there are typically four trips to and from the satellite orbiting the earth in space before the user gets data. This can make web surfing slower, prevent some applications (such as online gaming or real-time streaming) from working, and sometimes prevent users from accessing a virtual private network (VPN).

BRINGING INTERNET TO THE HEARTLAND

Several companies are working on bringing Internet access to rural areas using wireless technologies.

For example, Verizon provides 3G/4G services across the United States. Users are able to connect USB modems to their computer and connect to

(Continues)

Comparing Connectivity Methods in Enterprises

Enterprises can connect to the Internet through any of the same methods used by homes and SOHOs. However, a bigger concern for enterprises is connecting their offices.

Chapter 1 introduced wide area networks. As a reminder, a WAN is two or more local area networks (LANs) in separate geographical locations that are connected together. WAN links connect the LANs together.

Consider Figure 13.4, which shows a WAN connecting five locations together. It includes a company's primary location, a regional location, and three branch offices all connected together with four WAN links.

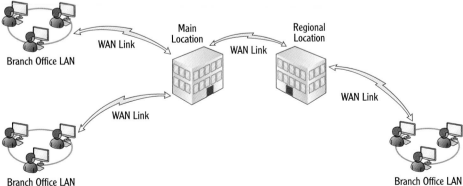

FIGURE 13.4 WAN connecting four LANs

The WAN links are usually slower than the speed of the LAN. For example, LAN speeds are often 100 or 1,000 Mbps today, but the cost of WAN links speeds that quick is rarely justified. Instead, a company will use a slower WAN link that is more affordable.

Table 13.2 introduces many of the WAN link methods used by enterprises today.

TABLE 13.2   Enterprise WAN connectivity

Chapter 12 described point-to-point wireless bridges. They can often be a cost-effective solution when compared to other methods.

Method	Speed	Availability
T1	1.544 Mbps	Widely available in the United States.
T3	44.736 Mbps	Used in the United States when higher bandwidths are needed.
E1	2.048	Used in Europe.
E3	34.368 Mbps	Used in Europe.
WAN DSL	Up to 24 Mbps	This is similar to DSLs used by home owners but is instead used for WAN links as business DSL or WAN DSL. When available, it is much more affordable than T1 and T3 lines.
ISDN	128 Kbps (BRI) 1.472 Mbps (PRI)	BRI uses two B channels and one D channel. PRI uses 23 B channels and one D channel.
P2P wireless bridge	Up to 54 Mbps	Widely available but limited by line of sight.
Ethernet WAN	Up to 10 Gbps	Available in some buildings, primarily in urban areas.

An organization often doesn't own these WAN links. Instead, they lease them as *leased lines*. The organization contracts with a communications provider for the line, and the provider guarantees a specific level of service identified in a *service level agreement* (SLA). The SLA defines expectations for performance and often identifies penalties if the service fails to meet the expectations.

Similarly, communications companies don't actually run a single dedicated line between the sites but instead use their existing infrastructure to provide the service.

Exploring Digital Signal Lines

Many of the signaling types used with WANs are based on digital signal (DS) levels. A single DS0 channel is 64 Kbps wide, and it can carry a single digitized voice phone call. T1 and T3 lines combine multiple channels together and are often used for WAN links.

Table 13.3 compares the most commonly used DS levels.

T1 and T3 lines are explored in more depth later in this section.

TABLE 13.3 Digital signal lines

Level	Speed	Comments
DS0	64 Kbps	One channel
DS1 (T1)	1.544 Mbps	24 DS0s (called T1 when carried on copper wire)
DS3 (T3)	44.736 Mbps	28 DS1s (called T3 when carried on copper wire)

T1 lines include an additional 8 Kbps used for overhead. In other words, it's 24 * 64 Kbps (1536 Kbps) plus 8 Kbps. 1536 Kbps + 8 Kbps = 1544 Kbps or 1.544 Mbps.

Europe uses a different standard identified as E-carrier. E-carrier signals use time slots instead of channels, and time slots are measured differently than channels. Table 13.4 shows the speeds of E1 and E3 lines and the number of time slots they use.

TABLE 13.4 E-carrier characteristics

Level	Speed	Comments
E1	2.048 Mbps	32 time slots
E3	34.368 Mbps	512 time slots

Using ISDN

Integrated Services Digital Network (ISDN) is a group of standards used for transmitting voice, data, and video. ISDN can be used as a WAN link.

Figure 13.5 shows an ISDN used as a WAN link to connect a main location with a branch office. Notice that the ISDN uses terminal adapters instead of modems.

ISDN uses bearer channels (B channels) and data channels (D channels). This is somewhat misleading since the B channels actually carry the data and the D channels provide signaling information such as caller ID, automatic number identification, and more. The B channels are 64 Kbps channels.

You may hear the term *ISDN modem*. However, since it doesn't modulate and demodulate signals, the ISDN terminal adapter is not actually a modem.

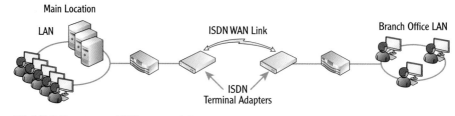

FIGURE 13.5 ISDN connectivity

There are two base types of ISDN service:

Basic Rate Interface (BRI)   A BRI uses two 64 Kbps B channels and one 16 Kbps D channel. This provides a 128 Kbps data link. BRIs can be used in both SOHOs and enterprises.

You may hear a PRI called a T1. However, a PRI is carried on a T1 (1.544 Mbps), but it isn't a T1 itself.

Primary Rate Interface (PRI)   A PRI uses 23 64 Kbps B channels and one 64 Kb/s D channel. This provides a 1472 Kbps data link for a total of 1.536 Mbps.

Using T1/T3 Lines and E1/E3 Lines

A *T1* combines 24 DS0 channels for a total of 1.544 Mbps. A *T3* combines 28 DS1 channels for a total of 44.736 Mbps. Figure 13.6 shows the basic connectivity using a T1 as a WAN link.

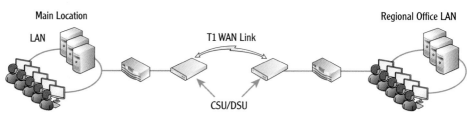

FIGURE 13.6 WAN connected with a T1 link

Both T1s and T3s use CSU/DSUs.

Notice that the WAN link is connected with a Channel Service Unit/Data Service Unit (CSU/DSU) at each end. The CSU/DSU translates the T1 signals from the WAN link to a format that the router can accept. This is similar to how a modem translates the digital and analog signals, though the technology is different.

The cost of T1 lines has been steadily dropping in recent years. However, the availability of other cheaper and quicker methods has reduced the demand for these lines.

In Europe, they use E1 and E3 lines instead of T1 and T3 lines. An E1 is 2.048 Mbps, and an E3 is 34.368 Mbps. Just as T1 and T3 WAN links are terminated with CSU/DSUs, E1 and E3 lines also use CSU/DSUs.

Ethernet WAN

The new kid on the block is Ethernet WAN. Although it's not widely available, it provides phenomenal speeds at relatively low cost when compared to T1 lines. Speeds range from 10 Mbps to 10 Gbps.

Ethernet WAN uses the same Ethernet standards used on Ethernet networks but over longer distances. It uses fiber-optic cables allowing connections to be up to 40 km apart.

As communications providers run more and more fiber-optic cable, the availability of Ethernet WAN connections will continue to increase.

◀

Ethernet WAN has limited availability and can only be found in larger cities.

Exploring Remote Access Services

Chapter 1 introduced remote access. As a reminder, a *Remote Access Service (RAS)* server give users the ability to access an organization's internal LAN from a remote location. Users can access a network from home, while traveling, or while visiting other locations such as customer sites.

The two primary methods of connecting to a RAS server are via dial-up or via a *virtual private network (VPN)*. You can configure Microsoft servers as either a dial-up or VPN server by adding the Network Policy and Access Services (NPAS) role and configuring Routing and Remote Access Services.

One of the important considerations when configuring a server to support RAS is security. You only want authorized people to access the remote access server, and you want to ensure transmissions can't be intercepted. You start by using authentication and then add encryption.

Figure 13.7 shows the different methods of authentication supported on a Microsoft RAS server.

Some of the common authentication methods used by Microsoft RAS servers are as follows:

◀

Chapter 9 showed how to add NPAS to create a router. You can also add NPAS to configure a Windows Server 2008 server as a RAS server.

PAP Password Authentication Protocol (PAP) passes the password across the wire in clear text. PAP is the least secure method since an attacker can intercept the password and read it.

CHAP The Challenge Handshake Authentication Protocol (CHAP) provides encrypted authentication. It uses Message Digest 5 (MD5) to encrypt the password instead of passing the password in clear text. Non-Microsoft clients can use CHAP.

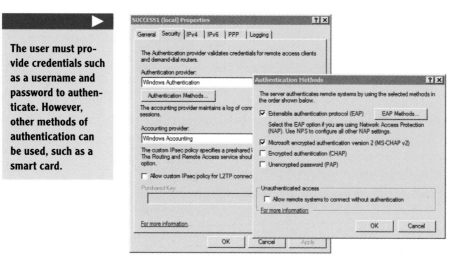

The user must provide credentials such as a username and password to authenticate. However, other methods of authentication can be used, such as a smart card.

FIGURE 13.7 Microsoft RAS authentication methods

MS-CHAPv2   The Challenge Handshake Authentication Protocol version 2 (MS-CHAPv2) provides more security for the authentication process when passwords are used. One important benefit is that MS-CHAPv2 provides mutual authentication. The server authenticates back to the client before the client passes the authentication data to the server.

EAP   The Extensible Authentication Protocol (EAP) supports additional methods including Protected EAP (PEAP) and smart cards. PEAP and smart cards use Transport Layer Security (TLS).

Connecting to RAS via Dial-up

A dial-up remote access server includes a modem and a phone line. Any user with a modem and a phone line can dial directly into the remote access server. However, just because a user can connect doesn't mean they are granted access.

Consider Figure 13.8. A dial-up user connects into the remote access server, and the dial-up server challenges the user for authentication. The user has to authenticate by providing credentials. The RAS server passes the credentials to a domain controller (or other identity database) for verifying the authentication. Once the user is authenticated, the user account is checked to see whether the user is authorized as a dial-in user.

REMOTE ACCESS VS. REMOTE DESKTOP

Remote Access and Remote Desktop are two different technologies used for different purposes. Remote Access Services provide access to an entire network from a remote location outside the network. Remote Desktop provides access to a specific system from a remote location but usually within the same network.

Administrators often use Remote Desktop to remotely access systems servers. The server is in a server room, that is the administrator is able to connect remotely from anywhere in the office.

Servers must be configured for Remote Desktop. The following graphic shows the System Properties for a Windows Server 2008 R2 server with the Remote tab selected.

The graphic shows that Remote Desktop is enabled for the server, as long as the computer is using the more secure Network Level Authentication.

One of the biggest drawbacks with dial-up RAS is the speed. Dial-up modems rarely get more than 50 Kbps, which can be painfully slow. However, virtual private networks (VPNs) are much quicker.

◄

Dial-up is rarely used for remote access today because of the speed.

Microsoft domains use domain controllers to authenticate clients. Only users with an account in Active Directory can authenticate.

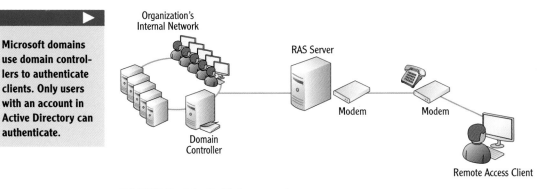

FIGURE 13.8 Dial-up remote access

Connecting to RAS via a VPN

A VPN provides access to a private internal network over a public network such as the Internet. You can configure a Microsoft server as a VPN server just as you can configure it as a dial-up server. The difference is that instead of a modem connected to a phone line, you need a NIC that is connected to the Internet.

Figure 13.9 shows a RAS server as a VPN server. The client first establishes a connection with the Internet and then uses a tunneling protocol to "tunnel" through the Internet. The tunnel encrypts the connection to protect the transmitted data.

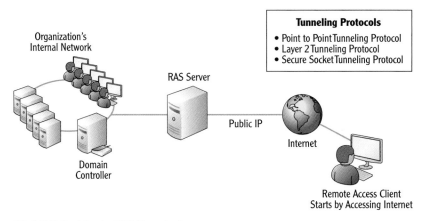

FIGURE 13.9 VPN Remote Access

The three primary tunneling protocols are the Point-to-Point Tunneling Protocol (PPTP), the Layer 2 Tunneling Protocol (L2TP), and Secure Socket Tunneling Protocol (SSTP). Table 13.5 introduces the three VPN tunneling protocols used with Windows Server 2008.

TABLE 13.5   VPN tunneling protocols

VPN Protocol	NAT Compatibility	Port	Comments
PPTP	Can traverse NAT	1701	Oldest of the three
			Uses Microsoft Point-to-Point (MPPE) encryption
L2TP	Cannot traverse NAT	1723	Uses Internet Protocol Security (IPSec) for encryption
SSTP	Can traverse NAT	443	Uses Secure Sockets Layer (SSL) for encryption
			Easy to configure

Microsoft introduced PPTP as a VPN tunneling protocol for VPNs. PPTP is an extension of Point-to-Point Protocol (PPP), which is used for dial-up networking. PPP within PPTP offers encryption and authentication for the VPN tunnel. In addition, Microsoft uses Microsoft Point-to-Point Encryption (MPPE) to encrypt PPTP transmissions.

L2TP is a tunneling protocol created by combining the Layer 2 Forwarding (L2F) protocol from Cisco and Microsoft's PPTP protocol. It is currently a standard used by many different vendors. The primary method of encrypting L2TP transmissions is with IPSec.

The one drawback with IPSec is that it can't pass through a NAT server. Because of how NAT translates addresses, it breaks IPSec. If the VPN server is behind a firewall that uses NAT, you either need to step backward and use PPTP or to go forward and use SSTP.

SSTP is the newest tunneling protocol. It uses SSL, which is a well-known, highly used, and respected security protocol. On the Internet, HTTP combines SSL as HTTPS to encrypt the majority of encrypted web pages.

Since SSL is used so often, it's common for the SSL port (port 443) to be open on network-based firewalls. In other words, an administrator doesn't need to manipulate the firewall to get SSTP to work, making it a little easier to configure.

Chapter 3 introduced IPSec, and Chapter 4 described it in more detail. Chapter 1 introduced Network Address Translation (NAT), and Chapter 9 covered it in more depth.

Comparing Client VPNs with Gateway VPNs

Up to this point, the VPN discussion has been focused on client-to-gateway VPN access. In other words, an end user connects to the Internet from home or another remote location and connects to the VPN. The user then has access to the internal network's resources.

However, you can also use a VPN as a WAN link. Consider Figure 13.10. It shows a main office and a regional office connected via a VPN used as a WAN link. The two VPN servers create a gateway-to-gateway VPN.

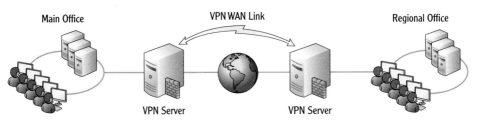

Main Office   VPN WAN Link   Regional Office

VPN Server   VPN Server

FIGURE 13.10 Gateway-to-gateway VPN

Users in the main office are able to access resources in the remote office over the VPN, and users in the remote office are able to access resources in the main office. A significant difference in this configuration from a client VPN is that the gateway-to-gateway VPN is transparent to the users.

In a client-to-gateway VPN, the user has to initiate the connection. However, in a gateway-to-gateway VPN, the connection is either always on or configured as a demand-dial connection. In a demand-dial connection, as soon as the user tries to access a resource in the other LAN, the VPN servers will create the connection.

Adding Remote Access Services to Windows Server 2008

These steps will also work on a Windows Server 2008 R2 server.

The following steps show how to add the Remote Access Services (RRAS) to Windows Server 2008.

1. Click Start ➤ Administrative Tools ➤ Server Manager.

2. Click Roles, and select Add Roles.

3. Review the information on the Before You Begin page, and click Next.

4. Select Network Policy and Access Services. Click Next.

5. Review the information on the Network Policy and Access Services page, and click Next.

6. Click the Routing And Remote Access Services check box. This will also select the Remote Access Service And Routing box. Your display will look similar to Figure 13.11. Click Next.

7. Click Install on the Confirmation page.

8. After a moment, the install will complete. Click Close.

9. You can launch the Routing and Remote Access console by clicking Start ➤ Administrative Tools ➤ Routing And Remote Access.

There is much more that you can do to configure and secure the RAS server. These steps only showed how to install it so that you can look around if desired.

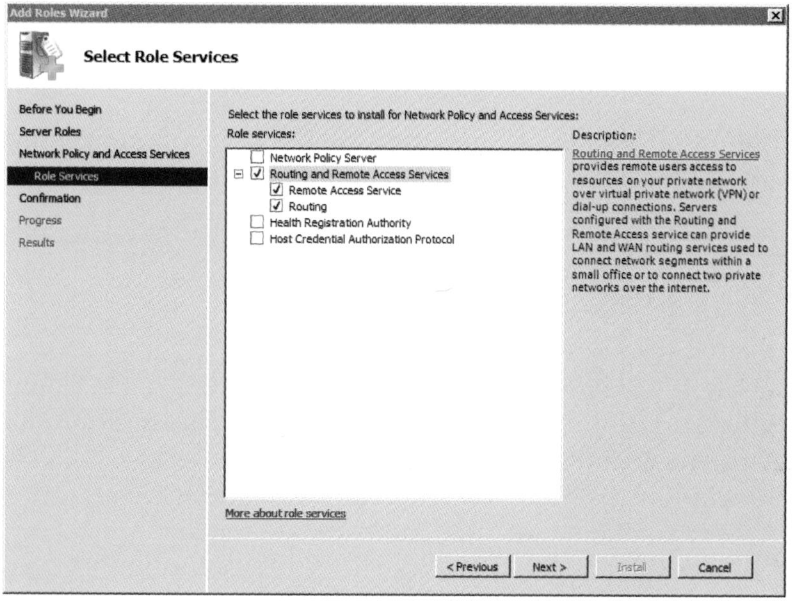

FIGURE 13.11 Adding RAS to a Windows Server 2008 server

Using RADIUS

If your organization includes multiple remote access servers, you might consider the addition of a Remote Authentication Dial-In User Service (RADIUS) server. The RADIUS server provides central authentication and logging.

As an example, consider Figure 13.12, which shows multiple VPN servers using a RADIUS server. You could have multiple VPN servers at different geographical locations such as regional offices. VPN clients can connect to any VPN server.

Each VPN server forwards all authentication requests to the RADIUS server. In a Microsoft domain, the RADIUS server forwards the requests to a domain controller. If the credentials are valid, the RADIUS server passes the information back to the VPN server. The VPN server then grants access.

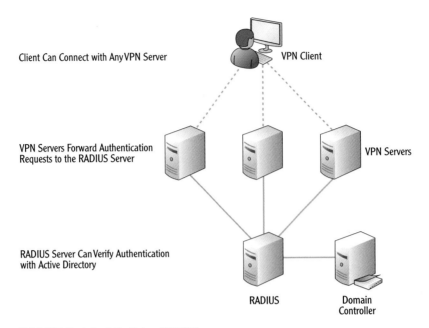

Client Can Connect with Any VPN Server

VPN Client

VPN Servers Forward Authentication
Requests to the RADIUS Server

VPN Servers

RADIUS Server Can Verify Authentication
with Active Directory

RADIUS   Domain
                Controller

FIGURE 13.12 Using RADIUS

The RADIUS server can also track all activity for each of the VPN servers with central logging. All connection attempts and usage data are logged on the RADIUS server for each of the VPN servers.

THE ESSENTIALS AND BEYOND

In this chapter, you learned about many of the different methods used to access the Internet and to create wide area networks. SOHOs often use DSL, broadband cable, and many other methods for Internet access. Enterprises use ISDN, T1 and T3 (in the United States), E1 and E3 (in Europe), and other methods to create WANs. A RAS server provides end users with the ability to access an organization's network even when they are away from the organization. VPNs provide access to the private network over a public connection such as the Internet, and they use tunneling protocols to protect the connection. Common tunneling protocols include PPTP, L2TP, and SSTP. When an organization has multiple RAS servers, they can use a RADIUS server for central authentication.

ADDITIONAL EXERCISES

▶ List the access methods used by at least three of your friends or fellow students.

(Continues)

THE ESSENTIALS AND BEYOND (Continued)

▶ Identify the speed of your Internet connection. **Warning:** It is not necessary to install software on your system to do this. Some attackers try to trick you into installing malicious software by describing it as a way to check your system for malware. You should only install software from a trusted source.

▶ List the different methods an enterprise can use to create a WAN.

▶ Draw a diagram that shows a gateway-to-gateway VPN used as a WAN link.

To compare your answers to the author's, please visit **www.sybex.com/go/ networkingessentials**.

REVIEW QUESTIONS

1. Which of the following methods can be used by small offices and home offices (SOHOs) for Internet access? (Choose all that apply.)

   A. Dial-up   **C.** DSL

   B. WAN   **D.** Broadband cable

2. How many B channels does an ISDN BRI use? (Choose all that apply.)

   A. One   **C.** Twenty-three

   B. Two   **D.** Twenty-four

3. Which of the following connection methods requires the client to be close to the central office of a telephone company?

   A. Dial-up   **C.** ISDN

   B. DSL   **D.** Ethernet WAN

4. True or false. T1 and T3 lines are used in Europe.

5. What is the speed of a T1 link?

   A. 1.544 Mbps   **C.** 34.368 Mbps

   B. 2.048 Mbps   **D.** 44.736 Mbps

6. What would you add to a Windows Server 2008 server to use it as a VPN server?

   A. Virtual Private Network Services   **C.** Routing and Remote Access Services

   B. Wide Area Network Services   **D.** Dial-up Remote Services

(Continues)

THE ESSENTIALS AND BEYOND *(Continued)*

7. Which of the following are valid tunneling protocols?

    A. PPTP   C. SSTP

    B. L2TP   D. WLTP

8. What is the primary purpose of RADIUS?

    A. VPN WAN link   C. Central authentication

    B. Dial-up WAN link   D. Central encryption

## CHAPTER 14

Troubleshooting TCP/IP

One of the primary reasons to study networking is so that you can trouble-shoot a network when problems occur. At this point, you're probably aware that many puzzle pieces must be in place when a user accesses network resources or just surfs the Internet. If any single piece is not exactly where it should be, the user will be asking for help. With a little bit of knowledge on troubleshooting, you can be the person who identifies the problem and fixes it. In this chapter, you'll learn about key troubleshooting tools.

▶ **Using the command prompt**

▶ **Checking TCP/IP configuration with** ipconfig

▶ **Troubleshooting connectivity with** ping

▶ **Identifying routers with** tracert

▶ **Verifying the routed path with** pathping

▶ **Viewing TCP/IP statistics with** netstat

▶ **Installing Telnet**

> All the trouble-shooting commands in this chapter use the command prompt.

Using the Command Prompt

Although the Windows graphical user interface (GUI) is easy to use for most end user tasks, it does have some limitations when troubleshooting network connectivity issues. In contrast, the *command prompt* can be very useful in troubleshooting basic problems. That is, of course, if you know how to use it.

> There are many other ways to launch the command prompt, but this method will work with most Windows systems.

You can launch the command prompt in just about any Windows system by clicking Start, selecting Run, typing **cmd** in the text box, and pressing Enter. You have a wealth of help available if you know how to ask. For example, you can just enter the Help command to identify the available commands.

Figure 14.1 shows the Command Prompt window with the results of the ping loopback command. The first command is using IPv6, and the second command is using IPv4.

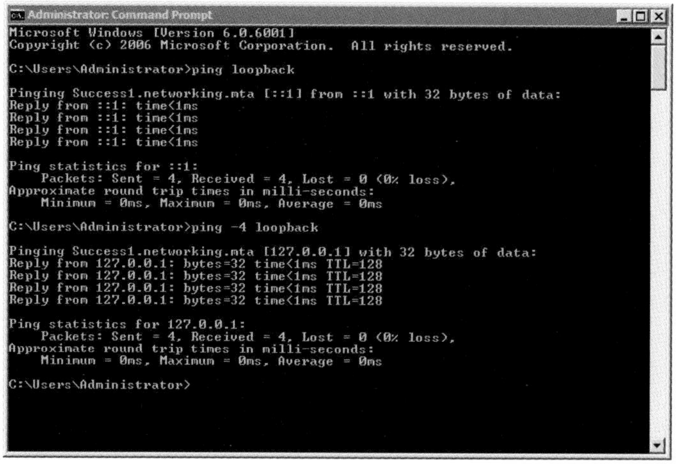

FIGURE 14.1 Viewing the Command Prompt window

Getting Help at the Command Prompt

Most commands have help available by typing in the command and adding a space, a slash (/), and then a question mark (?). For example, all the following commands will give you help:

- ▶ Ipconfig /?
- ▶ Ping /?
- ▶ Pathping /?
- ▶ Tracert /?
- ▶ Netstat /?
- ▶ Telnet /?

> ▶
>
> The telnet /? command will fail if Telnet is not installed on the system. Steps to install Telnet are included later in this chapter.

Sometimes the output can scroll past the screen before you have time to read it. You can use the More command with the command to show a single page at a time like this:

ipconfig /? | more

You can also redirect the output to a text file that you can read later. The following example sends the output to a text file named config.txt:

ipconfig /? > config.txt

Using Switches

Most commands support additional options. These options are added with switches. A switch is a forward slash (/) which would then be followed by the additional option. For example, if you enter `ipconfig` by itself, it gives minimal information. If you enter it as `ipconfig /all` (using the /all switch), it gives much more information. Entering the command with the `/?` switch will show you the switches supported by the command.

Although most commands use the forward slash (/) as a switch, some commands use a hyphen (-). Most Windows commands will accept either a forward slash or a hyphen. For example, the following two commands will both work the same way:

▶ `ipconfig /all`

▶ `ipconfig -all`

Understanding Case Sensitivity

With very little exception, command prompt commands are not case sensitive. In other words, you can enter them all uppercase, all lowercase, or any combination. For example, each of the following commands will provide the same results:

▶ `ping loopback`

▶ `PING LOOPBACK`

▶ `PiNg LoOpBaCk`

You'll often see commands shown with the first letter capitalized for readability. This doesn't mean it has to be entered that way. If a command is case sensitive, the documentation will usually stress it.

> The dash is more common in UNIX systems. The forward slash is more common in Microsoft systems. However, you'll see both in Microsoft systems.

> None of the commands presented in this chapter is case sensitive.

LAUNCHING THE COMMAND PROMPT WITH ADMINISTRATIVE PERMISSIONS

Some commands require administrative permissions to run. For example, if you try to release a DHCP lease using the `ipconfig /release` command in Windows 7, you'll see the following error if you haven't logged on as the administrator or started the command prompt with administrative permissions:

`The requested operation requires elevation.`

(Continues)

Launching the Command Prompt with Administrative Permissions *(Continued)*

If you're logged on with the system "administrator" account, the command prompt is automatically started with administrative permissions. However, if you're logged on with an account that is a member of the Administrators group, the command prompt does not start with administrative permissions.

The solution is to launch the command prompt with administrative permissions before executing the command. You can use the following steps in Windows 7 or Windows Server 2008 with administrative permissions:

1. Click Start.

2. Type **cmd** in the Start Search box.

3. The cmd shortcut will appear in the Programs list. Right-click cmd. Your display will look similar to the following graphic.

4. Select Run As Administrator. If prompted by User Account Control, click Yes to continue or enter appropriate administrator permissions depending on the prompt.

Checking the TCP/IP Configuration with ipconfig

`ipconfig` is one of the most valuable tools you have available to check and troubleshoot basic TCP/IP settings. You've already seen it in many of the chapters in this book, as shown in Table 14.1.

As a reminder, Listings 14.1 and 14.2 show the output of the `ipconfig /all` command with several key items highlighted.

TABLE 14.1 Use of `ipconfig` covered in previous chapters

Command	Chapter	Comments
`ipconfig /all`	3	Showed how to check the MAC address
`ipconfig /all`	5	Showed how to identify the IP address and DHCP status
`ipconfig /all`	6	Showed how to see whether your system is using Teredo for IPv6 compatibility
`ipconfig`	7 and 9	Showed how to identify the IP address of the default gateway
`ipconfig /displaydns`	10	Showed how to display the contents of the host cache
`ipconfig /flushdns`	10	Showed to remove the contents of the host cache
`ipconfig /all`	10	Showed how to determine the node type used for NetBIOS name resolution

Listing 14.1 identifies several pieces of key information shown by the `ipconfig /all` command. The Host Name value is the name of the computer. The Primary DNS Suffix value indicates that the computer joined the network .mta domain. The Node Type of Hybrid value indicates that NetBIOS names are resolved using WINS first and then broadcast.

Listing 14.1 `ipconfig /all` **Windows IP configuration**

```
C:\>ipconfig /all

Windows IP Configuration
```

◄

The NetBIOS name is created from the first 15 characters of the host name. If the first 15 characters of the host name are not unique, duplicate NetBIOS names will result.

```
Host Name . . . . . . . . . . . . : Success1
Primary Dns Suffix  . . . . . . . : networking.mta
Node Type . . . . . . . . . . . . : Hybrid
IP Routing Enabled. . . . . . . . : Yes
WINS Proxy Enabled. . . . . . . . : No
DNS Suffix Search List. . . . . . : networking.mta
```

Listing 14.2 shows the configuration of a network interface card (NIC) on the system. Some systems may have more than one NIC, and all of the NICs will be displayed.

Listing 14.2 `ipconfig /all` **NIC data**

```
Ethernet adapter Local Area Connection:

    Connection-specific DNS Suffix  . :
    Description . . . . . . . . . . . :
            Intel 21140-Based PCI Fast Ethernet Adapter (Emulated)
    Physical Address. . . . . . . . . : 00-03-FF-31-C4-CA
    DHCP Enabled. . . . . . . . . . . : No
    Autoconfiguration Enabled . . . . : Yes
    Link-local IPv6 Address . . . . . :
            fe80::1089:d255:6fa6:c8b%10(Preferred)
    IPv4 Address. . . . . . . . . . . : 192.168.3.10(Preferred)
    Subnet Mask . . . . . . . . . . . : 255.255.255.0
    Default Gateway . . . . . . . . . : 192.168.3.1
    DNS Servers . . . . . . . . . . . : ::1
                                        192.168.3.10
    Primary WINS Server . . . . . . . : 192.168.1.55
    NetBIOS over Tcpip. . . . . . . . : Enabled

Tunnel adapter Local Area Connection* 8:

    Media State . . . . . . . . . . . : Media disconnected
    Connection-specific DNS Suffix  . :
    Description . . . . . . . . . . . :
            isatap.{EE889A77-7A07-4D8B-A288-595E1FA01
800}
    Physical Address. . . . . . . . . : 00-00-00-00-00-00-00-E0
    DHCP Enabled. . . . . . . . . . . : No
    Autoconfiguration Enabled . . . . : Yes
```

The Physical Address value shows you the media access control (MAC) address of the NIC.

If it's a DHCP client, DHCP Enabled will be listed as Yes, and you'll also see the IP address of the DHCP server as long as the client was able to get an IP address from the DHCP server. In Listing 14.2, DHCP Enabled is set to No, so an IP address of a DHCP server is not available.

Autoconfiguration Enabled refers to Automatic Private IP Address (APIPA), and it is Yes by default. If the system couldn't get an IP address from the DHCP server and Autoconfiguration Enabled is sent to Yes, you'll see an IPv4 address that starts with 169.254. If Autoconfiguration Enabled is set to No, then APIPA addresses are not assigned when a DHCP server can't be reached.

A link-local IPv6 address always starts with fe80 and indicates that an IPv6 address isn't assigned, but IPv6 is enabled.

You can use the subnet mask with the IPv4 address to determine the network ID. In Listing 14.2, the IP address of 192.168.3.10 and a subnet mask of 255.255.255.0 indicates a network ID of 192.168.3.0. The network ID must be the same as other hosts on the subnetwork, including the default gateway. The default gateway and the IPv4 address share the same subnet mask.

The address of the Domain Name System (DNS) server is needed for most host name resolution. In Listing 14.2, the same computer is the DNS server. You can tell this from the IPv6 loopback address (::1) and the same IPv4 address (192.168.3.10) that is assigned to the computer. If the DNS server address information is misconfigured, you'll probably experience problems with name resolution.

A Windows Internet Naming Server (WINS) server resolves NetBIOS names. If the network includes a WINS server, the computer configuration should include the IP address in the Primary WINS server section.

If you have a NIC but it isn't connected, it will be listed as follows:

```
Media State . . . . . . . . . . . . : Media disconnected
```

This is an obvious sign that the cable isn't connected. If it does have a cable connected, check the link and activity lights on the NIC. If there are lights lit but the Media State indicates disconnected, check the cabling to ensure the following:

► The cable is seated completely in the NIC.

► The cable is seated completely in the wall jack.

► The cable is seated completely in the switch port (the switch will usually be in a separate room).

► Each of the cables is wired correctly.

► The cables are not bent excessively (beyond tolerance) when installing.

◄

An IP address starting with 169.254 in a network with DCHP should send alarm bells ringing in your head. The client is unable to get a DHCP address.

◄

The "Troubleshooting Connectivity with ping" section shows how to use ping to verify name resolution is working.

◄

Ethernet NICs have LED lights to indicate they are connected and have activity. Some have a single LED, and others have two LEDs.

Before replacing hardware, you should always reboot the system first. It's a simple step and cures many ills.

One of the simplest ways to check the wiring is to identify a known good path to the switch and use it. For example, if another computer is working, unplug the cable from that computer, and plug it into the computer you're troubleshooting. If the problem computer now works, you know it's the wiring. If it doesn't work, you know the problem is internal to the computer, and you may need to replace the NIC.

Although the ipconfig /all command is very valuable, the ipconfig command has other switches you can use. Table 14.2 shows these other commands with some comments.

TABLE 14.2 Important ipconfig commands

Command and switch	Comments
ipconfig /release ipconfig /release6	Releases an IPv4 lease (or an IPv6 lease with release6) obtained from a DHCP server. This doesn't have any effect if a system has a statically assigned IP address instead of a DHCP-assigned IP address.
ipconfig /renew ipconfig /renew6	Renews the IPv4 lease process (or IPv6 lease process with renew6) from a DHCP server.
ipconfig /displaydns	Displays host cache (includes names from hosts file and names resolved from a DNS server). This is useful to determine whether a name is in cache with a specific IP address.
ipconfig /flushdns	Remove items from host cache (removes items resolved from a DNS server but not items placed in cache from the hosts file).
ipconfig /registerdns	Registers the computer's name and IP address with a DNS server. This creates a host (A) record on the DNS server so that the DNS server can resolve the IP address for other computers.

The ipconfig /registerdns command will work in a Microsoft domain using a DNS server. It will not create a record on an Internet DNS server from a home computer.

Here's one way you can use the /displaydns and /flushdns switches. Suppose you are troubleshooting a problem where you can't connect to another computer. You know that the remote computer's IP address is 192.168.1.5. However, when you use ipconfig /displaydns, it shows the remote computer with a different IP address of 10.5.4.3.

Use ipconfig /flushdns   This should remove it from cache. If you enter ipconfig /displaydns but the faulty address is still in cache, it indicates it's in cache from the hosts file (not from DNS).

Try to Connect Again   If the ipconfig/flushdns command removed the entry from cache, try to connect to the remote computer again. If it's successful, the problem is resolved. If not, use ipconfig /displaydns to see what address is displayed. If it's still not the correct address (10.5.4.3 instead of 192.168.1.5), then DNS is giving the wrong address for the computer. In other words, the problem is with DNS.

Use ipconfig /registerdns   Go to the remote computer that you can't connect to, and enter **ipconfig /registerdns**. This should correct the record in DNS.

Flush DNS and Try Again   Go back to the original computer, and enter **ipconfig /flushdns** to remove the cache entries. Try to connect again, and it should be successful. If not, check the cache with ipconfig /displaydns. If it shows the wrong address (10.5.4.3 instead of 192.168.1.5), you need to let the DNS administrator know.

Troubleshooting Connectivity with ping

ping is a valuable command to check connectivity with other computers. It uses Internet Control Message Protocol (ICMP), which is the messenger service of the networking world.

THE HISTORY OF PING

Mike Muus wrote the original Ping program used with UNIX systems while studying radar and sonar in 1983. Sonar sends echo signals out, and the reply sounds like "ping," so he called his program Ping. He explained this at http://ftp.arl.army.mil/~mike/ping.html.

Somewhere along the line, someone decided that Ping was actually an acronym (PING) that stood for Packet INternet Groper. However, the source of this name is a little harder to find and verify.

You can ping an IP address or a host name. However, if you do use a host name, the first step in the process is that the ping will resolve the host name to an IP address. Listing 14.3 shows a basic ping command used to check connectivity with a server named DC1 in a network.

Listing 14.3 Successfullying pinging a computer

```
C:\>ping dc1

Pinging dc1 [192.168.1.112] with 32 bytes of data:
Reply from 192.168.1.112: bytes=32 time=1ms TTL=128
Reply from 192.168.1.112: bytes=32 time=1ms TTL=128
Reply from 192.168.1.112: bytes=32 time=1ms TTL=128
Reply from 192.168.1.112: bytes=32 time=1ms TTL=128

Ping statistics for 192.168.1.112:
    Packets: Sent = 4, Received = 4, Lost = 0 (0% loss),
Approximate round trip times in milli-seconds:
    Minimum = 1ms, Maximum = 1ms, Average = 1ms
```

Two very important point things occurred here, and both provide you with valuable information.

First, the computer named dc1 was resolved to the IP address of 192.168.1.112. You can see that in the first line after the ping dc1 command. If name resolution did not work, you would instead see this error:

```
Ping request could not find host dc1. Please check the name and try again.
```

Second, the ping command sent four packets to the server named dc1 and received four packets back. This reply verifies that the computer named dc1 is operational and able to respond to the ping request. If the server was not operational or not able to respond to the ping request, you would instead see a response similar to Listing 14.4.

Listing 14.4 Unsuccessfully pinging a computer

```
C:\>ping dc1

Pinging dc1 [192.168.1.112] with 32 bytes of data:
Request timed out.
Request timed out.
Request timed out.
Request timed out.
Ping statistics for 192.168.1.112:
    Packets: Sent = 4, Received = 0, Lost = 4 (100% loss),
```

Notice that even though the requests timed out, name resolution still worked. The ping command provides a reliable method to test name resolution. ping assumes the name (dc1 in the example) is a host name so attempts host name resolution methods first (such as DNS).

It's also important to realize that just because you receive a "Request timed out" response doesn't necessarily mean that the other computer is not operational. Secure networks and secure computers often have firewall rules blocking ICMP. If ICMP is blocked, the ping will fail even when the computer is operational.

The following are some other error messages you may see from the ping command:

◄

It's common for Windows 7 and Windows Server 2008 firewalls to block incoming ICMP traffic.

Destination Host Unreachable This usually indicates a problem with routing. The local computer may not be configured with the correct default gateway, the remote computer may not be configured with the correct default gateway, or a router between the two may be misconfigured or faulty.

TTL Expired in Transit The time to live (TTL) value starts at 128 on Windows Server 2008 and 64 on Windows 7. It is decremented each time the ping passes through a router (also called a *hop*). If the TTL value is lower than the number of routers the ping must pass through to reach its destination, the ping packet is discarded. However, it's very rare that a ping will need to go through 64 or 128 routers, unless there is a problem with routing.

Consider Figure 14.2 for an example of how to use the ping command to troubleshoot a system. It shows several systems on two subnetworks separated by a router. Imagine that Sarah is unable to connect with the server named FS1 and she asks you for help. You can use the ping command to check for several different situations.

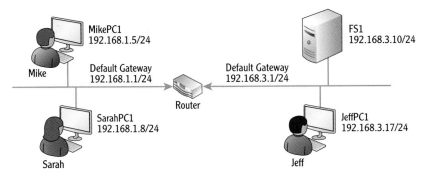

FIGURE 14.2 Using ping to test connectivity

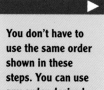

You don't have to use the same order shown in these steps. You can use any order desired as long as you are able to identify the problem.

The following steps show how you can troubleshoot the problem with ping:

1. Enter **ping localhost** or **ping 127.0.0.1**.

   By pinging the localhost or the loopback address (127.0.0.1), you can verify that TCP/IP is functioning correctly on Sarah's local system. You should get four successful replies. You can also use **ping -4 localhost** or **ping -6 localhost** to check IPv4 or IPv6, respectively.

2. Enter **ping 192.168.1.5**.

   This checks connectivity through a switch (or a hub) but not the router. You can also ping any other computer with the same network ID. If these pings fail, the problem is on this side of the router.

3. Enter **ping 192.168.1.1**.

   This pings the default gateway. Remember, you can use ipconfig to determine the IP address of the default gateway.

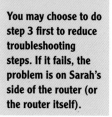

You may choose to do step 3 first to reduce troubleshooting steps. If it fails, the problem is on Sarah's side of the router (or the router itself).

4. Enter **ping 192.168.3.1**.

   This is the far side of the router. If successful, it indicates the router is successfully routing traffic. If it fails but you can ping 192.168.1.1 (the default gateway for 192.168.1.1), it indicates the router is causing the connectivity problem and may be misconfigured or faulty.

5. Enter **ping 192.168.3.10**.

   This pings the IP address of the server named FS1. If this succeeds, it indicates that the server is up and operational. Remember, though, if it fails, it could be because the server is blocking ICMP traffic.

6. Enter **ping fs1**.

   The first step of the ping should be to resolve the name fs1 to the IP address of 192.168.3.10. If it can't resolve the name, the problem is with name resolution. The primary name resolution methods to check are DNS, the host cache, and the hosts file.

Chapter 10 covered name resolution in depth, including DNS, the hosts cache, and the hosts file.

You can use other switches with ping as outlined in Table 14.3.

TABLE 14.3 Some ping switches

Switch	Comments
-4 Ping fs1 -4	Forces the use of an IPv4 address instead of IPv6.
-6 Ping fs1 -6	Forces the use of an IPv6 address instead of IPv4.

(Continues)

TABLE 14.3 *(Continued)*

Switch	Comments
-t Ping fs1 -t	Continuing pinging until stopped. You can press Ctrl+C to stop the pings.
-a Ping -a 192.168.1.5	Resolves IP addresses to host names. This requires that DNS has reverse lookup zones and associated pointer records, which are both optional. In other words, it may not work but doesn't indicate a problem.
-w Ping 192.168.1.5 -w 5000	This changes the timeout from the default of one second to five seconds (5,000 milliseconds). In cases when a computer is heavily loaded or under an attack, ping may fail with a timeout even when it is operational and ICMP is not blocked.

Identifying Routers with tracert

If your network includes multiple routers, you can use the tracert (pronounced as "trace route") command to trace the path a packet takes through these routers. The tracert command can verify the path throughout an entire network.

tracert is similar to ping in that it checks connectivity. However, it also includes information on all routers between your computer and the destination computer.

The tracert command also uses ICMP. Although this normally works well, the results may be incomplete if ICMP is blocked.

Listing 14.5 shows the results of the tracert command from a home computer to the computer hosting the Microsoft.com website. Notice in a few of the lines that the result indicates that the request timed out. This isn't because the path is faulty but instead because ICMP is being blocked.

Listing 14.5 Output of tracert command

```
C:\>tracert microsoft.com

Tracing route to microsoft.com [207.46.232.182]
over a maximum of 30 hops:

  1     3 ms    <1 ms    <1 ms   [192.168.1.1]
  2    10 ms     8 ms     9 ms   10.10.184.1
  3    11 ms    11 ms    10 ms   68.10.14.77
  4    14 ms    10 ms    13 ms   172.22.48.33
```

Although the primary troubleshooting value of tracert is on internal networks, you can also use it to view the routing path to computers on the Internet.

◄

◄

Attackers often use ICMP to launch attacks. It's common for Internet systems to block ICMP traffic to protect against these attacks.

```
 5     12 ms      9 ms      9 ms   nrfkdsrj02-ge600.0.rd.hr.cox.net
                                   [68.10.14.17]
 6     16 ms     16 ms     54 ms   ashbbprj02-ae4.0.rd.as.cox.net
                                   [68.1.1.232]
 7     15 ms     15 ms     17 ms   209.240.199.130
 8     17 ms     22 ms     18 ms   ge-3-1-0-0.blu-64c-1a.ntwk.msn.net
                                   [207.46.47.29]
 9     16 ms     17 ms     19 ms   ge-7-0-0-0.blu-64c-1b.ntwk.msn.net
                                   [207.46.43.113]
10     41 ms     78 ms     40 ms   xe-0-1-3-0.ch1-16c-1b.ntwk.msn.net
                                   [207.46.46.151]
11     44 ms     40 ms     51 ms   xe-7-0-0-0.ch1-16c-1a.ntwk.msn.net
                                   [207.46.43.146]
12     93 ms     90 ms     92 ms   ge-3-1-0-0.co1-64c-1a.ntwk.msn.net
                                   [207.46.46.118]
13     95 ms     93 ms     93 ms   ge-2-3-0-0.co1-64c-1b.ntwk.msn.net
                                   [207.46.35.151]
14     95 ms     95 ms     94 ms   ge-0-1-0-0.wst-64cb-1b.ntwk.msn.net
                                   [207.46.43.185]
15     93 ms     94 ms     94 ms   ge-4-3-0-0.tuk-64cb-1b.ntwk.msn.net
                                   [207.46.46.162]
16    142 ms     96 ms     97 ms   ten2-4.tuk-76c-1b.ntwk.msn.net
                                   [207.46.46.23]
17    107 ms    181 ms    101 ms   po16.tuk-65ns-mcs-1b.ntwk.msn.net
                                   [207.46.35.142]
18      *         *         *      Request timed out.
...
Trace complete.
```

> **The round-trip times are recalculated for each hop. Additional packets are sent for each router to calculate the round-trip time for that router.**

The tracert command identifies round-trip times for each hop listed in milliseconds (ms). Three different times are listed as tracert sends three separate probe requests by default for each hop. Shorter times indicate the trip is faster than longer times. You can see that the round-trips take progressively longer for each additional hop. Those routers are farther away.

It also lists the name of the routers when it can identify them. If tracert can't identify the name of the router, it just lists the IP address.

If the path between two systems is not working and tracert fails to complete, you can use the output to determine the location of the problem. For example, Listing 14.5 showed that the path was successful up to the 17th step. This indicates the 17th router from the source computer. The problem could be one of three things:

▶ The routing information on the 17th router is incorrect. This will prevent the data from reaching the 18th router.

▶ The 18th router is faulty.

▶ ICMP is blocked on the 18th router.

Table 14.4 lists some additional switches you can use with the `tracert` command.

TABLE 14.4 Some `tracert` switches

Switch	Comments
`-4` `tracert -4 microsoft.com`	Forces the use of an IPv4 address instead of IPv6.
`-6` `tracert -6 microsoft.com`	Forces the use of an IPv6 address instead of IPv4.
`-d` `tracert -d microsoft.com`	Suppresses IP address to name resolution. Only the IP addresses are listed.

Verifying the Routed Path with pathping

`pathping` is a combination of both `ping` and `tracert`. It starts by checking the route between the two computers similar to how `tracert` does so. It then uses `ping` to check for connectivity at each router.

It will send each router 100 echo request commands, and it expects to receive 100 echo replies back. It then calculates the percentage of data loss based on what it receives. For example, if it receives 100 replies, there is 0 percent packet loss. However, if it receives only 95 replies, there is 5 percent packet loss.

Listing 14.6 shows the output of a `pathping` command. Notice that in the first part of the `pathping` process, it checks the path similar to `tracert`. Lines 1 through 13 represent routers identified as hops. After it calculates the path, it then starts calculating the statistics by measuring loss. By default, the calculation process takes five minutes.

Listing 14.6: Output of `pathping` command

```
C:\Users\Dar>pathping microsoft.com

Tracing route to microsoft.com [207.46.197.32]
over a maximum of 30 hops:
  0  Laptop.hr.cox.net [192.168.1.114]
  1    [192.168.1.1]
  2  10.10.184.1
```

```
 3  68.10.14.77
 4  172.22.48.33
 5  nrfkdsrj02-ge600.0.rd.hr.cox.net [68.10.14.17]
 6  ashbbprj02-ae4.0.rd.as.cox.net [68.1.1.232]
 7  209.240.199.130
 8  ge-3-1-0-0.blu-64c-1a.ntwk.msn.net [207.46.47.29]
 9  xe-0-1-3-0.ch1-16c-1a.ntwk.msn.net [207.46.46.169]
10  ge-3-1-0-0.co1-64c-1a.ntwk.msn.net [207.46.46.118]
11  ge-1-0-0-0.wst-64cb-1a.ntwk.msn.net [207.46.43.163]
12  ge-7-1-0-0.cpk-64c-1b.ntwk.msn.net [207.46.43.228]
13  ten3-4.cpk-76c-1a.ntwk.msn.net [207.46.47.197]
14     *        *        *
Computing statistics for 325 seconds...
                 Source to Here   This Node/Link
Hop  RTT    Lost/Sent = Pct   Lost/Sent = Pct   Address
 0                                                 [192.168.1.114]

                                0/ 100 =  0%    |
 1   3ms    0/ 100 =  0%        0/ 100 =  0%    [192.168.1.1]
                                0/ 100 =  0%    |
 2   ---    100/ 100 =100%      100/ 100 =100%  10.10.184.1
                                0/ 100 =  0%    |
 3   11ms   0/ 100 =  0%        0/ 100 =  0%    68.10.14.77
                                0/ 100 =  0%    |
 4   ---    100/ 100 =100%      100/ 100 =100%  172.22.48.33
                                0/ 100 =  0%    |
 5   14ms   0/ 100 =  0%        0/ 100 =  0%
                        nrfkdsrj02-ge600.0.rd.hr.cox.net
                        [68.10.14.17]
                                0/ 100 =  0%    |
 6   25ms   0/ 100 =  0%        0/ 100 =  0%
                        ashbbprj02-ae4.0.rd.as.cox.net
                        [68.1.1.232]
                                0/ 100 =  0%    |
 7   21ms   0/ 100 =  0%        0/ 100 =  0%    209.240.199.130
                                100/ 100 =100%  |
 8   ---    100/ 100 =100%      0/ 100 =  0%
                        ge-3-1-0-0.blu-64c-1a.ntwk.msn.net
                        [207.46.47.29]
. . .
Trace complete.
```

The last few hops are similar to hop 8 and aren't listed. They are showing 100 percent loss since 100 packets were sent and 100 packets were lost. Again, this is likely because the routers are blocking ICMP, not because there is actual data loss.

If you have a large network with many routers, the `pathping` command can be useful to help you identify whether you are experiencing any data loss at specific routers. It could be that the routers simply have too much traffic for their capacity. You can either offload some of the traffic to another subnet or increase the capacity of the router.

Table 14.5 lists some additional switches you can use with the pathping command.

TABLE 14.5 Some pathping switches

Switch	Comments
-4 pathping -4 microsoft.com	Forces the use of an IPv4 address instead of IPv6.
-6 pathping -6 microsoft.com	Forces the use of an IPv6 address instead of IPv4.
-n pathping -n microsoft.com	Suppresses IP address to name resolution. Only the IP addresses are listed.
-q pathping -q 50 microsoft.com	Changes the number of queries per hop. By default, 100 queries per hop are used.

Viewing TCP/IP Statistics with netstat

You can use the netstat (short for network statistics) command to display information on any TCP/IP connections on your computer. You can use it show all the connections, ports, and applications involved with network connections. You can also use it to check TCP/IP statistics.

Table 14.6 shows the common netstat commands.

TABLE 14.6 Common netstat commands

Command	Comments
Netstat -a	Shows all connections and listening ports.
Netstat -b	Shows connections that all applications are using to connect on the network (including the Internet if the client is connected to the Internet).
Netstat -e	Shows Ethernet statistics.
Netstat -f	Shows fully qualified domain names (FQDNs).
Netstat -n	Shows both addresses and port numbers in numerical form.

Switches can be combined. For example, the netstat -ano command combines the output of the -a, -n, and -o switches.

(Continues)

TABLE 14.6   *(Continued)*

Command	Comments
Netstat -o	Includes the process that owns the connection.
Netstat -p protocol Netstat -p TCP	Shows connections for specific protocols. You can use any of the following protocols: IP, IPv6, ICMP, ICMPv6, TCP, TCPv6, UDP, or UDPv6. For example, netstat -p TCP would show connections for TCP only.
Netstat -r	Shows the routing table. This is the same routing table you can see with the route print command.
Netstat -s	Shows statistics for the protocols running on the system. This includes packets received, packets sent, errors, and more.
Netstat *interval* Netstat 15	Redisplays the statistics after waiting the interval period. The interval is specified in seconds as netstat 15 to wait 15 seconds before executing the netstat command again.

Listing 14.7 shows a basic listing of open ports for a computer running on a network without any Internet Explorer sessions opened. With a few web pages open in Internet Explorer, the number of open ports can easily fill a page.

Listing 14.7: Output of netstat **command**

```
C:\Users\Dar>netstat

Active Connections

  Proto  Local Address            Foreign Address          State
  TCP    192.168.1.114:135        WIN7-PC:49766            ESTABLISHED
  TCP    192.168.1.114:1030       WIN7-PC:49767            ESTABLISHED
  TCP    192.168.1.114:1060       MYBOOKWORLD:microsoft-ds
                                                           ESTABLISHED
  TCP    192.168.1.114:2078       beta:http                ESTABLISHED
  TCP    192.168.1.114:3389       Server08R2:56080         ESTABLISHED
  TCP    [fe80::41f0:f763:5451:198a%10]:135   Darril-PC:50506
                                                           ESTABLISHED
```

> Chapter 4 explained ports in depth. It includes a listing of many of the well-known ports in the range of 0 to 1023.
>
> ▶

The local address indicates the local computer (with an IP address of 192.168.1.114) and is in the format of *IP address:port*. The foreign address indicates the name or IP address of the remote computer. The State column indicates the state of the connection.

Some of the common states of a connection are as follows:

ESTABLISHED   Indicates that a TCP session is established

LISTENING   Indicates the system is ready to accept a connection

CLOSE_WAIT   Indicates that the system is waiting for a final packet from the remote system to close the connection

For a full listing of all possible session connections, check out RFC 793 (www.faqs .org/rfcs/rfc793.html). Some connection states are described in RFC 793 with a hyphen, but netstat displays them with an underscore. For example, RFC 793 uses CLOSE-WAIT, but netstat displays CLOSE_WAIT.

You may run the netstat command and see something that looks suspicious. For example, the Foreign Address of beta:http looks a little odd, and you may want to get more information about it. You can use the netstat -b command to identify the application or process using the port, as shown in Listing 14.8. The netstat-b command is one of the commands that must be run from an administrator prompt.

Listing 14.8 Using netstat -b to identify applications and processes

```
C:\>netstat -b

Active Connections

  Proto  Local Address           Foreign Address          State
  TCP    192.168.1.114:135       WIN7-PC:49766            ESTABLISHED
  RpcSs
  [svchost.exe]
  TCP    192.168.1.114:1030      WIN7-PC:49767            ESTABLISHED
  [spoolsv.exe]
  TCP    192.168.1.114:1060      MYBOOKWORLD:microsoft-ds ESTABLISHED
  Can not obtain ownership information
  TCP    192.168.1.114:2078      beta:http               ESTABLISHED
  [OUTLOOK.EXE]
  TCP    192.168.1.114:3389      Server08R2:56080        ESTABLISHED
  CryptSvc
  [svchost.exe]
```

If you have a little information about ports, you can use the output of the netstat command, the names of the applications, and the port numbers to determine what each of the ports is doing.

If you want to search RFC 793, you need to search with the hyphen. For example, you can search CLOSE-WAIT, but you won't find anything if you search on CLOSE_WAIT.

◄

◄

netstat can be useful in detecting spyware and malware. If the applications are unknown, they may be malicious.

Port 135   Port 135 is used for NetBIOS and Remote Procedure Calls (RPCs) in Windows systems. This shows an IPv4 connection (the first line) with another computer named Win7-PC in the network.

Port 1030   This is being used by the print spooler service (spoolsv.exe).

Port 1060   This port is being used to connect to a network drive (named MYBOOKWORLD) that is mapped to the system as an additional drive.

Port 2078   This is being used by Microsoft Outlook for a connection to the Internet.

Port 3389   CryptSvc is short for the Cryptographic Services service. Port 3389 is the port used by Microsoft for Remote Desktop Services (RDS). Combined, they indicate an RDS session is established with a remote computer named Server08R2.

That still may not be enough information if the application looks suspicious. You can use the following steps to get more information about any of these connections:

1. Enter **netstat** at the command prompt.

2. Review the listing, and determine whether there are ports you want to investigate more.

   Note the port number in the Local Address column. For example, you may want to investigate the beta:http line, which shows port 2078.

3. Enter **netstat -ano** at the command prompt.

   This provides a more detailed listing including the process ID (PID). Look for the line with your port number. The following code snippet shows the line for this port:

   ```
   Proto  Local Address      Foreign Address   State        PID
   TCP    192.168.1.114:2078 65.55.11.163:80   ESTABLISHED  5356
   ```

   The PID column shows a PID of 5356 for port 2078.

4. Launch Task Manager by pressing the Ctrl+Shift+Esc keys at the same time.

5. Select the Processes tab.

6. Click View, and click Select Columns.

7. Select the PID (Process Identifier) box. Click OK.

8. Look for the entry with the PID you're interested in. Your display will look similar to Figure 14.3.

Notice that it shows that the Image Name value (the process) is Outlook.

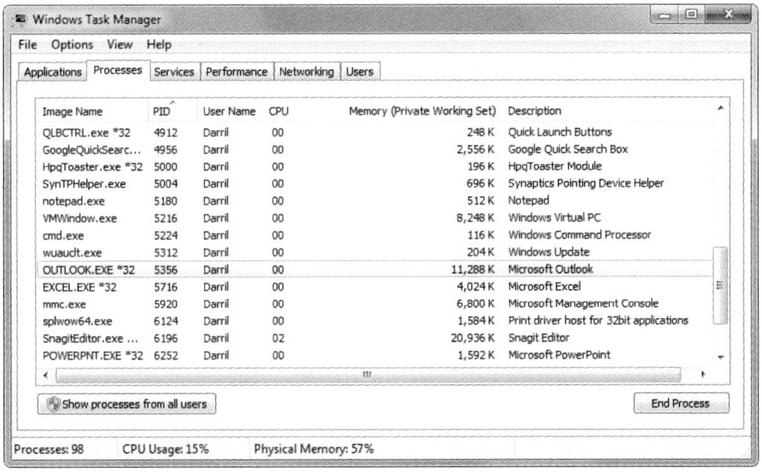

FIGURE 14.3 Locating the PID in Task Manager

9. Launch the Performance Monitor by clicking Start, typing in **perfmon**, and pressing Enter.

   a. In Windows Server 2008, the default display shows the resource overview. This provides the information you need.

   b. In Windows Server 2008 R2 and Windows 7, you need to launch the Resource Monitor by right-clicking Monitoring Tools and selecting Resource Monitor.

10. Look for the PID in the CPU, Disk, Network, and Memory sections. This allows you to get additional information on the process such as how much resources the process is consuming. Figure 14.4 shows the Resource Monitor on a Windows 7 system.

You can get more advanced in your searches to narrow down the source of connections. The goal of these steps isn't to make you a master at identifying all the resources that an open port may be using but instead to show you some of the possibilities. It gives you a chance to dig into your system and learn a little more about it.

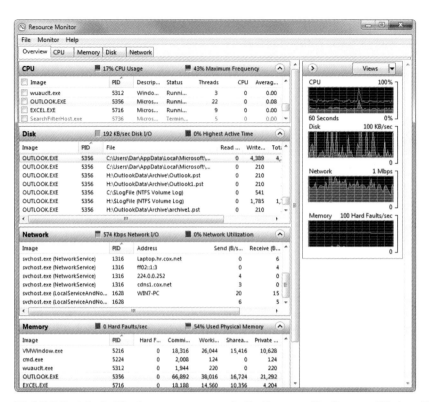

FIGURE 14.4 Viewing resource usage in the Resource Monitor on a Windows 7 system

Installing Telnet

Telnet is a lesser used tool for troubleshooting. It is not installed in Windows systems by default because of security risks, but it can be added. Attackers often use Telnet to check for open ports on a system that has Telnet enabled, so it is more secure to keep Telnet disabled unless it's needed.

When Telnet is installed on client and server computers, you can connect a Telnet client to a Telnet server. It provides a command-line interface that allows you to run Telnet commands from the Telnet client that are executed on the Telnet server. Commands include command-line programs, shell commands, and scripts.

Many programs that use Telnet can be configured to encrypt the traffic with Secure Shell (SSH). The ensures that attackers are not able read the traffic.

> **One of the risks with Telnet is that commands go across the network in clear text. An attacker with a sniffer can capture the traffic and easily read it.**

You can use the following steps to install both the Telnet client and the Telnet server on a Windows Server 2008 server:

1. Click Start ➢ Administrative Tools ➢ Server Manager.

2. Select Features. Click Add Features.

3. Scroll down, and select Telnet Client and Telnet Server, as shown in Figure 14.5. Click Next.

4. Click Install. When the installation is complete, click Close.

Telnet presents significant risks to computers in a network. You should not install Telnet on a computer in a production environment unless it's actually needed.

At this point, Telnet is installed. If you enter **telnet /?** at the command prompt, it will show the output of a help file. You can start a Telnet session from a Telnet client with the following command:

`Telnet TelnetServerName`

If you have more interest in Telnet, you can check out Microsoft's Telnet Operations Guide at `http://technet.microsoft.com/library/cc753164.aspx`.

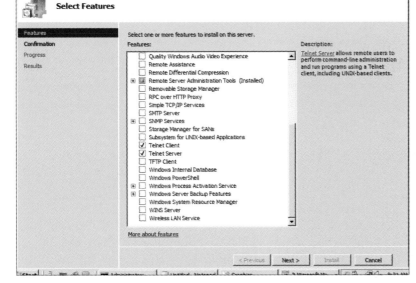

FIGURE 14.5 Adding the Telnet Client and Telnet Server features

THE ESSENTIALS AND BEYOND

In this chapter, you learned about many different methods for troubleshooting network and connectivity problems. You use these tools from the command prompt. Useful commands include ipconfig, ping, tracert, pathping, and netstat. You learned how to use these tools to check the configuration of a system and check its interoperability on a network. You also learned how Telnet can be added to a system if needed.

ADDITIONAL EXERCISES

▶ Remove all of the entries in your hosts cache that have been resolved by DNS.

▶ Identify your default gateway, and check connectivity with it.

▶ Identify the DNS server you are using, and identify how many routers are between your computer and the DNS server.

▶ Identify whether there is any packet loss on routers between your computer and your DNS server.

To compare your answers to the author's, please visit **www.sybex.com/go/ networkingessentials**.

REVIEW QUESTIONS

1. What switch can you use to view help for a command?

   A. /?   C. /hlp

   B. ?   D. /?Help

2. What command can you use to determine a computer's default gateway? (Choose all that apply.)

   A. ipconfig   C. netstat

   B. ipconfig /all   D. telnet

3. You want to verify a computer can connect with the default gateway. It has an IP address of 192.168.1.1. What command should you use?

   A. netstat 192.168.1.1   C. ping 192.168.1.1

   B. 192.168.1.1 Netstat   D. 192.168.1.1 Ping

4. You want to ensure that the ping command only uses IPv4. What switch should you use?

(Continues)

THE ESSENTIALS AND BEYOND (Continued)

5. You use the `ping` command to check connectivity with a server named DC1 and receive the following error: "Ping request could not find host dc1. Please check the name and try again."
   What does this error mean?

   A. DHCP is down.

   B. Name resolution didn't work.

   C. A router is not configured properly.

   D. The default gateway isn't configured.

6. You use the `ping` command to check connectivity with a server named FS1 and receive the following error: "Destination Host Unreachable."
   What is the most likely reason for this error?

   A. DHCP is down.

   B. Name resolution didn't work.

   C. A router is not configured properly.

   D. DNS isn't configured.

7. True or false. You can measure packet loss using the `tracert` command.

8. What tool can you use to view TCP/IP statistics including the number of packets that have been sent and received?

9. What is the command to view all open ports including known applications on a Windows Server 2008 system?

   A. `ipconfig /all`

   B. `pathping`

   C. `netstat`

   D. `netstat -b`

10. True or false. The Telnet client is installed by default in Windows Server 2008.

Answers to Review Questions

Chapter 1

1. **C** A firewall provides a layer of security for a computer that has a direct connection to the Internet. Routers connect subnets. Switches connect computers. A virtual private network (VPN) provides access to a private network over a public network.

2. **True** Wireless access points (WAPs) often provide connectivity for wireless clients to the Internet.

3. **A** A local area network (LAN) is a group of computers connected in a single connection. A wide area network (WAN) is a group of computers connected across two or more locations. A virtual LAN is an advanced implementation of a switch and wasn't covered in this chapter. A virtual private network (VPN) allows connectivity to a private network over a public network.

4. **bits** A lowercase *b* indicates bits. An uppercase *B* indicates bytes.

5. **B** A domain supports single sign-on where each user needs only one username and password. A workgroup requires users to have multiple usernames and passwords to access multiple computers. A wide area network (WAN) typically connects two or more LANs over separate geographical distances. A VPN provides access to the private network over a public network.

6. A group of computers connected together in a network

7. Typically two or more LANs connected together over a large geographical distance

8. **D** A virtual private network (VPN) allows connectivity to a private network over a public network such as the Internet. A domain controller hosts Active Directory but does not provide connectivity over the Internet. A local area network (LAN) connects multiple computers in a single location. A wireless access point (WAP) is used to provide connectivity to wired networks from wireless clients.

9.   **A, C** Remote access servers are either dial-up or virtual private network (VPN) based. Neither a wireless access point (WAP) nor a domain controller are types of remote access servers.

10. **False** Standards go through stages before they are considered standards, and many RFCs are submitted as Informational documents that do not go through stages to become standards.

Chapter 2

1.   **C** Broadcast traffic is sent from one device to all other devices in a subnet. Unicast goes from one device to another device. Multicast goes from one device to many devices. There is no such thing as allcast.

2.   **False** A switch passes broadcast.

3.   **C** Switches connect devices together, and routers connect subnets together. They are not the same. Switches pass broadcasts, but routers do not pass broadcasts.

4.   **True** Bridges can connect dissimilar physical topologies such as twisted pair on one network with fiber-optic connections on another network.

5.   **rules** The most basic hardware- or network-based firewall is simply a router with rules. These rules control both inbound and outbound traffic.

6.   **A software component that provides protection for a single system** Network-based firewalls include both hardware and software.

7.   **False** A crossover cable is used to connect similar devices such as a switch to a switch, or a switch to a router. A straight-through cable is used to connect a computer to a switch.

8.   **D** T568B defines the standard color code for twisted-pair cables.

9.   **a perimeter network (or DMZ)** A perimeter network provides a layer of protection for systems that are accessible from the Internet.

10. **An extranet** An extranet is accessible via the Internet but only to trusted entities.

Chapter 3

1.   **seven** The OSI Model has seven layers.

2.   **Various answers are possible.** One mnemonic is All People Seem To Need Data Processing for layers 7 down to layer 1. Another mnemonic is Please Do Not Throw Sausage Pizza Away for layers 1 up to layer 7.

3. **False** TCP is a connection-oriented protocol. UDP is connection-less.

4. **B** A unit of data at the Transport layer is a segment.

5. **C** A Media Access Control (MAC) address, or physical address, is composed of six pairs of hexadecimal characters. Valid hexadecimal characters are 0 through 9 and A through F.

6. **Network** Both IPv4 and IPv6 operate on the Network layer.

7. **TCP and UDP** The two primary protocols operating on the Transport layer are TCP and UDP. Several other Transport layer protocols exist, but these are the ones stressed in this chapter.

8. **True** Devices such as hubs on layer 1 have very little intelligence. Devices such as advanced firewalls on layer 7 have much more intelligence.

9. **C** Routers operate on the Network layer, layer 3.

10. **E** Proxy servers operate on the Application layer, layer 7 of the OSI Model.

Chapter 4

1. **B** TCP is a connection-oriented protocol. UDP is connection-less.

2. **True** UDP does not provide guaranteed delivery of data. Undetected data loss is possible.

3. **A, B, D** Streaming media and VoIP traffic all commonly use UDP since the overhead of TCP can slow traffic down.

4. **C** The Address Resolution Protocol resolves IP addresses to MAC addresses.

5. **SMTP, POP3, and IMAP4** Simple Mail Transfer Protocol (SMTP), Post Office Protocol version 3 (POP3), and Internet Message Access Protocol version 4 (IMAP4) are used for email.

6. **IPSec** Internet Protocol Security is used with L2TP (as L2TP/IPSec) for VPNs.

7. **IGMP** The Internet Group Management Protocol is used to manage multicast transmission.

8. **D** RDS uses port 3389. LDAP uses port 389. Secure LDAP uses port 636. PPTP uses port 1701.

9. **B** SMTP uses port 25. L2TP uses port 1723. RDS uses port 3389.

10. **C** Kerberos uses port 88. SMTP uses port 25. HTTP uses port 80. HTTPS uses port 443.

Chapter 5

1. **B** IPv4 addresses are in dotted decimal format. Each decimal must be between 0 and 255. You cannot use 256, since 256 is not a valid number in an IPv4 address.

2. **C** The first decimal in a Class C address is in the range of 192–224.

3. **False** The first one has a network ID of 192.168.1.0, and the second one has a network ID of 192.168.2.0.

4. **True** Both have a network ID of 10.0.0.0.

5. **Point B** The default gateway is the interface on the near side of the router for the subnet.

6. **C** The /26 in the IP address is CIDR notation indicating how many bits are a 1 in the subnet mask. The first octet has eight 1s, the second octet has eight 1s, the third octet has eight 1s, and the fourth octet has two 1s. The subnet mask is 255.255.255.192.

7. **B** The reserved IP address ranges are as follows:

   10.0.0.1 through 10.255.255.254

   172.16.0.1 through 172.31.255.254

   192.168.1.1 through 192.168.255.254

   IP addresses can't have numbers greater than 255 as in 10.80.*256*.1.

8. **C** The formula is $2^h - 2$ where h is the number of bits used in the host ID. Since 26 bits are used in the network ID, 6 bits are left for the host ID ($32 - 26 = 6$) and $2^6 - 2 = 62$.

9. **False** The first IP address has a subnet mask of 255.255.255.192 and a network ID of 192.168.1.64. The second IP address has a subnet mask of 255.255.255.192 and a network ID of 192.168.1.128.

10. **A** An address starting with 169.254 is an APIPA address. An APIPA address is assigned to DHCP clients when a DHCP server can't be reached. Manually configuring the default gateway or the DNS server IP address isn't needed for a DHCP client.

Chapter 6

1. **C** IPv6 addresses are expressed as groups of hexadecimal characters. Valid hexadecimal characters are 0 through 9 and *a* through *f*. Characters such as *x*, *g*, and *h* are not valid.

2. **E** Unique local addresses are assigned as private addresses. They have a prefix of fd hexadecimal.

3. **D** Internet Protocol Security (IPSec) is built into IPv6 and allows IPv6 to easily encrypt traffic.

4. **False** The IPv6 prefix of fd is for unique local addresses. Link-local addresses have a prefix of fe80.

5. **Teredo** Teredo is a tunneling protocol that encapsulates IPv6 packets within IPv4 datagrams. A lesser used protocol is 6to4, which can also be a valid answer.

6. **unique local addresses** Unique local addresses are assigned to hosts on private networks.

7. **A** Network Discovery uses ICMPv6 messages for router discovery.

8. **global unicast** Global unicast addresses are used on the Internet. They have a prefix of 2.

Chapter 7

1. **A, B** Electromagnetic interference (EMI) and radio frequency interference (RFI) can cause problems for networks.

2. **A** A short-duration increase in AC power is a power spike. A power surge is a relatively long-duration increase in AC power. Surge protectors can protect against power spikes and surges.

3. **False** An uninterruptible power supply (UPS) provides short-term power when power fails. The goal is to keep the system operational long enough to do a logical shutdown or to allow a generator to power up and stabilize before shifting from UPS power to the generator power.

4. **True** The shielding in shielded twisted pair (STP) provides protection against interference and cross talk.

5. **100** Twisted pair is limited to no more than 100 meters between devices. A repeater can extend the length of the cable.

6. **C** CAT 6 cable is rated at 1000 Mpbs. CAT 6E is rated at 10000 Mpbs.

7. **Twisted pair using four twisted pairs** The *T* indicates twisted pair, and currently used twisted-pair cables have four twisted pairs.

8. **A, B, C** Protocol analyzers can capture traffic going across a network. These are commonly called sniffers, and Microsoft's Network Monitor is one example of a protocol analyzer.

9. **A** 802.11g uses 2.4 GHz.

Chapter 8

1. **modular switch** You can expand a modular switch by adding modules.

2. **B** Ports on a 100 Mbps switch are labeled with F or Fa to indicate Fast Ethernet. The first port is 0, and the second port is 1. E is for 10 Mbps ports, and 1000 Mbps ports use Gi.

3. **False** A layer 2 switch creates separate collision domains, not separate broadcast domains.

4. **C** Switches create a separate collision domain for every device connected to the switch. Bridges creates separate collision domains but not one for every device. There's no such thing as a managed hub. Firewalls don't create separate broadcast or collision domains.

5. **False** A managed switch needs to be configured by an administrator to take advantage of the capabilities. Unmanaged switches work just by plugging them in.

6. **router** A layer 3 switch provides routing on layer 3 just like a router. It does so using hardware capabilities, so it is quicker than a router that routes using software capabilities.

7. **A** Switches create MAC tables to map MAC addresses to physical ports. Routers have routing tables to track subnetworks; although it's feasible to call a routing table a layer 3 table, it isn't an actual term, and it would track subnetworks, not computers. There's no such thing as a managed table.

8. **C** The minimum number of ports required for a VLAN is two. If the port has 48 ports, you can create as many as 24 VLANs.

9. **D** The five combined ports give a combined speed of 500 Mbps, and since full-duplex is being used, data can travel both ways, giving an effective throughput of 1000 Mbps (1 Gbps).

10. **Port security** Port security includes configuring the switch with specific MAC addresses and blocking access to unused ports.

Chapter 9

1. **A** The router knows only about directly connected routes by default.

2. **D** The easiest way is to add static routes to each router. Although you could add routing protocols such as OSPF or RIPv2 to create dynamic routes, it's much easier to just add static routes if you have only two routers and three subnets.

3. **False** Routers use the least cost path based on the metric to determine the best path.

4. **Routing table** A router stores all known routes in a routing table.

5. **A, B, C** Routing protocols allow clients to learn routes from each other dynamically. Common routing protocols on internal networks are RIPv2 and OSPF. ARP translates IP addresses to MAC addresses.

6. **False** Windows Server 2008 supports RIPv2 but not OSPF.

7. **B** A DHCP relay agent can be added to relay DHCP BootP broadcasts through routers that are not RFC 1542 compliant. RFC 1542-compliant routers can forward DHCP and BootP broadcasts. Adding another DHCP server would be an expensive solution and would work only if you had only two subnets connected. If you used this solution, you would need to add DHCP servers for every subnet.

8. **C** The IGMP Router and Proxy service can be added to a Windows Server 2008 server router so that it passes multicast traffic.

Chapter 10

1. **D** Host names are used on the Internet. Internal networks can have host names and/or NetBIOS names.

2. **B, D** Both host names and NetBIOS names are used on Microsoft networks, though the usage of NetBIOS names is being phased out. DNS resolves host names, and WINS resolves NetBIOS names.

3. **False** The primary name resolution method for NetBIOS names is WINS.

4. **True** Entries in the hosts file are automatically placed in the host cache (also called the *DNS resolver cache*). These entries can be viewed by entering `ipconfig /displaydns` at the command prompt.

5. **C** The `ipconfig /displaydns` command will display the host name cache. The `ipconfig /flushdns` command clears the cache. The `nbtstat` commands are used with NetBIOS names.

6. **False** WINS operates only on internal Microsoft networks to resolve NetBIOS names. WINS is not used on the Internet.

7. **A** The `ipconfig /flushdns` command removes entries from the host cache that have been resolved from a DNS server.

8. **Link-local multicast name resolution (LLMNR)** An IPv6 address with a prefix of fe80 is a link-local address. LLMNR is used for name resolution of link-local addresses.

Chapter 11

1.   **A** The Internet is considered the riskiest network security zone. Users with Internet access from anywhere in the world can attack resources placed directly on the Internet.

2.   **Network Address Translation (NAT)** NAT is a service that can run on routers and proxy servers. It translates public and private IP addresses, reduces the number of public IP addresses needed by a company, and hides internal computers.

3.   **C** A proxy server can restrict access to certain websites by using filters. The filter includes what websites are restricted and blocks them, or it includes what websites are allowed and blocks all others.

4.   **True** A perimeter network (also called a demilitarized zone or DMZ) provides a layer of security for Internet-facing servers.

5.   **A, B** Perimeter networks can be created with one or two firewalls. One firewall is cheaper, though a perimeter network created with a single firewall can be more complex to create. Although a third or fourth firewall can technically be added to a perimeter network, they would be redundant and don't follow perimeter network models.

6.   **C** Network discovery is a service that allows computers to discover other computers on the network.

7.   **An extranet** An extranet provides access to internal resources to trusted entities over the Internet.

Chapter 12

1.   **B, C** The SSID is a logical network name for a WLAN and has a maximum alphanumeric value of 32 bits. It doesn't identify the device type, and it doesn't identify the security encryption method.

2.   **False** Wireless networks (802.11 networks) use CSMA/CA. 802.3 networks use CSMA/CD.

3.   **D** 802.11a networks use 5 GHz. They have a speed of 11 Mbps.

4.   **A** IEEE 802.11b and 802.11g operate in the 2.4 GHz range. 802.11a operates in the 5 GHz range, and 802.11n is compatible with all three standards. None of the standards uses 4.1 GHz or 2.4 MHz.

5.   **C, D** 802.11n networks can use 2.4 GHz and 5 GHz. They have a speed of 300 Mbps.

6.   **B** 802.11b networks can be as fast as 11 Mbps.

7. **True** 802.11n networks use MIMO technology allowing them to operate at 300 Mbps and sometimes higher.

8. **D** WPA2 Enterprise Mode is the strongest. WPA2 Enterprise mode uses an 802.1x server, while WPA2 Personal mode only needs a preshared key.

9. **False** A WAP is only an access point, but a wireless router includes an access point and additional components such as a router, a switch, and DHCP.

10. **B** A Point-to-Point (P2P) wireless bridge can connect wired networks in two buildings 25 miles apart.

Chapter 13

1. **A, C, D** Dial-up, DSL, and broadband cable are all methods that a SOHO could use for Internet access.

2. **B** An ISDN BRI uses two 64 Kbps B channels and one D channel.

3. **B** DSL connections require the user to be close to a central office since the digital signal can't travel as far over telephone lines as an analog signal.

4. **False** E1 and E3 lines are used in Europe. T1 and T3 lines are used in the United States.

5. **A** A T1 is 1.544 Mbps. An E1 is 2.048 Mbps, an E3 is 34.368 Mbps, and a T3 is 44.736 Mbps.

6. **C** The Routing and Remote Access Services service is part of the Network Policy Access Services role. You can configure it as a VPN or a dial-up server.

7. **A, B, C** PPTP, L2TP, and SSTP are all valid tunneling protocols.

8. **C** RADIUS is used for central authentication and logging. It cannot be used as a WAN link and doesn't provide encryption.

Chapter 14

1. **A** The /? switch provides help for almost any command. The format is command /?, as in `ipconfig /?`.

2. **A, B** Both `ipconfig` and `ipconfig /all` will show the default gateway.

3. **C** The `ping` command checks connectivity with remote computers. You can follow the computer name with the IP address.

4. **-4** You can use the `ping -4 computername` or `ping -4 IPAddress` command to ensure that ping uses IPv4.

5. **B** The error indicates that the host could not be resolved to an IP address. It could be a problem with DNS (or another type of name resolution), or it could be the host name is not entered correctly in the ping command.

6. **C** The error usually indicates a problem with routing. It could be that a router is not configured correctly or that one of the two systems does not have its default gateway configured correctly.

7. **False** tracert will identify the routers in the path, but it will not measure packet loss. pathping can measure packet loss.

8. **netstat** netstat (network statistics) can show statistics for protocols running on a system.

9. **D** netstat -b shows all the connections that all applications are using to connect to the network. netstat (without the -b switch) does not list the applications.

10. **False** Telnet is not installed by default in Windows Server 2008. You can add Telnet as a feature.

Microsoft's Certification Program

Since the inception of its certification program, Microsoft has certified more than 2 million people. As the computer network industry continues to increase in both size and complexity, this number is sure to grow—and the need for *proven* ability will also increase. Certifications can help companies verify the skills of prospective employees and contractors.

Microsoft started with the Microsoft Certified Professional (MCP) program that validated individuals' knowledge and expertise on a wide variety of products. It has expanded these certifications into multiple categories:

Microsoft Technology Associate (MTA)   The MTA certifications are entry-level certifications that are available only at academic institutions. They validate an individual's knowledge and basic understanding of key technology concepts. The three IT professional series certifications are Networking Fundamentals, Security Fundamentals, and Windows Server Administration Fundamentals. There are also several developer certifications. You must take and pass one exam to earn each MTA certification.

Microsoft Certified Technology Specialist (MCTS)   The MCTS is the next level of certification. For people who are not in an academic institution, these certifications can be the first certifications they earn. The MCTS certification program targets specific technologies instead of specific job roles. You must take and pass one to three exams to earn an MCTS certification in different technologies.

Microsoft Certified IT Professional (MCITP)   The MCITP certification is a Professional Series certification that tests network and system administrators on job roles rather than only on a specific technology. The MCITP certification program generally consists of one to three exams in addition to obtaining an MCTS-level certification.

Microsoft Certified Professional Developer (MCPD)   The MCPD certification is a Professional Series certification for application developers. Similar to the MCITP, the MCPD is focused on a job role rather than on a single technology.

The MCPD certification program generally consists of one to three exams in addition to obtaining an MCTS-level certification.

Microsoft Certified Master (MCM)   The MCM program is for experienced IT professionals who want to deepen and broaden their technical expertise on specific Microsoft server products. It includes three weeks of highly intensive classroom training, three computer-based tests, and one lab-based exam for each of the MCM certifications. There are five separate MCM certifications.

Microsoft Certified Architect (MCA)   The MCA is Microsoft's premier certification series. Obtaining the MCA requires a minimum of 10 years of experience and passing a review board consisting of peer architects.

Certification Objectives Map

Table A.1 provides objective mappings for the Microsoft Technology Associate (MTA) Networking Fundamentals Exam (98-366). It identifies the chapters and sections where the 98-366 exam objectives are covered.

TABLE A.1   Exam 98-366 objectives map

Objectives	Chapter and section
Understanding Network Infrastructures	**Chapters 1, 5, 8, 11, 12, and 13**
• Understand the concepts of Internet, intranet, and extranet. This objective may include but is not limited to VPN, security zones, firewalls.	Chapter 11: Understanding Risks on the Internet, Exploring an Intranet, Understanding Firewalls, Identifying a Perimeter Network, Understanding Extranets
• Understand local area networks (LANs). This objective may include but is not limited to perimeter networks, addressing, reserved address ranges for local use (including local loopback IP), VLANs, wired LAN, and wireless LAN.	Chapter 1: Networking Small Offices and Home Offices, Networking Enterprises Chapter 5: Exploring the Components of an IP Address Chapter 8: Comparing Managed and Unmanaged Switches Chapter 11: Identifying a Perimeter Network Chapter 12: Exploring Basic Wireless Components

(Continues)

TABLE A.1 *(Continued)*

Objectives	Chapter and section
• Understand wide area networks (WANs). This objective may include but is not limited to leased lines, dial-up, ISDN, VPN, T1, T3, E1, E3, DSL, cable, and so on, and their characteristics (speed, availability). Item idea: Map T1, and so on, to a LAN or WAN.	Chapter 1: Networking Enterprises Chapter 13: Comparing Connectivity Methods used in Homes and SOHOs, Comparing Connectivity Methods in Enterprises
• Understand wireless networking. This objective may include but is not limited to types of wireless networking standards and their characteristics (802.11A,B,G,N including different GHz ranges), types of network security (WPA/WEP/802.1X, and so on), Point-to-Point (P2P) wireless, wireless bridging.	Chapter 12: Comparing Networking Standards and Characteristics, Comparing Network Security Methods, Using Wireless Networks, Understanding Point-to-Point Wireless
• Understand network topologies and access methods.	Chapter 13: Exploring Remote Access Services Chapter 11: Exploring an Intranet, Understanding Firewalls, Identifying a Perimeter Network, Understanding Extranets
Understanding Network Hardware	**Chapters 2, 7, 8, and 9**
• Understand switches. This objective may include but is not limited to transmission speed, number and type of ports, number of uplinks, speed of uplinks, managed or unmanaged switches, VLAN capabilities, Layer 2 and Layer 3 switches, security options, hardware redundancy, support, backplane speed, switching types, MAC table, understanding capabilities of hubs vs. switches.	Chapter 2: Understanding Network Hardware Chapter 8: Connecting Multiple Computers Together, Understanding Physical Ports, Comparing Hubs and Switches, Comparing Managed and Unmanaged Switches, Exploring Switch Speeds, Understanding Security Options

(Continues)

TABLE A.1   *(Continued)*

Objectives	Chapter and section
• Understand routers. This objective may include but is not limited to transmission speed considerations, directly connected routes, static routing, dynamic routing (routing protocols), default routes, routing table and how it selects best route(s), routing table memory, NAT, software routing in Windows Server.	Chapter 2: Understanding Network Hardware Chapter 9: Connecting Multiple Networks Together, Routing Traffic on a Network, Identifying Transmission Speed Considerations, Software Routing in Windows Server 2008, Understanding Other Routing Protocols
• Understand media types. This objective may include but is not limited to cable types and their characteristics, including media segment length and speed, fiber optic, twisted-pair shielded or nonshielded, CATxx cabling, wireless, susceptibility to external interference (machinery, power cables, and so on), susceptibility to electricity (lightning), susceptibility to interception.	Chapter 7: Identifying Problems with Connectivity, Exploring Cable Types and Their Characteristics
Understanding Protocols and Services	**Chapters 3, 4, 5, 6, 9, 10, 13, and 14**
• Understand the OSI model. This objective may include but is not limited to OSI Model, TCP Model, examples of devices, protocols, applications and which OSI/TCP layer they belong to, TCP and UDP, well-known ports for most used purposes (not necessarily Internet), packets and frames.	Chapter 3: Understanding the OSI Model, Understanding the TCP/IP Model, Mapping Devices on the OSI and TCP Models, Mapping Protocols on the OSI and TCP/IP Models Chapter 4: Understanding Ports

(Continues)

TABLE A.1 *(Continued)*

Objectives	Chapter and section
• Understand IPv4. This objective may include but is not limited to: subnetting, IPconfig, why use IPv6, addressing, IPv4 to IPv6 tunneling protocols to ensure backward compatibility, dual IP stack, subnetmask, gateway, ports, packets, reserved address ranges for local use (including local loopback IP).	Chapter 5: Exploring the Components of an IPv4 Address, Exploring an IPv4 Address in Binary, Subnetting IPv4 Addresses Chapter 6: Understanding the Dual IP Stack Chapter 9: Connecting Multiple Networks Together
• Understand IPv6. This objective may include but is not limited to subnetting, IPconfig, why use IPv6, addressing, IPv4 to IPv6 tunneling protocols to ensure backward compatibility, dual IP stack, subnetmask, gateway, ports, packets, reserved address ranges for local use (including local loopback IP).	Chapter 6: Exploring IPv6 Addresses, Exploring the Components of an IPv6 Address, Understanding the Dual IP Stack
• Understand name resolution. This objective may include but is not limited to DNS, WINS, steps in the name resolution process.	Chapter 10: Exploring Types of Names Used in Networks, Exploring Types of Name Resolution, Identifying the Steps in Name Resolution
• Understand networking services. This objective may include but is not limited to DHCP, remote access.	Chapter 5: Comparing Manual and Automatic Assignment of IPv4 Addresses Chapter 6: Comparing Manual and Automatic Assignment of IPv6 Addresses Chapter 13: Exploring Remote Access Services
• Understand TCP/IP. This objective may include but is not limited to tools such as `ping`, `tracert`, `pathping`, **Telnet**, `ipconfig`, `netstat`, reserved address ranges for local use (including local loopback IP), protocols.	Chapter 14: Using the Command Prompt, Checking the TCP/IP Configuration with ipconfig, Troubleshooting Connectivity with ping, Identifying Routers with tracert, Verifying the Routed Path with pathping, Viewing TCP/IP Statistics with netstat, Installing Telnet

INDEX

Note to the reader: Throughout this index **boldfaced** page numbers indicate primary discussions of a topic. *Italicized* page numbers indicate illustrations.